LINCOLN CHRISTIAN COLLEGE AND SEMINARY

W9-BUK-715

UNDERSTANDING AND CHANGING YOUR MANAGEMENT STYLE

UNDERSTANDING AND CHANGING YOUR MANAGEMENT STYLE

Robert C. Benfari

Jossey-Bass Publishers
San Francisco

Copyright © 1999 by Jossey-Bass Inc., Publishers, 350 Sansome Street, San Francisco, California 94104.

All rights reserved. No part of this publication may be reproduced, stored in a retrieval system, or transmitted, in any form or by any means, electronic, mechanical, photocopying, recording, or otherwise, without the prior written permission of the publisher.

Jossey-Bass books and products are available through most bookstores. To contact Jossey-Bass directly, call (888) 378-2537, fax to (800) 605-2665, or visit our website at www.josseybass.com.

Substantial discounts on bulk quantities of Jossey-Bass books are available to corporations, professional associations, and other organizations. For details and discount information, contact the special sales department at Jossey-Bass Inc., Publishers.
(415) 433–1740; Fax (800) 605–2665.

For sales outside the United States, please contact your local Simon & Schuster International Office.

Manufactured in the United States of America. The text is printed on acid-free recycled paper containing a minimum of 10 percent postconsumer waste.

Library of Congress Cataloging-in-Publication Data

Benfari, Robert.
   Understanding and changing your management style / Robert C. Benfari.
     p. cm.
   Includes bibliographical references and index.
   ISBN 0–7879–0858–4
   1. Executive ability. 2. Management. I. Title. II. Series.
HD38.2.B459   1999
658.4'09—dc21   99-27759

FIRST EDITION
HB Printing 10 9 8 7 6 5 4 3 2 1

CONTENTS

98571

PREFACE

"Usually, the bad boss doesn't know himself or herself and doesn't have any idea of being a bad boss. The [bad] boss doesn't really have regard for people, doesn't trust them, thinks they need to be kicked in the butt to get things done, thinks he has to throw a tantrum once a day to keep people in line, doesn't understand how teams work, how to delegate, and can't communicate well, and doesn't try too hard."

—JAMES GALVIN, FORMER COMMANDER OF NATO AND
DEAN OF TUFTS UNIVERSITY'S FLETCHER SCHOOL OF LAW AND DIPLOMACY

For managers and leaders at all levels, the constant bombardment of daily challenges, problems, and triumphs of getting work done often obscures the underlying concern about what it takes to excel as a manager and a leader. We know that managing and leading well pays off not just in favorable business outcomes but also in more satisfying working relationships. The way we manage—our management style—is fundamental, yet it so often seems enigmatic. Some people seem to lead and manage effortlessly, as though born to the work, while others struggle with it, often damaging business results and the morale and spirit of their coworkers. They become the "bad bosses" that James Galvin describes in the quote above. Even some of the most talented managers may find that they are overwhelmed with the challenges from time to time. What makes the difference? Is there a way to gain greater understanding of our natural strengths and play to them, while at the same time gaining more awareness of possible weaknesses and developing strategies for growth and change? The answer, of course, is "yes." That is why I wrote this book.

The Purpose of the Book

In my course at Harvard, "Understanding Your Management Style," I have developed a curriculum based on my personal experience with thousands of managers who attended my workshops. In addition, I have conducted interviews and observed good and bad practices of both effective and dysfunctional managers. From these experiences and from a review of the current literature, I have come up with an integrated model to help managers at any level to better understand and then take steps to change their management style. My model, called the Integrated Management Style Model (shown in Appendix A), rests on several key building blocks. By becoming aware of these building blocks and then isolating and defining them, managers can lay the groundwork for understanding themselves and thereby work more effectively with other people as a manager and a leader.

Why an Integrated Management Style?

The Integrated Management Style Model is designed to help us analyze how we react to a whole constellation of aspects of management, including conflict, stress, and difficult people, and to become aware of what may have previously been unconscious behavior.

By uncovering the patterns of our behavior, we move from being reactive to being in charge of our lives. Once we are aware, we can initiate a program for positive, proactive behavior. But the process must begin with an understanding of the essential building blocks of management style. This is not a theoretical endeavor but a highly practical one with potentially enormous personal and organizational consequences.

The Building Blocks of Management Style

The first building block of management style—our psychological type—explains how we use our energy, how we perceive the world, and how we judge our perceptions. Once we understand which type we are (out of a total of sixteen possible types), we have a better sense of our "hard wiring," the in-born psychological makeup that affects so many of our preferences for how we like to work, how we tend to manage, and how we interact with other people.

Needs, the second building block, are almost as fundamental as psychological type but are more affected by our upbringing and life experience. Through needs we express our approach to and desire for competence and accomplishment. Needs affect how we function as managers in exercising power, handling tasks, and relating to colleagues, as well as how we relate to our superiors and subordinates, how we take on tasks, and what kind of tone and style we use as managers.

Closely related to our needs is our power orientation—the methods we use to influence other people. Power and influence can take many forms, from coercion to expertise to information and much more. Knowing the different sources of power and how to use them appropriately, especially with other psychological types, can mean the difference between an organization where managers spend their time in power struggles and one in which managers exert a positive influence on each other and with superiors and subordinates to get the work done.

The next building block concerns our approach to conflict and problem solving. Just as our power orientation may be conditioned by our environment and life experiences, we may have learned dysfunctional or ineffective ways of handling conflict and solving problems. Given that problem solving is a huge component of management and that conflict is inevitable from time to time, understanding our reactions to both of these elements and taking a proactive approach to developing better skills can make a big difference in business results and the quality of organizational life.

Proactive managers understand the importance of the next building block—values, those often unspoken but essential rules that govern the way we operate and do business. In many instances, we are driven by these forces without a clear understanding of what they fully mean to us. In the Integrated Management Style Model, understanding and clarifying our personal values are essential to our sense of why and how we do our work.

The final building block of management style is our reaction to the stresses of our environment and all the pressures of daily living, including dealing with difficult people and situations. In order to minimize defensive and negative approaches to handling stress, we need to understand it, its origins, and ways of engaging with it in a positive manner.

All of these elements come together in a unique constellation in each manager. The process of recognizing your personal configuration of these elements and becoming aware of what you need to do to maximize strengths and overcome weaknesses is the essence of what this book is about. Contrary to what you may have heard or read before, good management is not in-born in some, nor is so-called bad management a fixed state for others. Changing your management style is possible once you understand what can be changed (and what cannot) and are willing to do the work to shift your assumptions, perceptions, and behavior.

Another Important Ingredient: Your Practical IQ

This book is based in part on the concept of what Robert Sternberg of Yale University called "Practical IQ." Unlike academic or intellectual intelligence, practical intelligence concerns the kind of "street smarts" that affect how we approach our work and handle interpersonal relationships. In many ways, Practical IQ is similar to psychologist Daniel Goleman's emotional IQ, but it takes into account the development of conceptual acumen as well (for finding opportunity, handling uncertainty, and seeking out challenges). Practical intelligence, I believe, develops through understanding ourselves and others and knowing when to modify our behavior to be effective. A large part of the goals of this book is to build the necessary skills that put management style under our own control. It is an essentially optimistic outlook.

The Path Through the Book

Each chapter is designed to guide you through the theoretical and practical applications of the Integrated Management Style Model using examples and cases to illustrate the principles. It moves from the most innate of the elements—psychological type—through the rest of those building blocks that are more amenable to change. In the appendixes, you will find a series of assessments and inventories that you can use to determine where you stand at a given point in time on each of the building blocks. The idea is that once you know where you stand, you can use the techniques for change that each chapter presents. The most fruitful way of working through the book is to take the assessments in the appendixes before you start your journey. That will make the chapters more personally relevant for you. The last chapter is devoted to helping you pull all the elements of your management style together into a coherent picture and to assist you in developing an action plan for the kinds of changes you want to make.

Acknowledgments

I would like to thank Cedric Crocker and Byron Schneider of Jossey-Bass who thoughtfully and patiently helped put this project into reality. I would like to give special acknowledgment and thanks to Sheryl Fullerton who actively and creatively helped me mold the final product. Her help was immeasurable. Her efforts proved that there is a cooperative win/win solution to most problems.

Now on to the journey.

ABOUT THE AUTHOR

Dr. Robert C. Benfari, A.B., M.B.A., Ph.D., has been on the faculty of Harvard University since 1967. In addition he is visiting professor at the University De La Empresensa (Argentina). Dr. Benfari is trained in psychology, organizational behavior, and behavioral medicine. He is president of BGL Ltd., a consulting firm.

Among others, Dr. Benfari's consulting clients included AT&T, IBM, the U.S. State Department, Raytheon, the United States Navy, and the Perez Center for Peace.

Affiliations

Dr. Benfari is a member of the American Psychological Association, and he is a licensed psychologist in the state of Massachusetts. He has spoken at Harvard commencement and in 1994 received a Distinguished Teaching Award from the university. From 1970 to 1983, Dr. Benfari was the principal investigator at Harvard for the Multiple Risk Factor Intervention Trial. He served on the steering and executive committees and acted as a consultant to the national trial on behavioral and organizational issues.

UNDERSTANDING AND CHANGING
YOUR MANAGEMENT STYLE

WHAT MAKES A GOOD MANAGER?

Dave had been a star at Enerjetics, a fast-growing Internet software firm in North Carolina. He had come on early in the start-up phase as a key software engineer and was responsible for the creation of their first highly successful product. A year later, in recognition of his contributions, he was promoted to manage several teams who were developing their next generation of products.

Now, eleven months later, the tension around Dave and his performance as a manager had grown to the point where Mark and Carol, the co-founders of Enerjetics, could not ignore it anymore. Several key programmers and tech people were threatening to leave, the marketing people were complaining that Dave was not giving them what they needed, and Janice, the HR director, was spending a lot of her time on damage control. Dave had been through several targeted—and expensive—management seminars, but he still kept doing things the same way with increasingly problematic results. Janice finally told Mark and Carol that Dave needed to be moved out of management, to another role that suited him better. When Mark and Carol broke the news to Dave, he was astounded. "What are you talking about?" he said. "We're doing great on the teams. We're on schedule with the products, they're looking good, the code is solid. What the hell is the problem?"

What Makes a Good Manager?

The story of Dave as a manager-in-trouble at Enerjetics is a familiar one, especially in companies where technical and engineering people "come off the bench" to head up teams of people doing a variety of jobs. Maybe you have been in Dave's shoes or witnessed a promising colleague struggling with new or different managerial responsibilities. Many people get promoted into management because they have been doing a great job. But that previous success may not transfer to their new jobs. The reasons for the discrepancy can be blamed on all kinds of factors: insufficient management training, poor fit between person and job, lack of talent or aptitude, to name just a few. Sometimes it seems as though good managers are just born that way, while others seem destined to find management a difficult and frustrating assignment. But it does not have to be that way.

Effective management is not an enigma, nor is it simply a matter of better training and development. The way that we manage—our management style—is a mixture of conceptual skills and interpersonal factors. When you understand those skills and factors, how they fit together, and how (and whether) they can be changed or developed, it is possible to assess your own strengths and weaknesses and devise a strategy for improving your management style. The purpose of this book is to foster a deeper understanding of the most significant ingredients of effective management and to show you how you can choose to shift your own management style so that you will not only achieve more of what you want but also eliminate the barriers that are keeping you from enjoying your work as a manager. It assumes that there are just a few but highly potent ingredients that need to be understood individually and in combination; the best managers are highly aware of them and have learned how to integrate them into a coherent management style. It also assumes—based on extensive social and behavior scientific research—that we can change our management style, that good managers are made, not just born (although a few of them seem to be).

The keys to understanding and improving your management style are really quite simple:

1. Understand the contributions of nature (innate qualities such as personality) and nurture (learned behavior such as how we handle conflict) to management style. We'll look at nature–nurture in more detail later in the chapter, as well as in other chapters. Because innate qualities may not be modified in the same ways that learned behavior can be, managers have to know the limits to the changes they may want to make in themselves and others.

2. Realize that the different ingredients of management style interact in complex but fully understandable ways. Our basic response to stress, for example, can

affect our ability to solve problems or manage conflict. Managers who are aware of the ingredients and their interaction will be more likely to avoid— or at least head off—difficult situations.

3. It is important to assess where you stand on the various components of management style. There will be a number of tests or inventories in this book that you can use to help you assemble a coherent picture of your strengths and weaknesses. You can then plan strategies for modifying particular elements that will lead to improved performance for you and your staff.

4. Develop what we might call "practical intelligence," the conceptual and interpersonal skills and mindset that allow you to achieve goals you personally value. It is the kind of intelligence that makes things work—that lets us seek out and meet challenges, to be motivated, to complete tasks, to work well with other people (even difficult ones). When accompanied by self-awareness and the ability to see situations objectively, practical intelligence can be essential in helping us strengthen our weaknesses and maximize our strengths. (We will come back to this topic in more detail in Chapter Three.)

The Six Building Blocks of Management Style

Before we delve into the specific elements of management style, it is worth emphasizing that some qualities or behaviors are innate, while others are learned. This point, a variation on the old nature versus nurture debate, is important for managers because it addresses the issue of what behavior can be changed. Behavior that is more a product of our inborn nature can be temporarily shifted to meet a particular situation, but is not amenable to permanent change. Psychological type (which is fundamentally an orientation to be directed more inwardly or outwardly), for example, is fixed. Needs (for recognition, social contact, security, and so on) are also relatively resistant to change, although they can be mediated, as we will see in Chapter Five. Both personality and needs affect our general response to life, as well as our ability to learn new behaviors and to modify old patterns.

Within the realm of learned behavior, we are strongly influenced by our experiences and the specifics of our life situations. Being born into and growing up in different kinds of families or in a specific culture or religious tradition dramatically affect our perceptions and assumptions about people, about right and wrong, about how we should interact with one another, and about how we get other people to do what we want. For example, a woman who grows up in a culture and in a family that assumes women are equal to men may have a difficult time managing a team of men and women in another country or subculture where the role of women is one of subservience.

Through our experiences we build up what might be thought of as scripts that tell us how we should act and that are so much a part of us that we tend to follow them automatically. These scripts incorporate all of our learned behavior and profoundly influence our personal as well as professional lives, particularly the way we manage—everything from our values to the way we handle conflict and solve problems.

This book is based on a model of management style that emphasizes the interaction between nature and nurture—that is, between individuals, their environments, and the innate qualities they were born with. It focuses on six key elements:

Innate Elements	*Learned Elements*
Psychological Type	Power Bases
Needs	Styles of Problem Solving and Handling Conflict
	Values
	Styles of Handling Stress

Let's take a brief look at each of these six elements, keeping in mind that we will discuss them again in subsequent chapters. Although we look at them one at a time here, none of them can be considered solely in isolation. The combination and integration of these elements create your overall management style.

1. **Psychological Types: Innate Temperament and Preferences.** Based on the Myers-Briggs Type Indicators (MBTI), psychological types describe a person's temperament or attitudes. One dimension, for example, indicates whether your energy is primarily focused inward (introvert) or outward (extrovert). Because psychological types originate more in nature than nurture, they cannot be permanently changed, although they can be adjusted to respond to particular situations. Learning the different types and their orientations allows us to appreciate our own and others' strengths and weaknesses and to predict others' behavior and adjust our reactions to them.

2. **Needs: The Drivers of Behavior.** The concept of need implies something that we want to fulfill—something we lack but seek or something we have and wish to keep. We all share physical needs such as air, water, food, and safety, as well as social needs for companionship, boundaries, our own turf, and the sense of being part of a group. At work, other needs (for achievement, dominance, affiliation, and so on) drive us. The particular individual constellations of needs are an important and to some extent innate part of who we are and

how we express our personalities. Understanding how needs affect our behavior (and that of everyone around us) is often the first step to unlocking what can seem like perplexing behavior patterns and to harnessing those needs toward constructive outcomes.

3. **The Bases of Power: The Uses and Abuses of Influence.** Power—the ability to influence the beliefs, emotions, and behaviors of other people—affects every relationship and all actions in every organization in one way or another. Some people have an uncanny instinct for using power effectively (and positively), while others use it in negative ways to manipulate, misinform, and subvert. Both positive and negative power operate out of our instinctive need for dominance, out of our desire to control our lives and situations. By acquiring the right skills, even someone who has a low need for dominance or lacks a natural sense of how to use power can develop better ways of influencing others. Acquiring power and using it effectively are vital to success in organizations, to productive relationships, and to the manager's sense of self-esteem and desire for self-fulfillment and competence.

4. **Conflict Styles: Getting to Resolution.** While we all come equipped with a basic "fight-or-flight" response to conflict, neither of those reactions is effective in organizational settings. We cannot turn on our opponents and beat them up, nor can we run away from them, although most people tend to try to either avoid or dominate conflict—neither of which is helpful in finding resolutions. In this book, the approach to changing the way we handle conflict concentrates on shifting out of old patterns and training in steps that lead to win/win strategies. Because conflict is such a pervasive element of organizational life, understanding and changing our approach to resolving it are crucial for managers who want to become more effective.

5. **Values: Clarifying Ideals and Beliefs.** Values are our individual and collective sense of ideals and what we think is worthwhile and important. Unlike the more innate factors that influence management style, values are clearly learned and determined by culture, social institutions such as family and religion, and personal experience. Values can change as society, our situation, our self-concept, and our self-awareness change. We explore values in this book because managers must know what is important to them when it comes to leadership, power, professional ethics, respect, responsibility, equality, and so on. They must be able to define and clarify their personal value structures and modify them as desired. In particular, managers in a democratic society cannot divorce their actions in the business realm from their own personal values or from commonly held social values.

6. **Stress: Responding to Pressure.** Response to stress is akin to how we handle conflict. Although it may be based in the primordial "fight-or-flight" response, life experiences and individual differences affect our response to both

internal and external stressors. The challenge in responding to stress is to go beyond the primitive "fight-or-flight" reaction and use more sophisticated and proven methods for recognizing our own tendencies and alter them so that we deal with stress without coming apart.

Putting It All Together

Although it is useful at one level to consider the six elements of management style individually, they are most valuable when seen as an integrated whole. That is the goal of the Integrated Management Style Model (see Appendix A). It assumes that managers can get a clearer and more practical picture of themselves and their behavior by looking at all six elements and their interactions.

Needs, for example, are intimately related to the way a manager solves problems and handles conflict. If you have strong needs to dominate *and* to work autonomously, you are going to find it difficult to collaborate with your colleagues in resolving a disagreement about how to deal with a missed deadline. Or if you are an introvert with an orientation to details rather than to the big picture, you are going to be stressed in dealing with a boss who constantly talks about vision and seems short on command of how that vision will be realized. In both cases, however, if you understand these aspects of yourself and your behavior and have learned ways to shift your perceptions and your actions, you can consciously change your response. You do not have to go through the roof in the next team meeting about that deadline or be accused of browbeating your colleagues. You do not have to let your boss drive you crazy; there are actually ways to get that extroverted fuzzy thinker to nail down some specifics for you. The Integrated Management Style Model is designed to help you understand all the ingredients of your own style (and the styles of those you work with), bring them together into a coherent whole, and develop strategies for using all this information to improve your performance and increase your satisfaction as a manager.

What's Coming Up

Before we take up each of the six elements of management style in detail, the chapters in Part One will discuss four general, overarching topics that explore how those elements interact and give us an overall model for changing them. Chapter One revisits the six elements in more depth in order to explore which of them can—and cannot—be changed. Chapter Two takes up the most fundamental of the six elements—psychological type—in order to help you gain a fuller and more realistic picture of each one. An understanding of the characteristics of each psychological type is essential to the rest of our discussions of management style. (If you take the Myers-Briggs Type Indicator before you read this chapter, it will have more value for you.) Chapter Three examines practical intelligence, that crucial combination of conceptual, interpersonal, and influence skills that are essential to effective management. Practical intelligence is in effect the "oil" in the management motor, lubricating all the other elements and making sure that the engine is running smoothly. Part One ends with Chapter Four, which explores the assumptions, perceptions, and feelings that drive our behavior as managers and presents a method for changing our mindset as the first step in altering behavior that does not serve us—and our coworkers and bosses—effectively.

Building on the model for change developed in Part One, Part Two devotes a chapter to each of the individual management style factors: needs, power bases, problem solving and conflict management, values, and stress. The chapters are designed to help you assess where you stand in relation to each element and to offer guidance for developing your ability to function effectively within it. The final chapter helps you put together a matrix of all the elements of your personal management style and uses case examples to show how other managers have used the Integrated Management Style Model not only to do their jobs better but to experience more satisfaction and harmony in their work and personal lives.

PART ONE

A MODEL FOR CHANGE

CHAPTER ONE

THE DYNAMICS OF MANAGEMENT STYLE: WHAT CAN BE CHANGED?

Charlie Ott liked knowing that he had acquired a reputation as one of the most benevolent yet productive department managers at Burch, O'Brien & Powell, a direct marketing and advertising firm where he had worked for more than eight years. Over time, most of his subordinates had tolerated his command-and-control style because he treated them well, protecting them from outside intrusions and what they all liked to think of as "meddling" by other departments. He had recently been promoted to a new position where he was put in charge of three big accounts, with two middle managers (responsible for a number of teams) and a secretary reporting directly to him. He was supposed to be more hands-off than he had been in the past but monitor the progress of a variety of projects and activities as the teams worked to complete them. Because BO&P had recently committed to a flat matrix structure for the organization, Charlie's authority was limited to budgeting, scheduling, and overall workflow; teams and their leaders were responsible for giving him progress reports and meeting with him periodically to keep him informed on how they were doing.

But Charlie was frustrated. He liked knowing specifically what was going on, liked getting involved and giving advice. He was not all that comfortable trusting his managers (one of whom had just joined BO&P) to make sure the projects went well. He felt anxious about things slipping through the cracks, although so far not too many problems had cropped up. Charlie heard from his boss that both team leaders and his direct reports were complaining about him going around them to get more information about what the teams were doing and even trying to change their plans midstream. But as crucial deadlines neared on several of the projects, Charlie told his boss, "Look, Dave, you know I always deliver. I pride myself on that. I like this new team approach, but I still think I need to be more involved. And I'm not always so sure that these teams—and even my managers—are as on top of things as they should be."

"I know, Charlie, I know," Dave answered. "You have always done a great job. But I promoted you into this new position not so you could keep tracking details but because I thought you could really watch the big picture and motivate and train these talented young managers. People are feeling undermined and morale is kind of shaky—and that's not good given that we're right on top of these deadlines. I want you to lay off, pay attention to budgets and schedules, and let these guys do their jobs. I've seen the progress reports; they're on track and they're really creative. So just relax, OK?" As he said this, Dave could see Charlie's face was full of doubt and frustration. He didn't seem to be listening. Had he made a mistake in promoting Charlie?

Is Charlie just in the wrong job? Is he failing as a manager? Should he be put into a more hands-on position? Or is there a chance that with the right guidance he could change his approach to his new position—and even to management? The answer is not simple. The scenario in which Charlie and Dave find themselves is common. A management style that may have been effective at one level or setting does not work as well when someone moves into a new position, where the demands and structure are different. The key question is not just about a mismatch between person and position but about a perennial debate regarding human nature. Does the root of such problems lie in personality, which may be unchangeable, or in other factors that might be more amenable to change? For managers, the answer is crucial. As we discussed in the Introduction, some aspects of management style are innate, while others are learned behavior. Innate qualities such as personality type are more fixed but not entirely resistant to change, while learned aspects, with the right kind of targeted effort, can be modified.

In the midst of their frustration and conflict, Charlie Ott and his boss do not have the objectivity to see clearly what parts of his behavior Charlie can reasonably change and what he cannot. Charlie especially seems to have lost the ability to stand back and assess his situation and understand what factors affect the way he operates, including his ability to change. He may try to tinker with his management style, but when he finds that his attempts to do better fail to produce the results he wants, he will feel even more frustrated and out of control. This leads to increased and prolonged stress, with its attendant unhealthy effects. Without a more conscious, structured approach to change, Charlie is in a no-win situation.

In this chapter, we examine a central aspect of working with management style: understanding which of the six factors can be changed and how such change can be accomplished. This is the first step in gaining the objectivity to avoid situations like Charlie Ott's. Use the Integrated Management Style Model to begin to develop a more conscious and flexible management style.

Our Assumptions About What We Can Change

Our current beliefs about what we can and cannot change in ourselves did not materialize on their own in the twentieth century. They are the product of a long series of debates about human nature and character throughout history that have ranged from the idea that all is determined from birth, to all can be modified with the right methods. Those who have defended the idea that nature is the great determining force in our lives have used everything from theology to animal research to support their position. An equally potent school of thought maintains that our actions and choices determine our fates. Science has shown that we can manipulate nature to some degree and that we are not entirely bound by natural constraints. Most of the self-help movement that is flourishing today is based on the assumption that we can use our free will to change our predicaments, from alcoholism to weight loss to self-empowerment to response to stress.

Yet thinkers have emphasized the importance of learning in behavior, the idea that we can modify our behavior with the right application of external reinforcement and punishment. That model (known as behaviorism) tends to minimize the importance of internal factors in learning thought and our ability to reinforce our actions and attitudes ourselves. For managers who want to be more aware of their management style and alter it to make themselves more effective, learning is the key. Understanding how to promote learning—and where and how it will be most effective—is the focus of the rest of this chapter.

What—or Who—Are the Agents of Change?

In a sense, all styles of behavior, including management styles, stem from a combination of personality, past experience, and attitude. Our reactions to problematic situations and individuals are based on the sort of people we are—whether we are extroverts or introverts, for example, or whether we meet conflict head-on or shrink away from it. Some of us almost instinctively make the right moves, but most of us do not. Nevertheless, we can all learn how to alter aspects of our management style in order to become more effective in dealing with bosses, peers, and subordinates.

The question of *how* such change can take place still remains. Can a person, by his or her own insight and actions, change circumstances or is a prompt from the outside necessary to instigate the change? In his book *What You Can Change and What You Can't,* Martin Seligman describes two opposing views: those of the "booters" versus the "bootstrappers." The "booters" believe that change can only result when an external force or agent acts upon an individual. The psychotherapist, using the tricks of the trade, gently moves the client to insight and change. The behaviorist manipulates reinforcements and shapes the individual's actions. The "bootstrappers," in contrast, believe explicitly that the change agent is the self: we lift ourselves up by our bootstraps. Essential to the bootstrappers is the concept of the "maximal self," where we have ultimate control of our lives, versus the "minimal self," where we are controlled by our nature and fate and thus need external help to make changes.

As Seligman points out, self-improvement bootstrapper techniques do work. As we drive ourselves to change, we are more fulfilled. However, there are limits. The truth about change lies somewhere between the total plasticity of bootstrappers and the total passivity of booters. There are things that we can change and things that we cannot just as there are ways of coping with situations that help us to control ourselves. It is hard to disagree with Seligman's assertion that "much of successful living consists of learning to make the best of a bad situation."

Applying Seligman's approach to management style and organizational culture, the things we *can't* change include:

- Our boss or our subordinates if they do not want to
- The course of the national economy (unless you are head of the Federal Reserve Bank)
- The macro environment of our organization—not even CEOs can do that
- Our own deep-rooted dispositions (more on this in Chapter Two)

But we *can* change:

- The coping mechanisms we use to deal with uncertainty, to manage stress and difficult people, and to control our own negative thoughts
- Skills and behaviors such as decision making, planning, and problem solving that help us function more effectively
- Our level of optimism, which has to do with our convictions that we can change our lives for the better, including the ability to dispute negative thoughts about ourselves and others
- Five of the six building blocks of management style we discussed in the Introduction (needs, conflict and problem solving, use of power, personal values, and approach to handling stress)

The sixth building block—personality type—cannot be changed, but we can work with it to enhance our strengths and lessen the effects of our weaknesses.

Change and the Building Blocks of Management Style

The six factors that make up management style encompass a wide range of behaviors and propensities and profoundly affect all sorts of interactions. The six include:

- Psychological type (how we perceive and judge the world around us)
- Need patterns (what drives us and how we gain a sense of personal satisfaction and competence)
- Power bases (how we influence others)
- Style of handling conflict and solving problems
- Personal values and their effect on organizational behavior
- Methods of handling stress

These six elements have been known and studied for a long time, but too often separately from one another. In this book, the goal is integration of the elements: identifying and looking at our own configurations in order to understand and determine whether we might want to rearrange them to create a different management style. That is the reason we call the model the Integrated Management Style Model. Whether we *can* reconfigure depends upon the extent to which a given building block can be reshaped. We have to consider the factors that most affect the probability for successful change. Let's look at each of the six now in more depth and examine whether and how they can be changed.

Psychological Type: Innate Temperament and Preferences

The four main psychological types we will use here are drawn from the Myers-Briggs Type Indicators (MBTI), a popular personality test that came into use after World War II and that is based on Carl Jung's psychological theories. The psychological types are useful in drawing a map of a person's temperament or attitudes but are not necessarily definitive; that is why they are only one element in assessing management style. Taking the MBTI and finding out your type is a highly useful way to begin thinking productively about management style because it helps you understand your preferences and innate tendencies.

There are four aspects of psychological types:

1. **Extroversion versus introversion.** This dimension indicates how we use our psychic energy. Extroverted people are oriented to the objective, outer world and to people, things, events, and institutions. Introverted people are oriented away from the outer world toward a subjective, internal awareness.
2. **Sensing versus intuition.** This dimension indicates how we perceive the world around us and our environment. Sensing people focus on details, facts, and data derived from the five senses. Intuitive people focus on possibilities and the big picture, go beyond the facts, and use their "sixth sense."
3. **Thinking versus feeling.** This aspect describes how we judge situations. Thinking types use impersonal, logical, and analytical approaches to judge situations. Feeling types base their judgments on individual value systems and focus on the personal impact of their judgments on others and on themselves.
4. **Perception versus judgment.** This aspect indicates whether we use sensing versus intuition (the perceptive function) or thinking versus feeling (the judgment function) to deal with the outside world.

Psychological type is more nature than nurture. Parents often observe that their children seem to be born with distinctive temperaments that do not change much over their lives, and recent research indicates that patterns of shyness and assertiveness emerge at an early age. Similarly, the research on the sensing versus intuitive function reveals underlying physiological differences between them. For example, brain scans of the intuitives show more interaction between the hemispheres, while scans of sensing types demonstrate fewer such crossovers.

Once we realize that psychological type is innate and strongly established early on in life, it is clear that changing behavior that stems from it must be approached with an appreciation for what can and cannot be modified. Whether you are trying to change some aspect of type in yourself or in someone you manage, that attempt could be stressful. It is more realistic and effective to avoid attempts at major, long-term change and to focus instead on encouraging adjustments that are designed to respond to particular situations. For example, if you are an introvert who is uncomfortable in public speaking roles, you can take a course in public speaking and improve those skills. If you are an intuitive, you can learn to deal with details and time management in a specific job setting. Neither one will change your underlying natural stance; you may adapt and bend for short periods of time or in specific situations, but your fundamental nature will stay the same. Just as a parent who tries to help a shy, introverted child to become extroverted may be thwarting a natural pattern of behavior, with possibly disastrous consequences, bosses who demand conformity to their preferences create stress for their subordinates.

For managers and leaders, the rational and humane approach is to understand and accept the reality of different psychological types. Conflicts that emerge from a clash between psychological types can be turned into a positive force if managers understand how to balance roles and responsibilities to play to everyone's strengths. In Charlie Ott's case, for example, he is probably an introverted-sensing-thinking-judging type. He likes to get information in the form of data, would rather work things out on his own rather than in groups, and is more analytical in overall approach. That explains, at least in part, why he has a difficult time when he must rely on teams and his managers to get things done, especially if they have a different and (at least from his point of view) less detailed approach to their work. The concept of psychological types not only explains why people behave in different ways but also explains why it is so difficult to change basic behaviors.

Although we cannot permanently change our psychological type, we can train ourselves to modify it temporarily when circumstance dictates flexibility. An introverted thinker like Charlie, for example, can develop different ways of satisfying his need for detailed data and analysis that do not put extra burdens on his subordinates and their staffs. And Dave could work with Charlie to help him keep the big picture in mind, knowing that this is not the strong suit for Charlie's type.

Needs: The Drivers of Behavior

The concept of need implies that we are missing something—either we lack something we seek or have something we wish to keep. We all have physical needs such as air, water, food, and safety, but we also have social needs for companionship, intimacy, boundaries, our own turf, and the sense of being part of a group. We differ in our individual configurations of needs, but they are an important part of our identity and our personalities. At work, for example, people vary in their need for autonomy—the desire to be independent and to be left alone. Some people need a high degree of autonomy, while others would rather work in association with others, with more supervision. Understanding how needs affect our own behavior (and that of everyone around us) is often the first step to understanding perplexing behavior patterns and to harnessing those needs toward constructive outcomes. If, for example, you know your boss has a high need for autonomy, you can let him or her choose the time of your meetings and avoid creating interruptions or asking for too much direction.

Although psychologists have described as many as forty different needs that determine personal satisfaction and competence, this book will focus (in Chapter Five) on those that most affect the way we manage people and tasks. Needs can affect other management style factors, even psychological type, because they can intensify or diminish the effects of our preferences. Thinking, for example, can be softened by a need for nurturance or introspection or can be sharpened and heightened if combined with a high need for aggression.

Though needs are to some degree innate, they are not fixed. When they threaten to overwhelm our behavior, they can and should be changed. Strengths, for example, can become weaknesses if they are overplayed. A person with a high need for achievement and dominance who tries to control the task in a small problem solving group can save everyone a lot of grief by learning how to mediate those needs. When we become aware of our patterns of needs and understand their interaction with other aspects of management style, we can set the stage to manage and mediate them.

The Bases of Power: The Uses and Abuses of Influence

Power—the ability to influence the beliefs, emotions, and behaviors of other people—informs every relationship and all actions in every organization in one way or another. It is a key ingredient of a manager's sense of self-esteem, as well as to the healthy functioning of the entire organization. When we think of power, we often think of the chain of command—who gets to tell other people what to do. But even peers in an organization try to influence one another, just as subordinates try to influence their bosses by, for example, demonstrating their technical expertise in urging their solution to a particular problem.

Some people seem to have an unerring instinct for using power effectively (and positively), but it is not entirely clear why they are so skillful in influencing others. Other people use power in negative ways to manipulate, misinform, and subvert. They seem to believe that others are to be used like fuel in the furnace of power or cleared away like worn out gears for more efficient replacements. Others seem largely oblivious to how they are using power or deny its importance. Still others believe that power poisons and thereby shun its use. They may use power on a subconscious level, but probably in an ineffective way. Our use of power depends on our assumptions, perceptions, and feelings about it, which themselves are shaped by our values, culture, and experiences. The most effective managers recognize the reality of power—both its uses and abuses—and try to build a repertoire of skills such as influencing people.

In a sense, power is neutral until it is used. In a lopsided power relationship, one person wields power while the other receives it. If the one who receives it feels that he or she is being exploited, manipulated, or controlled, it will be a negative experience. However, if both people feel that they are sharing in the interaction, they will see the act of using power as positive. Both positive and negative power operate out of our instinctive need for dominance, out of our desire to control our lives and situations.

There are a number of kinds of power, which we will examine in detail in Chapter Six; they are based in a variety of factors such as access to information or even good old-fashioned coercion. Classifying power in these ways makes it easier to identify and understand its bases and to develop new skills in using different forms of influence.

The use of power is based on the requirements of the job. Someone with a set of command and control needs, like Charlie Ott, is likely to impose his authority on subordinates and peers. But clearly, in Charlie's case, this was inappropriate. He would have been better off exerting his influence through his considerable expertise and the valuable information he could share with his managers and their teams. Our instinctive use of power, based on psychological type and needs, may not work. By knowing our psychological type and understanding our needs and the way our preferences for using power interact with the other building blocks of management style, we can identify pitfalls and shape the kinds of power we use as managers.

Conflict Styles: Getting to Resolution

Conflict, like power, is an unavoidable part of work and management. While we all are born with a built-in "fight-or-flight" response to conflict, neither of those reactions is effective in the workplace. Most of us have learned to mediate that inherent response in some way (not always productively) during our upbringing. Some families, for example, may handle disputes with a free-for-all, where everyone tries to browbeat each other into submission. Others may discourage any open discussion of disagreement altogether. Some cultures may foster discussion and consensus-seeking as ways to resolve conflicts while others reach for their weapons (or lawsuits) as a way of settling disagreements. In any case, most people's experience has taught them to try to avoid or dominate conflict—neither of which is helpful in finding resolutions. In the majority of situations we tend to react on the spot (usually not very effectively) rather than anticipating problems and conflicts and dealing with them proactively.

Our use of problem solving and conflict resolution strategies as managers can be changed by modifying our assumptions and making shifts in our thinking and our actions. Unlike psychological type and, to a lesser extent, needs patterns, problem solving and conflict resolution are two of the most malleable management style factors. In particular, conflict resolution has a set of prescribed rules and procedures (which we will talk about in Chapter Seven) that can structure the process and lead to a wise solution rather than to a watered-down compromise, destructive win/lose tactics, or even worse, problem and/or conflict avoidance.

Values: Clarifying Ideals and Beliefs

Values are a mixture of how we feel and what we believe based on our assumptions about life. Explicitly or implicitly we value things, people, events, and ideas as good or bad, pleasant or unpleasant, beautiful or ugly, appropriate or inappropriate, true or false, virtuous or immoral. We learn values through some kind of experience of pain or pleasure, deprivation or gratification, goal attainment or frustration or failure, social approval or disapproval, love or hate. Even very short-term experiences may influence our values concerning both people and ideas.

The same processes that create our personal values as individuals also contribute to the values we hold as managers or as organizations. Among the ways in which values and beliefs can be created and changed, the following are noteworthy:

1. **Creation of values.** A new standard or belief is developed out of experience and becomes effective, at some level, in regulating behavior. For much of this century, the old command and control style of management was thought to be best, but recent management thinking explored more lateral, less hierarchical self-managing teams and organizational structures. As our old assumptions came into question, new practices affected our values, just as our values were affecting those practices.
2. **Erosion of values.** When there is a slow change in assumptions, perceptions, and feelings, fewer and fewer people promote, support, teach, or defend a specific value. For example, there has been a long-standing belief in male superiority. As women assume positions of power in organizations, this old belief is challenged. The old value erodes and is replaced by one that more accurately reflects reality.
3. **Application and extension of values to additional groups of people.** In the old hierarchical system of organizations, a few people located at the top of the pyramid made all the decisions for everyone else. The new organization values diversity and input from all levels. This shift of privilege extends decision making to previously disenfranchised groups.
4. **Values clarification.** Values become more complex and change as individuals and organizations attempt to integrate and rationalize them. For example, in many organizations freedom and equality co-exist in an uneasy

tension. Carrying individual freedom too far may clash with the values of fairness and equality. Too much emphasis on equality erodes individual freedom. Unless this basic paradox is recognized and dealt with, both individuals and the organizational culture will oscillate between emphasizing one value without regard for the impact of the other. Clarification puts the two values into context with each other.

The task at hand for managers is to scrutinize and clarify their values so that they form a coherent pattern that fits the needs and orientation of the organization and society as a whole.

Unlike the more innate factors that influence management style, values are learned and determined by culture, social institutions such as family, school, and religion, and personal experience. Our individual and collective sense of our ideals, what we think is worthwhile and important, and how we are willing to act on those beliefs are not immutable, but they must be respected as the result of a powerful combination of societal demands and personal needs. If a company says that it values both responsibility and individual development, for example, that dovetails well with general United States cultural values about individual initiative and freedom. Those same values, however, would not be expressed in the same way or to the same extent in a traditional Japanese firm that emphasizes group effort and harmony.

We explore values in this book because managers must be able to define and clarify their personal value structures and modify them as desired. In particular, managers in a free market, democratic society must be concerned with some fundamental values: fairness (creating a level playing field), integrity (knowing right from wrong), and honesty (building future trust).

Stress: Responding to Pressure

The pressures within our occupations, impending corporate mergers, globalization, the volatility of the stock market, downsizing, and a multitude of concerns about ourselves, our families, and our lives are all stressors. Although our reactions to stress may be based in the primordial "fight-or-flight" response, we modify it through our life experiences. Some of us are particularly likely to become stressed, while others apparently live stress-free lives. Some managers, for example, might see the pressure of meeting deadlines as a positive challenge and develop priorities that help them guide the workload, while others might perceive deadlines as a threat and react with harried, hostile, and aggressive behavior. To understand stress, then, we have to learn how to account for the role of individual differences in responding to both internal and external stressors. All of us can reduce our stress levels by changing dysfunctional reactions into positive coping mechanisms.

The most common stressors—dealing with difficult people (such as a boss or subordinate), work overload, time pressure, fear of failure, anxiety, and so on—are all amenable to psychological intervention, as we will see in Chapter Nine. We may not be able to change a looming deadline or eliminate a boss who is difficult to work with, but we can learn to be more aware of our habitual responses and use that consciousness to change our mindset about the stressors in our lives. Being able to do so is crucial not only for developing a more effective management style but also for enjoying a better quality of life.

Conclusion

Although the six building blocks of management style do not cover every aspect of management behavior, they do account for the most significant and useful components and variations. Considered individually, they shed light on key areas of management, but the way they fit together is essential. It would be useless for someone like Charlie Ott to look at his psychological type without also being aware of the needs that drive him most strongly, the deficits he may have in problem solving and conflict resolution, his use of power, and the other factors of management style.

When it comes to changing management style, it is usually a matter of learning or enhancing skills based on acquired knowledge and desired behaviors. Fundamental, innate factors such as personality type need not overwhelm behavior. It is in fact the only element of the six that is considered to have such a dramatic effect on managerial performance. Using proven techniques for changing our minds and our behavior, we can learn to moderate our needs and values, our methods of solving conflicts and problems, the ways we find and use power, and the ways we handle stressful situations. Because we can change our minds and our thinking and master the skills that will change our behavior, we can find greater satisfaction in every area of our lives.

CHAPTER TWO

PERSONALITY AND PSYCHOLOGY: WHAT'S YOUR TYPE?

Since the Myers-Briggs Type Indicator, or MBTI, was introduced to the business world in the 1980s, it has become one of the most used assessment instruments in organizational development. The concepts behind the MBTI, based on Carl Jung's theory of psychological type, are useful in understanding management style, team building, conflict resolution, and career choices.

The MBTI's enormous appeal stems in part from its simplicity. Its hundred-plus questions assess personality with incredible success. Like a miracle diet or a quick fix to save a marriage, the MBTI has lured some enthusiasts into expecting it to cure complex problems that it cannot. But it nevertheless remains a valuable tool if its complexities—and limitations—are understood. Psychological-type theory has an essential role to play in understanding management style, in career counseling, and in handling conflicts in organizations, but it must be put in perspective. Anomalies and inconsistencies arise when the test becomes the sole source of information. Carl Jung saw psychological types as templates or patterns of general personality features, not as true representatives of complex individual psychologies.

Jung's now-classic treatise *Psychological Types* is the backbone of the MBTI. After World War II, mother and daughter Katherine Briggs and Isabel Briggs Myers designed the MBTI and made available for the first time a reliable and valid instrument for determining psychological type. The MBTI appealed to both the imagination and the pragmatism of training and personnel development staff in a wide variety of businesses and institutions. Moreover, because the psychological types described in the MBTI applied to everyone, they were not seen as manifestations of pathology. Instead, under the value-free descriptions and rules of the types, everyone came out a winner. The discovery of one's type—the "a-ha!" experience—was positive and enlightening. Type theory, when not abused by overzealous converts, became a way that healthy people could learn something valuable about themselves. It is also central to understanding and creating a more effective management style.

What Psychological Types Really Measure

The psychological type theory measures four attributes of personality:

1. Our attitudes and orientation: inward versus outward
2. Our perception function (how we perceive the world): sensing versus intuiting
3. Our judgment function (how we judge the world): thinking versus feeling
4. Which function we use in dealing with our outer world: perception versus judgment

These four attributes do not, of course, constitute the whole of a person—or a management style. The Integrated Management Style Model, as we have already seen, is designed to look at other critical aspects that cannot be predicted by psychological type. The thorough overview of the concepts behind the MBTI and the specific types in this chapter is designed to clarify its possibilities (and limits) as a part of developing and integrating the different aspects of management style.

Attitudes and Orientation: Extroverts and Introverts

Jung used the term "attitude" to refer to the ways that individuals direct their psychic energies. In the *extroverted attitude* (designated as "E" in the MBTI), conscious energy flows outward from the person toward people, things, or events in the external world. As Jung said, the extrovert's "entire consciousness looks outwards to the world, because the important and decisive determination always comes . . . from without. And it comes to him from without only because that is where he expects it." In the *introverted attitude,* in contrast, energy is directed inward, away from objects and toward a subjective, internal awareness. Jung described the introverted person as feeling so constantly overwhelmed by the objective world that he or she retreats toward inner subjective truths. Naturally, introverts are aware of external conditions, but they use their subjective impressions as the deciding factors. Introverts turn inward, away from external objects, which are of secondary importance, toward their own inner world.

It is interesting to note that Jung was introverted and that he had a particular affinity for the plight of other introverts, who are statistically outnumbered by extroverts. He believed that the preponderance of the extroverted attitude has at times had a negative influence on history. "We must not forget—although extroverted opinion is only too prone to do so—that all perception and cognition is not purely objective," he wrote. "The world exists not merely in itself but also as it appears" to the individual.

Jung believed that introversion and extroversion are innate, inherited attitudes that unfold regardless of environmental influences and that we ignore the existence of these attitudes at our peril. He insisted that the attitudes exist in all of us, like an affinity for left- or right-handedness. Moreover, he pointed out, it is impossible to be an introvert and an extrovert at the same time. Even if we deliberately shift our focus, we still maintain a preferred attitude. Any attempt to convert an introvert into an extrovert, for example, would cause a distortion of that person's nature that could result in abnormal, maladaptive behavior. In other words, we must accept our basic attitude, as well as those of others.

Jung also proposed that although we cannot change our attitude, we can develop or make use of its opposite if we accept both our predominant attitude and its opposite. Healthy integration lies in knowing who we are and how to synthesize the less-differentiated aspects of our personalities. Most conflicts in organizations arise out of the difference between the detail-oriented (sensing) and the big-picture (intuitive) people. The detailed-oriented people are weak in grasping the big picture, while the intuitives seem entirely too casual about details. Each type needs to understand their own preferences, know when the opposite attitude is required, and shift accordingly.

The Functions: Judging and Perceiving

Jung used the word "function" to designate specific forms of psychic activity and behavior that are consistent regardless of circumstances. According to Jung, the human personality contains four functions:

- The *rational functions*, used for purposes of judging and evaluating situations, people, and events, are either thinking (represented as "T") or feeling ("F"). Thinking uses principled reasoning, logic, and impersonal analysis employing criteria for evaluating the reasonableness, quality, and validity of data. In contrast, feeling uses empathy for another person or personal values to make a judgment; a feeling person calculates subjectively whether a judgment is important or unimportant, valuable or useless.

- The *irrational functions,* used for purposes of perception are sensing ("S") and intuition ("N"). These functions simply receive and process information without evaluating or judging it. Sensation is sense perception, or perception mediated by the bodily senses, that focus on concrete, tangible realities in the present. Sensing types of people distrust ideas that cannot be supported by the facts. Intuition relies on perception through the unconscious mind. An intuitive individual can arrive at a perception or a judgment without being aware of the concrete basis for it. Intuitive types of people can make leaps from the past or the present to future possibilities, and they can perceive complex connections among various phenomena, whereas sensing people prefer to work through the details to reach their conclusions.

To understand the operation of the functions, it is necessary to see them as polarities. Sensing is the opposite of intuition, and thinking is the opposite of feeling. Because they are opposites, not part of a continuum, thinking and feeling cannot operate simultaneously. Nor can sensing work simultaneously with intuition. Underlying Jung's theory is the supposition that everything that exists eventually changes into its opposite. Youth becomes old age, decay follows creation, winter follows spring. The same is true in the human psyche. Even as one function dominates our conscious life, its equally strong opposite function develops in our unconscious. Only one function occupies the stage at any given time, while the opposite function waits in the wings. If the opposite function never has an opportunity to play out its role, it may burst onstage, following a cue from our unconscious. In organizations there is usually a preponderance of thinking (T) versus feeling (F) types. Most of the time, the feeling function is suppressed. Under stress, the value-laden feeling function can erupt during a heated meeting. For example, suppose that several people are attending a meeting to discuss the company's position on day care. One of the members (a thinking type) has strong family-oriented values that are apparent only to people close to him. When the group decides against company-provided day care, he blows up and spends fifteen minutes on a diatribe against what he sees as the unfeeling decision. The decision violated his latent feeling values so that his personality erupted in a way that shocked his colleagues, who saw him as an analytical—not emotional—individual.

Because perception and judgment are independent and polar functions, there are four possible combinations of them: sensation and thinking (ST), sensation and feeling (SF), intuition and thinking (NT), and intuition and feeling (NF). Each of these four combinations has distinctive characteristics. When joined together with either the extroverted or the introverted attitude, they in turn produce eight possible combinations. The extroverted types are EST, ESF, ENT, and ENF, and the introverted types are IST, ISF, INT, and INF. Myers and Briggs expanded these original eight types to sixteen by adding an "orientation" variable to indicate which kind of function (perceiving or judging) a person used most often in dealing with the outer world. A judging (J) orientation means that the person uses either thinking or feeling in conscious interaction with the external world. A perceiving (P) orientation means that the person uses either sensing or intuition in these interactions. Thus, the sixteen MBTI personality types include those whose judging function (be it thinking or feeling) is dominant (ESTJ, ENTJ, ESFJ, ENFJ, INTP, INFP, ISTP, and ISFP) and those whose perceiving function (be it sensing or intuition) is dominant (ENTP, ENFP, ESTP, ESFP, ISTJ, INTJ, ISFJ, and INFJ). Readers who are unfamiliar with the MBTI will want to consult the "Assessment of Psychological Type" test in Appendix B to see which personality type best describes them.

In our psychological development, one of the functions (judging or perceiving) becomes dominant, while the other (what Jung called the "inferior function") recedes into our unconscious. It does not disappear, but can and will break through, often at inappropriate times. As we grow up, we identify with our dominant (and favored) function. For example, if we have feeling as our dominant function, thinking becomes the least preferred. In context of business, the feeling executive would be overly concerned for the welfare of the people and the fairness of decisions based on values. The feeling manager would, most likely, be in favor of ethics training and clearer definitions of organizational values. That person might see thinking as backward, cold, hard, and impersonal.

Our dominant function and inferior functions are opposites, but we also have two other functions (which Jung called "auxiliary") that complement the dominant function. For example, if the dominant function is sensing, then the auxiliary function will be either thinking or feeling. Intuition will be the inferior function. The two most prevalent combinations of functions in organizations are sensing plus thinking (ST) and intuition plus thinking (NT). In either of the combinations one is dominant and the other complementary. Sensing can lead or back up thinking as can intuition. The problem-solving styles are a result of the synergistic interplay between the complementary functions. The ST problem solvers seek out and evaluate details, while the NTs search for concepts to evaluate.

Using Psychological Type to Understand Each Other

How one uses psychic energy, whether as an extrovert or an introvert, is important, because each attitude uses the dominant function differently. The extrovert projects the dominant function onto the external world, while the introvert uses it in his or her subjective internal world. We are more likely to see a dominant function in action when dealing with an extrovert, while with introverts we are more likely to see their auxiliary function. For example, suppose we have Jason, an extrovert, who focuses on facts and concrete detail and talks about them constantly; it is fairly easy to see that his dominant function is sensing (S). His coworker Leslie is an introvert; when she voices her opinion it involves the same level of detail as Jason's opinions. But in this case Leslie's auxiliary function, sensing (S), is not dominant. She uses her dominant function internally, and we rarely see it. Because their dominant or favored function is submerged, introverts are hard to fathom. If Leslie's dominant function was feeling (F), we could easily violate her hidden set of values without realizing it. An interesting point is that among close friends, family, and trusted colleagues, introverts reveal themselves and act like extroverts. But in unfamiliar territory they retreat into their introverted attitude.

Knowing another's dominant function is the key to understanding and influencing that individual. For example, a manager seeking constructive criticism on a written report is likely to receive the most objective and rigorous evaluation from a person whose dominant function is thinking. By the same token, a thinking type person who needs to counterbalance the effects of a calculated decision would be wise to seek the empathetic perspective of a feeling type person. Managers who lack knowledge of psychological types commonly impose their dominant functions on colleagues and subordinates, with rejection and conflict as frequent results. The flowery, vague ideas and plans of an intuitive type of person are not likely to impress a sensing type, no matter how exciting those plans are. The constant attention to detail and data can squash an intuitive's creativity— or at least lead to frustration and lack of cooperation.

Using the Sixteen MBTI Types in Management

By now, it should be obvious that any proactive strategy requires that a manager know his or her own psychological type and dominant function. That information allows us to accept our strengths and gifts and work on integrating the less-developed parts of our psyche. We can see how we fit into our respective environments and move toward more harmonious relationships. Jung considered this recognition and commitment to be the essence of self-development.

Knowledge of psychological types also helps us come to terms with people whose styles are different from our own. Once we recognize and accept our own attitudes, functions, strengths, and pitfalls, we can understand why we always seem to be in conflict with a particular colleague or why our boss never appreciates certain aspects of our work. We can accept the quirks and foibles of people that we once barely tolerated. As we strive toward greater balance within ourselves, we can appreciate that others are also engaged in the same task.

For a manager, the next step after recognizing others' differences is to work toward integrating people of varying psychological types in such a way as to take best advantage of their individual strengths. Skillfully done, this can create a dynamic synergy among psychological types. Building this team synergy and observing it in operation is one of the most exciting aspects of organizational development. In the rest of this chapter, we will delve more deeply into the management implications of the sixteen MBTI types.

Extroverted Thinking Types: ESTJ and ENTJ

Both of these extroverted types judge their environments through thinking, their dominant function. They draw their conclusions from objective external information. The external world is their reality, and they demand that everyone conform to their view of it. Extroverted thinkers interpret their environment through logic and careful organization. Their analytical approach to problem solving sometimes seems impersonal and cold, but in emergencies their decisiveness is welcome. When a decision must be put on the table, they willingly supply one.

Because these types' dominant function is thinking, feeling is their inferior side, which often causes trouble both for themselves and others. When the inferior feeling side remains ignored and unconscious, it can explode. As Marie Von Franz, one of Jung's closest colleagues, wrote, "The extroverted thinking type has . . . a kind of mystical feeling attachment for ideals and often for people. But this deep, strong, warm feeling hardly ever comes out."

ESTJ: Sensing and Thinking. ESTJs use introverted sensing as their auxiliary function. They observe the world through their five senses, but they must apply the orderliness of thinking to their impressions before they have meaning. Because their sensing function is introverted, it primarily serves their extroverted thinking function, giving them a matter-of-fact approach to problems. In optimal circumstances extroverted thinkers are principled, idealistic, dedicated, and rational. In a maladaptive mode, they are dogmatic, single-minded, intolerant, reclusive, and cold. If their perception, sensing or intuition, functions are underdeveloped, ESTJs may leap to premature decisions before they have gathered and digested data. This is a major problem for extroverted judging types. Strongly developed ESTJs generally distrust intuition and feeling. There are no mystics among ESTJs. (See Table 2.1.)

TABLE 2.1   ESTJs AT A GLANCE

Strengths	Under Stress	Areas to Develop
In touch with the external environment	Become rigid or dogmatic	More appreciation for impacts
Good at organizing and carrying out standard procedures	Become intrusive, "know-it-all" experts	A more balanced approach to judgment so they can evaluate information carefully without making hasty decisions
Able to evaluate others but can be abrupt	Tend to be poor listeners	
Loyal to organizations	Become obsessive with details	Express their inner feelings and frustrations
Dutiful and faithful to mates, colleagues, and bosses		More appreciation for the big picture

ENTJ: Intuition and Thinking. ENTJs use introverted intuition to guide their inner lives. With them, vision and a sense of possibilities enter the picture. The ENTJ's dominant judgment function is based upon grasping the meaning of facts and things, and their unique associations. An ENTJ would be at home with an ESTJ in offering opinions, but the two would violently disagree about whether their opinions were based on fact or fiction. ENTJs have been called natural "commandant" types who insist on ruling by their particular vision. In organizations, they are the ones who look to the future and conceive new ventures. If their sensing function is not brought into play, however, their formulations may be nothing but pure fantasy. Successful ENTJs are able to balance their visions with relevant facts. (See Table 2.2.)

Extroverted Feeling Types: ESFJ and ENFJ

Extroverted feeling types are in tune with their environment, especially with other people. They use their judging function—feeling—to evaluate each situation according to an individualized set of values. Instead of principled reasoning, the criterion behind their values is whether something has relative status or personal worth for them according to their individual values. Cold logic is not part of the picture. There are many do's and don'ts in their life scripts, and what is right and what is wrong is their mantra. Extroverted feelers are excellent at sizing up or creating an atmosphere, for example, in social situations such as weddings. Because thinking is the function most likely to disturb feeling, they suppress it.

TABLE 2.2　ENTJs AT A GLANCE

Strengths	Under Stress	Areas to Develop
Depend on logical, empirical, objective reasoning	Become distant and critical	Control domineering attitude
Intolerant of inefficiency	Ignore the feelings or wishes of others	Develop appreciation for others' ideas
Good at strategic planning and developing vision for the organization	Dogmatically take charge	Factor in the needs of others in making decisions
Good at taking charge of projects	Become abrasive and aggressive	Pay attention to details and specifics before acting
Supporters of organizations they believe in		

They make friends easily and vent their feelings often. But their feelings and statements are not always appropriate. Anyone who exclaims on a dreary, rainy Monday, "Oh, what a beautiful day!" is overdoing it.

ESFJ: Sensing and Feeling. Because introverted thinking is their inferior function, extroverted feeling types have no patience with philosophical ramblings, and they back away from conversations that require careful analysis. If suppressed too much, the inferior thinking function can erupt in a volley of negative criticism, some of which is apt to be illogical or crude. When that happens, the individual is overpowered by the inferior function. But when extroverted feeling types try to integrate their inferior thinking function, they sometimes overdo it and become dogmatic and conventional. Inexperienced in critical analysis, they embrace a new idea without reservation, swallowing it whole.

Good judges of people and situations, ESFJs keep in tune with their environment by using sensing as their auxiliary function. They are service-oriented and can be extremely self-sacrificing. Because their sensing function is introverted, their keen awareness comes from internally scanning details and images from the external world. (See Table 2.3.)

ENFJ: Intuition and Feeling. ENFJs, on the other hand, use introverted intuition as their auxiliary function. Instead of focusing on present realities, they look at future possibilities. They find great satisfaction in creating growth experiences for themselves and others. They also place high value on trust and cooperation. If this value

TABLE 2.3   ESFJs AT A GLANCE

Strengths	Under Stress	Areas to Develop
Personally involved with projects and people Value-driven judgment Enjoy social projects Respect and obey rules and regulations Community-oriented Respect tradition and values	Doubt themselves and focus entirely on satisfying the needs of others Worry and feel guilty Become controlling in their push for harmony—"We *will* all get along!" Become overly sensitive, imagining sleights where none were intended	Logic and analytic skills, because thinking is their inferior function Clarify and prioritize their values Look at the big picture Greater appreciation for standard procedures and authority

is violated, ENFJs can become formidable enemies. They are very expressive individuals, but they often assume that others understand them, despite their unusual value-based judgments. Their quest for perfect work relationships can get them into frustrating situations, because they base their perceptions of individual potential on intuition, not facts. A well-developed ENFJ can be a positive group leader, however, creating a productive atmosphere and tuning into the needs of group members. There are not enough of these types in organizations. (See Table 2.4.)

Extroverted Intuitive Types: ENTP and ENFP

Extroverted intuitives use their dominant function to sort through the choices their external world presents. They have a great sense of anticipation. If they have fully developed intuition, they are successful in predicting the future. They focus their energy outward toward what will happen next, and they see many alternative possibilities for objects, people, and situations. In the 1950s, it was probably an extroverted intuitive who noticed some children playing with a thin metal tire hoop and created a similar hoop out of plastic—thereby inventing the Hula Hoop. This ability to sniff out possibilities makes extroverted intuitives entrepreneurial and innovative. Some extroverted intuitives get no further than the search, however. Their weak decision-making ability or poor organization prevents them from completing tasks or following through on their inspirations. In that case, they can be little more than gadflies, lighting on one idea, then moving on to another, then another.

TABLE 2.4   ENFJs AT A GLANCE

Strengths	Under Stress	Areas to Develop
Tolerant and trustworthy (as long as personal values are not violated) Devote considerable energy to building relationships Develop people in the organization well Can lead or follow Can read people well Excellent hunch player	Worry, feel guilty, and doubt themselves Become insistent and controlling in their desire for harmony Become overly sensitive to criticism—real or imagined	Thinking function Pay attention to details and specifics Recognize the role of others' values Balance intuition with facts and not just personal values

The inferior function of extroverted intuitives is introverted sensing. They give scant attention to details and tend to overlook essential facts. Because their inferior sensing function is introverted, they pay excessive attention to bodily sensations or to minor, misplaced facts. They notice insignificant details, imagining that those details have personal importance. A twinge in the lower back can portend a grave illness. An astrological forecast can paralyze their decision-making ability on the day when the company needs it most. In such instances, the inferior function has taken over, crippling an otherwise spontaneous and creative individual. Extroverted intuitives need to develop their sensing function and bring it out of its unconscious lair so that it can do good rather than harm.

ENTP: Intuition and Thinking. ENTPs use thinking as their auxiliary function, putting a critical spin on their intuition. They tend to be interested in projects involving things rather than people. They are good at the innovation and integration of various systems. Their judgment function, which is secondary, is logical and analytical. They are always on the lookout for new and better ways to do things. Entrepreneurship is one of their specialties. They are fun to work with because they can not only play with ideas but critically evaluate them. They make excellent "devil's advocates." The ENTP is a good member of a brainstorming group. But the ENTP's weak point is lack of thorough preparation. They are great at generating ideas but poor at following through. This may be why many

TABLE 2.5   ENTPs AT A GLANCE

Strengths	Under Stress	Areas to Develop
Good at functional analysis of their ideas	Become brash, rude, and abrasive	More careful attention to details required to implement insights
Tolerant of ambiguity	Criticize others, especially those whom they see as inefficient or incompetent	Look carefully at the impact
Develop new ideas and procedures		Balance enthusiasm with reality checks
Sensitive to possibilities	Become rebellious and combative	
High need for competency	Become scattered, unable to focus	Ensure that steps for implementation and follow-up are in place
Understand that design is a means to greater productivity		

entrepreneurs fail just when an innovation most needs good management. When careful follow-through is needed, a good ENTJ, ESTJ, INTJ, or ISTJ is a more welcome partner than an ENTP because their over-reliance on intuition gets in the way of closure. (See Table 2.5.)

ENFP: Intuition and Feeling. Because ENFPs use feeling as their auxiliary function, they shift from objects and analysis to people and values. When presented with a task such as developing a more marketable product, they consider their real task to be developing their own potential and that of their colleagues. Enthusiastic crusaders, they are engaged in a lifelong quest for perfection, authenticity, and spontaneity. They are delighted when their quest inspires their fellow workers; when it does not, they may become depressed and even vindictive. As intuitives, they look for information to confirm their preconceived biases. When their cloudy judgment interacts with their inferior thinking function, they may draw erroneous conclusions. When their judgments of people and situations are correct, they are brilliant; when they are wrong, they are disastrous. ENFPs like to work in free-wheeling environments and have difficulty adjusting to institutional or organizational constraints. They are the bane of organizers and those who enforce policy. Placed in a suitable role, an ENFP can inspire the development of human potential in an organization. (See Table 2.6.)

TABLE 2.6   ENFPs AT A GLANCE

Strengths	Under Stress	Areas to Develop
Value intense emotional experiences	Become scattered, have trouble focusing, and are easily distracted	Attend to follow-through phase of their plans
Keen, penetrating observers of the human scene	Become rebellious, excessively nonconforming	Clarify and prioritize their values
Optimistic and confident in their abilities	Ignore deadlines and procedures	Pay attention to details and specifics
Strong need for novelty and new possibilities	Become overwhelmed by detail and lose their normal perspective	Do not overextend themselves by hasty commitments
Can be charismatic leaders Independent and autonomous according to internal values		

Extroverted Sensing Types: ESTP and ESFP

Extroverted sensing types are masters at observing external details. They focus on people and things, and they remember exactly what someone wore on a particular occasion and what they said and did. Recognition of details and events is primary, while recognition of their significance is secondary. The extroverted sensing type is the most accurate eyewitness, whereas the introverted intuitive is the worst. Extroverted sensing types are practical, down-to-earth people. They reject intuitive fantasizing, preferring to focus on the present. They bring a splash of reality to any situation or discussion. When their pedestrian tendencies are extreme, they seem to be spoilsports and obstructionists. Materialism is their forte; they revel in a world of things. Every detail of a management-by-objectives program enthralls them. They are the realists of organizations who stockpile reams of information. But to be useful, their facts need sorting and categorizing.

Intuition is the inferior, dark side of extroverted sensing types. They regard with great skepticism anything that is only a hunch. Their undeveloped intuition may break through in suspicious thoughts about people or events—thoughts that are more often wrong than right. Because their intuitive function is not refined, when used at all it is egocentric. Marie Von Franz pointed out that when extroverted sensing types let go of their egos through drink or weariness, they sometimes tell fantastical, imaginative tales. They are apt to deny having done so when

TABLE 2.7 ESTPs AT A GLANCE

Strengths	Under Stress	Areas to Develop
People of action who love the "game" Good observers of motives Good at trouble shooting and negotiating (if the skills are developed) Entrepreneurial promoters of new activities in an organization Witty and charming in groups and social activities Deeply pragmatic	Have trouble accepting structure and meeting Focus entirely on excitement and external activity Put enjoyment of life ahead of important obligations	Select more carefully among the vast array of deadlines compiled details Learn to focus on the big picture as well as the details Refrain from impulsively accepting data Refrain from impulse for immediate gratification

their egos come back in charge again. Von Franz also cited examples of no-nonsense extroverted sensing types who rush with complete abandon into esoteric eastern religious sects or new wave movements. This illustrates the pull of opposites.

ESTP: Sensing and Thinking. Thinking is the auxiliary function of ESTPs. They are logical in gathering data and resourceful in using it, keeping information logically sorted and ready for action. Because their perception function is finely tuned, they are on the lookout for change, anticipating their neighbor's next move. They are excellent negotiators and "firefighters." Because of the dominance of their sensing function, ESTPs live fully in the present but can focus the energy of their auxiliary function on future plans. Their organizational abilities are not as refined as those of an ESTJ, and some of their actions and judgments may be hasty. (See Table 2.7.)

ESFP: Sensing and Feeling. ESFPs use introverted feeling as their auxiliary function. Empathetic and hypersensitive, ESFPs are naturally friendly people. They seek company and have an uncanny sense of tact, sympathy, and social ease. For them, life itself is a performance into which they throw their artistic and aesthetic talents. But ESFPs are not strong at analyzing events or at offering criticism. They shy away from any form of conditional negative feedback—a serious weakness for them as managers. (See Table 2.8.)

TABLE 2.8   ESFPs AT A GLANCE

Strengths	Under Stress	Areas to Develop
Warm and optimistic	Become distracted and overly impulsive	More logical and analytical skills
Generous in giving assistance to others	Have trouble accepting and meeting deadlines	Clarify and prioritize prioritize values
Love working with people	Overpersonalize others' actions and decisions	Greater tolerance for ambiguity and complexity
Enjoy the good life		
Rely heavily on personal experiences and common sense		Develop a clear sense of obligations
Good at handling personnel crises in organizations		

Introverted Thinking Types: ISTP and INTP

With introverted types, the dominant function is directed inward, and what is seen in their dealings with the outside world is the secondary or auxiliary function. Thus, introverted thinking types use thinking internally. They are the people of ideas and principles. Taking a logical, systematic approach to the world is their raison d'être, but they guard themselves against others knowing that this is how they operate. Because their auxiliary function is perception, they come across as quiet and reserved. Their judgment function does not surface unless they are required to explain the logic behind a particular plan, whereupon they unveil a highly systematic scheme. In problem-solving groups, introverted thinkers are the silent minority who need to be prodded for their input. Jung described naturalist and explorer Charles Darwin's classification of external factors as the prototype of extroverted thinking and philosopher Emmanuel Kant's inner critique of knowledge as the prototype of introverted thinking.

The inferior function for introverted thinkers is feeling. Their judgments are black and white. "You could compare the inferior feeling of an introverted thinking type," wrote Von Franz, "to the flow of lava from a volcano; it only moves five meters an hour but it devastates everything in its way. But it also has the advantages of a primitive function, for it is tremendously genuine and warm. When an introverted thinker loves, there is no calculation in it." Unfortunately, the introverted thinker hates with an equal lack of calculation.

TABLE 2.9 ISTPs AT A GLANCE

Strengths	Under Stress	Areas to Develop
Action is self-directed Fearless, with devil-may-care attitude Masterful executors of the "tool"—high mechanical aptitude Lead by example Egalitarian in outlook; love freedom Good at arts and crafts	Become cynical and negative Withdraw their attention and energy Put off decisions	Attend to the big picture—focus on long-term ramifications Greater empathy for others Slow down reaction time to avoid hasty decisons

ISTP: Sensing and Thinking. ISTPs use sensing as their auxiliary function; they gather facts and details from the real world to make internal judgments. Because they deal with external matters through their perceptive function, they sometimes seem laid-back. They have a penchant for economy of effort. Most of their psychic energy is expended on subjective assessments about what facts mean to them. They view action as an end in itself, and they want the freedom to follow their own assessments. ISTPs are the most taciturn of types; talking is not their thing. They are also patient, accurate, good with their hands, and appreciative of the outdoors. (See Table 2.9.)

INTP: Intuition and Thinking. INTPs are quite different in demeanor from ISTPs. Both use thinking as their dominant function, but the INTP deals with the outside world through ideas and possibilities, gathering insights from the environment. Of all the psychological types, INTPs exhibit the highest precision in thought and language. They are good at detecting inconsistencies in thought and logic. INTPs are the natural architects of ideas, using logic, perceptiveness, and ingenuity. Because of this talent, they are sometimes viewed as intellectual snobs or even as dilettantes. Although they are good at developing ideas, they are weak at putting them into practice. Action is not their strong suit. They generously supply problems with new alternatives and clear reasoning. (See Table 2.10.)

TABLE 2.10   INTPs AT A GLANCE

Strengths	Under Stress	Areas to Develop
Great precision in thought and language	Become cynical and negative	More effective communications with others
Able to see distinctions and inconsistencies in situations	Become sarcastic and destructively critical	Think more carefully about the impact of their actions
Abhor redundancy and incoherence	Isolate themselves and put off action	Greater appreciation for details
View the world as something to be understood	Engage in verbal sparring and arguments	Consider others' needs and values
Architect of systems		
Adaptable until their principles are violated		

Introverted Feeling Types: ISFP and INFP

The dominant function for introverted feeling types is inward-directed feeling. Because they have highly differentiated sets of values but rarely express them, they are poorly understood. Their intuitive function communicates in a somewhat distant manner, while their feeling function remains buried deep within. Directed by their introverted feeling, they display an uncanny sense of ethics and moral propriety that they seldom verbalize. As idealists, they put a tremendous amount of energy into philanthropic causes. Intensely loyal to their inner values, they seem driven by internal forces. In fact, without a unifying value system, the introverted feeling type is like a floundering ship. But armed with a strong, personal set of values, he or she is the backbone of organizations.

The inferior function of the introverted feeling type is thinking. Pushed by the inferior function, introverted feeling types drive to amass data and can become overwhelmed. While a well-differentiated extroverted thinker is an organizer and an astute evaluator of information, the introverted feeling type is not. Von Franz recommended that the introverted feeling type should always check thoughts against facts and should reevaluate them often.

ISFP: Sensing and Feeling. ISFPs use extroverted sensing as their auxiliary function and are therefore in tune with their world, using relevant facts and details

TABLE 2.11 ISFPs AT A GLANCE

Strengths	Under Stress	Areas to Develop
Good at sensual appreciation—art, decorating	Withdraw from people and situations	See the big picture—focus on long-term ramifications
Unconditionally kind	Passively resist structures and rules	Clarify and prioritize values as basis for judgment
Prefer to have their fingers on the pulse of life	Are excessively self-critical	More logical and analytical skills
Express themselves through action	Feel unappreciated and undervalued	More effective communication skills—verbalize reasons and rationales
Can practice their artistry for hours in devotion to performance		
Graceful and attentive		

to meet the requirements of their jobs. They see the needs of the moment and respond accordingly. They like to express themselves and their values through actions instead of words and work devotedly at projects that satisfy this need. (See Table 2.11.)

INFP: Intuition and Feeling. Because extroverted intuition is their auxiliary function, INFPs have more insight into their actions than ISFPs do. But their intuition is shy, almost reticent. They have a deep sense of traditional values, and they like to pledge themselves to a cause. Because of their feeling function, they seek continuity and coherence, but they are vague about what those qualities entail. They are able to interpret symbols and view situations from a broad perspective.

With their good sense of mood or atmosphere and a strong interest in people and their potential, INFPs make good novelists and character actors. In organizations they are adaptable and sensitive. Impatient with conditional or hypothetical possibilities, they prefer their own real or imagined truths. (See Table 2.12.)

Introverted Intuitive Types: INTJ and INFJ

Introverted intuitives deal with the external world with the logic and analysis of thinking. Their dominant function, however, is introverted intuition. Jung saw the introverted intuitive as a peculiar combination of mystical dreamer and eccentric

TABLE 2.12   INFPs AT A GLANCE

Strengths	Under Stress	Areas to Develop
Have a profound sense of honor based on personal values	Have difficulty expressing themselves verbally	See the big picture—focus on long term ramifications
Unconditionally kind	Withdraw from people and situations	Clarify and prioritize values as basis for judgment
Prefer to have their fingers on the pulse of life	Do not give enough information to others, especially about important values	More logical and analytical skills
Express themselves through action		More effective communication skills—verbalize reasons and rationales
Prefer the valuing process over the logical		
Adaptable and open to new ideas		
Patient with complicated situations, but impatient with details		
Make unusual sacrifices for values they believe in		
Calm, pleasant, and caring		

artist. Introverted intuitives must sometimes be brought back to reality and asked what their ideas mean. Their perceptions tend to be single-minded, and their views unshakable. As introverts, they see their visions clearly, but they are not always aware of how others perceive them. Introverted intuitives need to develop their judgment function—either thinking or feeling—in order to balance and plan out their inner visions. Jung himself was an introverted intuitive, as are many of today's Jungian analysts.

The inferior function of introverted intuitives is sensing. They are not in close touch either with their own physical senses or with those of others. Von Franz pointed out that the introverted intuitive is vague about facts, plucking from the environment whatever they need to verify their preconceived conclusions. So others—and even they themselves—may need to question their facts. When unchecked by their judgment function, they can deceive themselves. In extreme introverted intuitives, facts present themselves as isolated islands of information, unrelated to any structure or larger meaning. As they selectively and subjectively process information, introverted intuitives often make wildly incorrect assumptions.

INTJ: Intuition and Thinking. Because INTJs have thinking as their auxiliary function, thinking keeps their visions in balance, making them logical, critical, and decisive, although they may not communicate the premises behind their judgments. Ironically, many CEOs in American industry are INTJs. A *Wall Street Journal* article stated that the occurrence of INTJs among CEOs is twenty times greater than among the general population. It seems as if most INTJs become either Jungian analysts or CEOs! As managers move up the corporate ladder, their communication skills become more crucial—except, apparently, for INTJs. They seem to be promoted on the strength of their insights and determination, regardless of their inability to communicate well. A manager working with an INTJ can ward off potential conflicts and misunderstandings by frequently reviewing roles and objectives. (See Table 2.13.)

INFJ: Intuition and Feeling. INFJs are more aware than INTJs of their impact and influence on others. They are less concerned with moving an organization or institution toward a future vision than with learning the meaning of events. They are something of an enigma, for although their feeling function is directed to the outside world, they are reluctant to share their private intuitions. Interested

TABLE 2.13   INTJs AT A GLANCE

Strengths	Under Stress	Areas to Develop
Extremely self-confident	Become aloof and abrupt; do not give enough information about internal processing	More attention to details
See reality as malleable and changeable		Do not assume that people are mind readers
Single-minded in purposes	Are critical of those who do not see their vision quickly	Look at the impact of decisions and actions on others
Anti-authoritarian—influenced by deeds not position	Become single-minded and unyielding in pursuing goals	
Use intuition to grasp coherence		Avoid quibbling over abstractions
High achievers in school and in the organization		

TABLE 2.14   INFJs AT A GLANCE

Strengths	Under Stress	Areas to Develop
Have strong empathetic abilities	Do not give others information used to arrive at a decision; can seem arbitrary	Clarify and prioritize values as the basis for judgment
Vivid imaginations; use intuition productively	Base judgments on little data, on a sense of "knowing" that has little basis in reality	More effective communication skills—verbalize reasons and rationales
Good one-on-one interactions		Pay more attention to details and specifics
Good at public relations	Withdraw energy and insight	Greater openness to other perspectives
Good interpersonal skills	Become resentful and critical	
Good at jobs requiring solitude and concentration		

in what others think and feel, they reveal little about themselves. Although they are concerned about the general welfare, they are not as communicative as ENFJs. (See Table 2.14.)

Introverted Sensing Types: ISTJ and ISFJ

Introverted sensing types take in their environment through their dominant sensing function. Placid but absorbed, they interpret the world through their five senses. To those who do not know them well, introverted sensing types may seem entirely unaffected by external events, as if little from the outside world penetrates their consciousness. This appearance is deceptive, for their acute perception and memory make them tremendous organizational assets. When their auxiliary function—thinking or feeling—is in operation, they pour out details and impressions that others never thought existed. Their patient attention to detail and shades of meaning is without parallel. Introverted sensing types deal with external matters through their judgment function, presenting encapsulated evaluations of events and information. They like to have things, people, and facts under control. Their business and personal affairs are organized to a degree that is hard for extroverts to fathom. They make up for their lack of spontaneity by their dependability and carefulness. But if anything useful is to come from their deeply stored impressions, introverted sensing types must develop their judging function.

The inferior function of the introverted sensing type is extroverted intuition. Sensing types are in danger of seeing no further than the present. When intuition

TABLE 2.15   ISTJs AT A GLANCE

Strengths	Under Stress	Areas to Develop
Decisive and practical	Become rigid about time, schedules, procedures—"go by the book"	More appreciation for the impact of their decisions on others
Guardians of time-honored institutions		
	Critical and judgmental of others	More balanced approach to judgment, so that information is evaluated carefully without quick decisions
Interested in thoroughness, details, and practical procedures	Find it hard to delegate and to trust others to do the job correctly	
Patient with work and procedures within an organization		Express inner feelings and frustrations
		More appreciation for the big picture
Persevering and dependable		
Quiet and serious		

occasionally does break through, it is apt to be unreliable, certainly not the basis for action. But this type may throw caution to the wind when intuition takes over. A prudent, dependable financial accountant will squander hard-earned money on a whim, for example. At the other extreme, an intensely rigid individual, distrustful of all intuition, will create tremendous internal conflict by suppressing all dreams and imagination. Introverted sensing types tend to resist interventions such as brainstorming. They can describe sensations in vivid and exquisite detail, but they cannot take the next step and draw meaning from those sensations.

ISTJ: Sensing and Thinking. ISTJs have extroverted thinking as their auxiliary function. They are rational, impersonal, logical, conclusive, and ready to act on their impressions. Tact and empathy are not their strong suit, just as they are not for the extroverted thinker. Often ISTJs fail to consider the impact their decisions have upon others. The ISTJ needs to balance the secondary function with empathy and feeling. (See Table 2.15.)

ISFJ: Sensing and Feeling. ISFJs are tactful and considerate. They use extroverted feeling when dealing with the outside world, and they consider all the nuances of their actions. Their personal values determine their actions, and to those who share their values, they are extremely loyal, becoming fierce defenders of their organizations' welfare and of the status quo. (See Table 2.16.)

TABLE 2.16 ISFJs AT A GLANCE

Strengths	Under Stress	Areas to Develop
Devoted and loyal to institutions that foster their values	Become rigid in supporting hierarchy, authority, and procedures	More appreciation of the unusual
Caring and dependable	Feel unappreciated, resentful; complain a lot	Express inner feelings and frustrations
Extraordinary sense of responsibility	Overly focused on immediate impacts of decisions on people	More appreciation for the big picture
Work with single-minded purpose on tasks		More logical and analytical skills
Respect traditional procedures and go by the book		
Conserves resources		

Strengthening and Developing Psychological Type

Jung assumed that psychological type is a constitutional given, that each one has its own natural pattern of growth. As we have discussed, however, imbalances can develop that prevent us from utilizing all our potential. The goal for psychological type is not to change it but to strengthen it. An extrovert should not want to become an introvert or a sensing type should not want to become an intuitive type and so on.

Understanding the natural strengths and weaknesses of each type as described in the sections above allows us to move on to strengthening our types. In doing so, keep the analogy of the on/off switch in mind. Extroverts have their extroverted switch on most of the time, just as introverts have their introverted switch on. But both can use the opposite pole. In the extreme cases where the preferred switch is always on, we must work diligently to strengthen the opposite pole. In normal cases of type, it is a matter of developing wholeness. The following suggestions are designed to help each type to develop their inherent strengths and integrate their lesser functions.

The Task for Introverts: Becoming Comfortable Outside

- Attend assertiveness training classes, or join a discussion group in which everyone has to talk about what is on their minds.

- At parties, conferences, or dinners, introduce yourself and interact actively with others.
- Meet with subordinates, peers, and bosses, and ask them what they need from you.
- Ask yourself, "What did I leave out in the conversation?"
- Attend some drama classes or role-playing seminars held by adult education programs.
- Attend presentation or speaking skills classes.
- See a Marx brothers film. Harpo, Groucho, and Chico are the archetypical extroverts.

The Task for Extroverts: Becoming Comfortable Inside

- Learn the relaxation response, set out at the end of Chapter Four.
- Read Proust and Thoreau. Both these authors painstakingly explore their inner worlds.
- Set aside one hour of quiet time each day.
- Take a long walk in the woods alone and contemplate nature.
- Take a course in imagery rehearsal, which trains you to explore your inner self.
- Learn active listening techniques.
- Keep a diary of your inner thoughts.

The Task for Intuitive Types: Develop Sensing

- Learn to cook from recipes.
- Learn a sport such as sailing that demands specificity: terms, exactitude, and precision.
- Learn computers, the most sensing of all electronics.
- Listen to jazz for the fun of it.
- Use your hands; paint, sculpt, or fix up the house.
- Plant a garden.
- Use your eyes to focus on details in nature.
- Learn to master a balance sheet.

The Task for Sensing Types: Develop Intuition

- Visit a museum with a good collection of abstract paintings and write about their personal meaning to you.
- Construct a personal five-year plan with strategic options.

- Listen to classical music. Try to grasp the complexity, and weave it into an interpretation of what the music means to you.
- Write an explanation of why a rose is not just a rose.
- Watch a Fellini or a Bergman movie or *My Dinner with André*. Fellini and Bergman are extremely abstract and symbolic in their film themes. *My Dinner with André* is a dialogue between a prototypical sensing type (Wally) and a full-blown intuitive type (André). The film is useful for both sensing and intuitive types. The sensing type should try to understand and empathize with André and the intuitives do the same with Wally.
- Read poetry, especially the Lake Poets (Wordsworth, Coleridge, and Southey), and note their use of allegory, metaphor, and symbolism.

The Task for Thinking Types: Develop Empathy and Personal Values

- Write about your most cherished values.
- Ask a very close friend about his or her most cherished values.
- Develop a more personal style. Write a letter (not to be sent) to a subordinate who gives you trouble. In the letter try to walk a mile in his or her shoes. Stay away from impersonal factual and critical comments.
- Attend an AA meeting to see others' personal pain.
- Interview a friend about certain critical issues. Share your views with that person.
- See Charlie Chaplin in the movie *The Kid*. The film is full of pathos and feeling.
- Ask yourself when you have to make a decision, "Did I consider the impact of the decision on others' welfare?"

The Task for Feeling Types: Develop Balanced and Logical Judgment

- Hear both sides of an issue before judging.
- Pay attention to reacting less personally to criticism.
- Take a course in critical thinking.
- When making a decision ask yourself, "Did I go through an impersonal analysis of the facts in the case before imposing my values on the decision?"
- Develop power bases. Power is not evil.
- Learn effective performance appraisal skills.
- Seek out a thinking type to explore the following problem:
  In an attempt to offset the shortage of water in several large cities, plans are being completed to dam major rivers, thus creating artificial lakes as reservoirs. Naturalists complain that wildlife in these areas will not be able to adjust and

will be severely affected. In several cases whole villages may have to be moved to higher ground, leaving farms and traditions behind them. How would you and the thinking type approach the problem?

A Case of Balancing Psychological Type

I first met Sam in the early 1990s, when he and I attended a retreat on organizational development. At that time he was a technical director for a government research and development laboratory. During the retreat I had considerable opportunity to observe Sam, and I began to feel I knew his management style quite well. Knowing that Sam had just returned from an MBTI workshop, I offered to predict his type.

> "Okay, give it to me," he said.
> "You're an ENTP," I said.
> "Right on three, wrong on one," said Sam.
> "Oh, you're a J, not a P—right?" I said.
> Sam laughed and said, "No, I'm an NTP, but I'm introverted, not extroverted."

I was floored. Sam had exhibited a high level of extroverted energy in meetings and group presentations. That I had so misjudged his attitude jarred my professional ego. I objected, "But I've seen you perform. You come off as a full-blown extrovert. What's the explanation?" I was hoping he would say that he did not understand the difference between the two attitudes, or that he had been tired when he took the test—or maybe that he was a borderline extrovert. But what Sam revealed gave me both humility and insight into psychological types.

He said that long before he took the MBTI, he had known intuitively that he was an intense introvert. When he took the test, his score on the introversion/extroversion dimension was strongly in the introverted direction. He had taken the test as it should be taken, as a reading of his actual—not his ideal—preferences. In high school, college, and graduate school he had been true to his introverted self. But early on in his professional career, he had realized that he did not want to be an isolated trench scientist and that management had great appeal for him. His need for power drove him toward management, where he could express it. He said that he had seen many successful introverted managers but that the best ones were those who could take on an extroverted attitude when necessary.

Sam then deliberately mapped out the program of self-development that he had undertaken to overcome his intense introversion. He had taken assertiveness training and communication courses, and he had attended public speaking workshops. The result of this intensive effort was the vibrant, outgoing Sam whose extroverted manner had deceived me. He had willfully adapted his attitude to this kind of situation. He went on to confess that after every group meeting or presentation, he retreated to the solitude of his office, closed the door, and sighed, "Thank God that's over!" He then returned to his true introverted attitude, gathered his inner resources, and recouped the energy he had expended on being an extrovert.

Sam's story illustrates two points. The first is that it is possible for us to understand the reasons for our behavior. The second is that it is possible for us to modify and control our behavior if we are so inclined and motivated. Motivation is the key. No personality is cast in stone. We can use cognitive behavioral techniques (which we will discuss in Chapter Four) to develop our weaker functions. Workshops can help us develop intuitive thinking, just as time management and planning workshops can strengthen the sensing function. All four of the functions can be developed if the motivation is there. Sam's case demonstrates that other sides of the self can evolve to supplement—not replace—natural tendencies. Despite all his training and deliberate efforts, Sam knows and accepts that he is still an introvert.

Sam undertook all these personal interventions before he knew his MBTI type. Through self-analysis he decided what he wanted and how to get it. He assessed his strengths and weaknesses and learned how to adjust to various situations. His natural introverted attitude helped him to see the need for him to make these changes. He recognized that most problems deserve a tailored response not a blind, reactive one.

Sam also worked intuitively to develop his inferior function. As an INTP, his dominant function was introverted thinking; his inferior function was feeling. Sam realized that unfettered thinking could get him in trouble. No one gets far with the proverbial foot in the mouth. He knew that brilliant thinking types like General George S. Patton were often their own worst enemies, delivering tactless statements without regard for their impact. Development of his feeling function could overcome this self-destructive tendency. Today Sam is in better touch with his feelings and has persuasive language skills.

The changes that Sam made were behavioral, not psychological. He is still an INTP, well aware that too much development of his inferior function can cause psychic overload. But he is capable of interacting with the outer world with a far greater range of behavior than he had before. He has developed behavioral skills the way some people improve their golf swing or learn to ski. Sam's goal in life is to be a successful technocrat in the best sense of that word. He likes science and its rational, positive approach to the world's problems. He is an idealist, with just the right smattering of pragmatism. Power plays an important role for him; he wants control over himself and his environment. If Sam had carried his drive for control to an extreme, it would have become an obsession with all of an obsession's negative consequences. But early in life, Sam developed a keen sense of social responsibility that tempered his drive for power. He genuinely wants to improve the world. In spite of his conscious behavior modification, he comes across not as manipulative or phony but as authentic and sincere.

Psychological Type and Key Management Activities

The psychological types dramatically affect how we approach the central activities of management. One of the key skills, delegation, is the universally required ability to maintain responsibility yet relinquish authority. Some managers give subordinates the responsibility to act but do not give them corresponding authority. This is not delegation. Delegation, when done well, extends the tasks from what a person can do to what she or he can control; releases time for more important work; develops subordinates' initiative, skills, knowledge, and competence; and allows decisions to be made at the appropriate level. Most managers agree that decisions ought to be delegated to the lowest possible level where they can be made intelligently and where the relevant facts and required judgment are available. Often, in practice, they violate this rule by micromanaging or just telling their subordinates what to do. Or they make the mistake of dumping the decision without enough guidance or taking it back and doing it themselves. All of these mistakes have negative consequences. The cardinal principle in delegation lies in the type of decision that must be made. A policy decision clearly belongs in the hands of top management. Operating decisions, however, where the problems are best solved by those with special expertise, should be made by middle and lower management.

The personality type of both the boss and the subordinate can have a profound effect on whether effective delegation takes place. In sensing type bosses, because of their proclivity for detail, the tendency is to micromanage or hover over the task and take initiative away from their subordinates. Intuitive types may not explain all the details or responsibilities to the subordinate because they believe they have given a broad enough picture. Introverts may not fully communicate all the necessary information they have; their delegation will be patchy and inconsistent. Extroverts may wander with their thoughts and not be concise in their communications. (This problem is less likely with extroverted sensing types than with extroverted intuitive types.) Impersonal and hypercritical thinking types can arouse anxiety and uncertainty in an insecure subordinate. Feeling types may seek harmony and avoid conflict, which will come back to haunt them later on. Judging types may push too hard for the outcome and operate out of a crisis management mode. Perceptive types may procrastinate by mulling over the problem or task and not delegate until a crisis explodes.

Although delegation is certainly not the only key management activity, it can serve as an excellent illustration of how the sixteen personality types tend to manage their work and their relationships. Other activities will show variations on these themes, which are fundamental to effective management style.

ESTJs give subordinates mountains of detailed information without regard to its importance, so the big picture will be out of focus. They like to organize and plan all the procedures, which they focus on to the exclusion of overall strategy. Then they hover and push for closure. They can be abrupt and hypercritical of others' performance, with delegation sometimes taking the form of giving orders and demanding results. In my management sample of more than 1,000 middle- and upper-level managers in a Fortune 100 company, 22 percent were ESTJs as compared to 14 percent in the population.

ESFJs are sensitive to rules and regulations and, paradoxically, to the needs of people as well, so when it comes to delegation they will be caught between these two poles. They may hover over subordinates to make sure they follow guidelines and to offer support. They are extremely social and may tend to oversell their kindness. ESFJs are a minority in management—only 2 percent of my sample as compared to 14 percent in the general population.

ENTJs have a sense of self-importance. They give orders, rather than truly delegate, so control and authority remain in their hands. They hand out criticism with no regard for the feelings of others. Twelve percent of my management sample were ENTJs, whereas there are 5 percent in the general population.

ENFJs are very involved with the group as a leader and as a participant; sometimes becoming over-involved with too many tasks. "Reverse delegation"— taking on or sharing subordinates' responsibilities can be the result. ENFJs must learn to dissociate from over-identification with others. Only 1 percent of my management sample were ENFJs, as opposed to 5 percent in the general population.

ESTPs, more entrepreneurs than managers, do not attend to details as much as to action. Follow-up is not their strong suit. This could be why only 2 percent of the executives in the management sample were ESTPs, as opposed to 14 percent in the general population.

Active and entertaining *ESFPs* make work a happy place. They are performers of the highest quality in their social interactions. But they must be on guard about dumping work on their subordinates without providing them with adequate guidelines. They will pay more attention to the human side than the task side. That is why only 1 percent of management jobs are held by this type as compared to 14 percent in the population.

ENTPs ponder the scope of the problem and expend much time in defining the possibilities. They have no great sense of urgency when trying to accomplish a task. Because of the tremendous number of options and alternatives they generate, subordinates may be confused about what an ENTP really wants. Clear expectations may not be given. ENTPs make up about 10 percent of the management jobs whereas they are 5 percent of the population.

ENFPs are careful not to criticize subordinates or to overburden them. But because they are so concerned about the human side of the equation, the task may suffer. ENFPs must separate the people from the problem, outline the task at hand, and be assertive in giving instructions and handing over authority. There is no time urgency for the ENFP; schedules may slip and priorities get ignored. ENFPs are rare in management jobs, only 1 percent were found in the sample as compared to 5 percent in the population.

ISTJs focus on details, giving out only what they perceive as important information. They are likely to be very impersonal and not give rewards when the subordinate does a good job. A subordinate who does not live up to the expectations of an ISTJ will pay for it. An extraordinary 21 percent of a management group in one of my studies were ISTJs, compared to 5 percent in the general population.

For *ISFJs*, communication is a problem. They are uncomfortable in a position of authority because they respect it and prefer to follow rather than give directions. Therefore, they are less likely to delegate and tend to do jobs themselves. They are underrepresented in management. Of the managers in my population sample, 2.3 percent were ISFJs as compared to 5 percent in the population.

INTJs think about the big picture but do not fully communicate their vision, believing that subordinates can read their minds. Subordinates have difficulty dealing with INTJs because they do not like others to criticize their grand design. Like ENTJs they tend to give orders and not delegate; the difference between the types is in the amount and structure of their communications. The INTJs made up 14 percent of the management but only 1.5 percent in the population.

INFJs strive toward harmony in the organization and respect the feelings of others. This is commendable, but INFJs have a tendency not to give constructive criticism when it is warranted; as a result, subordinates may not grow under their tutelage. INFJs fix their subordinates' mistakes themselves and remain silent. Less than 1 percent were found in the management sample as compared to 1.5 percent in the population.

ISTPs immediately attack the problem, leaving little room for subordinates to interact in defining the problem or devising a solution. The ISTP is more a troubleshooter than a manager. ISTPs made up 5 percent of the management sample and this matched the rate in the population.

ISFPs are rarely found in management. They do not plan and prepare; rather, they like to perform in the fine arts. The atmosphere of the organization is a damper on their soul. Delegation would be a hard task and an alien operation for the prototypical ISFP. Less than 1 percent were found in the management sample as compared to 5 percent overall.

INTPs examine the task and ruminate over the possibilities. But after they have scanned all the possibilities, they give the subordinate a carefully drafted list of how to approach the task. The problem for the subordinate is that the INTP has suggested too many options, leading to dead ends and poor time management. INTPs comprised 5 percent of the management sample as compared to 1.5 percent overall.

INFPs are impatient with details; they focus on the big picture, overlooking some needed facts and pushing on with the job. Therefore, in delegating to others, some vital aspect may be missing. INFPs do not get involved unless they feel that a project fits in with their values. In this respect, priorities may not be respected. Less than 1 percent were found in the management sample as compared to 5 percent in the population.

Psychological Type and Values

There are people who believe so strongly in the power of pure reason (the thinking function) that they disregard feeling, that is, values. That is why thinking types often have a difficult time articulating their values. Because 80 to 90 percent of business executives are thinking types, this deficit presents a serious problem for integrating personal values with organizational ethics. Most thinking types are not accustomed to allowing their feeling values to surface and be examined for consistency and appropriateness. Therefore, engaging in value clarification is all the more important for the thinking type manager.

The thinking types try to rationalize and intellectualize most moral dilemmas by trying to remain outside the situation. By distancing themselves, they can remain detached from personal involvement. For example, the stockbroker in the film *Twelve Angry Men* tries to suppress any empathy for the defendant, accused of murder, because he believes in the power of logic and reason. His personal values never surface. The facade is broken when he sees a contradiction in a witness's testimony. At that point he realizes that if he had paid more attention to the person and the emotions lying beneath the surface of his logic, he would have seen the situation more clearly.

In contrast, feeling types use their personal values to judge the world. They are constantly ruminating about how their values fit in with given circumstances and whether they agree with the fit. With introverted feeling types, where the feeling value is in the inner world, you may not be aware of a particular value until you violate one of their cherished beliefs. Then you can expect an outburst of emotion that may take you aback. You will be asking yourself what you said that set them off. If you were cognizant of their values, you may have avoided the confrontation or at least delicately bridged the subject. On the other hand, extroverts show their values on their sleeves and espouse them in public. What you see is what you get with an extroverted feeling type.

Conclusion

Harry and Sheila were discussing their experience after a two-day MBTI workshop sponsored by their company. Sheila made an observation that Phil, her boss, fit the ENTJ type right to the letter of the law. He was assertive, outspoken, one-minded at times, and very decisive. Harry commented that was very true, but that Stan, another ENTJ, was much mellower and tended to avoid confrontations and liked to work with teams. He went on to question the validity of the type concept. After all, they are both ENTJs, but one was consistent and the other was an anomaly. Sheila then said, "Now that you bring that up my husband is an INTJ and he tells me everything I need to know. No surprises like Kate. She is inscrutable as the usual INTJ. What gives?"

The questioning that goes on with most people who have gone through an MBTI experience is often like this. How do we explain these inconsistencies? The answer is simple—the participants in our scenario differ on other critical factors like their needs, use of power, and conflict management style. The MBTI is limited to understanding how we use our psychic energy, how we perceive and judge the world—and that's it! Our understanding of our fellow team members and ourselves will not be complete until we examine these other factors as well.

Before we go on to those other factors, we will look at two other critical aspects of understanding and changing management style. In Chapter Three, we examine practical intelligence (the skills, knowledge, and mindset that are essential ingredients of management savvy) and in Chapter Four we look at cognitive restructuring (the "technology" for shifting our way of viewing the world and our behavior once we have identified what we want to change). Equipped with our understanding of this overall model for change, we can then move on to the other building blocks of management style in Chapters Five through Nine.

CHAPTER THREE

PRACTICAL INTELLIGENCE: HOW DO WE MAKE IT WORK?

After graduating from an engineering program at an Ivy League university with a 3.86 grade point average and excellent recommendations, Stacey was hired by a high-tech Fortune 500 company. They welcomed her eagerly, full of great expectations for her future with the organization. In Stacey's first year, she performed at a high level in a job that required individual contribution and little teamwork with other engineers or groups. At that point, her boss decided to promote her to a first-line supervisory position and assigned her to a cross-functional group that was working on a subunit of integrated systems. Because the company was organized as a matrix organization, there were many tasks in this large, multi-million-dollar program that had to be completed across work groups. Teamwork was not only necessary within Stacey's own group, but also with other groups in the organization.

Within just a few months, Stacey's boss, John, began receiving complaints about her behavior and performance. Coworkers and other managers acknowledged that she was brilliant at her specialty, but felt she displayed many irritating and dysfunctional behaviors. They described her as self-centered and insensitive, and accused her of hoarding results, being uncooperative with people outside her group, and lacking awareness of the big picture. One of her peers reported, "She just doesn't have street smarts."

John tried to remedy the situation by talking to Stacey about her problems with other people, but that only exacerbated the situation. After another six months of frustration and failure in trying to deal with the situation, John finally wrote Stacey off as a failed promotion and transferred her back to her previous position.

This scenario and its consequences are unfortunately not uncommon in organizations. No one knows exactly how often it happens, but the rate of such failure is high enough that it is not only frustrating but also damaging to morale and productivity. When John and his coworkers tried to explain what had happened, they came up with several possibilities:

1. Stacey was a "bad" choice and did not live up to expectations.
2. The job was beyond her capabilities.
3. The system did not apply the right measurements when it selected employees.
4. The system did not develop Stacey's potential.
5. The system did not know what skills were needed to succeed in an interactive team environment.
6. A combination of the above.

Those are typical responses, but they are all personal, focused around Stacey's innate qualities, her behavior, or the way the system evaluated and trained her. If we analyze the situation from an organizational perspective, however, the blame shifts from Stacey to the skills that she needed to perform well. There are in fact three interrelated factors that hold the key to a manager's personal effectiveness:

- Conceptual Skills: Knowing a job's technical, cognitive, and human skill requirements
- Influence Skills: Knowing your strengths and weaknesses as a manager, particularly in getting others to do what is needed
- Interpersonal Skills: Understanding the strengths and weaknesses of others (subordinates, peers, and bosses) and knowing how to work effectively with them.

These three components add up to what is known as *practical intelligence,* which is entirely different from traditional academic intelligence. Stacey was promoted on the basis of her grade point average and her references, which reflected past performance in the narrow range of abilities that are valued in an academic setting but that could not predict her future performance as a manager. She was lacking that constellation of practical skills (which can be learned) that are essential to a manager's success. The six building blocks of the Integrated Management Style Model that we have already discussed, form the operational core of developing practical intelligence. In this chapter, we look more closely at practical intelligence, its components, and its significance for a range of managerial tasks and responsibilities.

Your Practical IQ

As a general overview, practical intelligence and "Practical IQ" (the way it is measured) involve skills and knowledge as well as a mindset that allow a manager not only to perform well but also to relish the challenges of life in an organization. A manager with a high Practical IQ has the ability to:

- Seek out, create, and enjoy challenges—to live with uncertainty.
- Maintain appropriate levels of control through decision making.
- Be self-motivating.
- Complete tasks and work together with others as a team.
- Give support to, cooperate with, and understand others (including difficult people).

Enhancing your Practical IQ involves an awareness of its three main components: the conceptual, the interpersonal, and the ability to influence others. In the rest of the chapter we look at those three components in detail.

Problems and Opportunities: Enhancing Conceptual Skills

In his studies of intelligence, Robert Sternberg of Yale University has isolated three types of intelligence that have practical implications for the performance of everyday managerial tasks. The first, called *componential intelligence,* relates to how we analyze and process information internally. That is what standard IQ tests measure. Stacey had excellent componential intelligence, which made her good at her first job as an engineer. When her new job demanded different skills, however, her componential intelligence did not help.

When a job or task requires that we combine disparate experiences and insight, Sternberg calls that type of intelligence *experiential thinking.* Someone with this skill will be good at linking past experiences with new experiences and coming up with creative insights about them. Some people have both componential and experiential intelligence, while others score high in only one. If someone scores high in only one type and is placed in a job that requires others as well, as was the case with Stacey, performance may very well suffer. Peter Lynch, the highly successful manager behind the Fidelity Funds, undoubtedly has experiential intelligence about the stock market, which he has seen through several major downswings. A new broker starting out in the roaring 1990s has only experienced a bull market and may block out the possibility of market corrections and the severity of other factors such as falling emergent markets. The best and the brightest of managers have high levels of experiential thinking.

The capacity to interact with the environment and to read situations correctly from their context is what Sternberg calls *contextual intelligence*. People who have this intellectual skill are usually called "street smart." They may not possess a very high level of componential or experiential IQ, but they know how to play the game well and can manipulate their environment, including other people. When Stacey's coworkers complained that she was not street smart, they were pointing out her lack of ability to understand what was going on, especially with the interdepartmental struggles and turf wars that often occur on large and complex matrix teams.

Similarly, the expert salesman who can read the body language of the potential customer knows when to make the pitch for the final close. The grifter who can measure "the mark" for the scam is a case of the negative use of contextual intelligence. Some of the best examples of the use of contextual intelligence are portrayed in film roles. Tom Cruise's role in *The Color of Money* depicts a contextually wise character.

Most schools focus heavily on developing componential IQ and base admittance on tests that measure it. So the fact that componential IQ gets emphasized to the detriment of the other two types probably accounts for the lack of relationship between standard tests, grade point averages, and job performance. Most jobs require the application of a combination of all three. As Sterling Livingston, former professor at Harvard Business School, points out, a manager's job involves very little use of analytical (componential) skills and heavy application of experiential skills. Effective managers must be able to use their experience and knowledge to identify opportunities as well as understand problems and how to solve them.

Knocking on Opportunity's Door

For managers, the pertinent question is not how to do things right but how to find the right things to do—that is, how to find opportunities. An elegant solution to the wrong problem wastes valuable resources and limits the effectiveness of all involved. Opportunity finding is the ability to scan the environment, see the areas in which the most can be gained, and focus on the opportunities. Using a mixture of experiential and contextual intelligence, an ability to find opportunity can only be developed as we interact with our environment. Some people are born with more of an ability to look for opportunities, but it can be developed with the appropriate training. Most of the emphasis on entrepreneurial development that one sees in the business literature is directed at setting up organizational climates that foster their members' opportunity-finding skills.

One of the best examples of opportunity finding is when Bill Gates and Paul Allen started a software firm in the 1970s that anticipated the rise of the PC in the future marketplace. Software at that time was written for the large mainframe computers used in industry. Most programmers worked within the companies to write individualized programs for specific needs. But Gates and Allen developed the DOS operating system that would work for personal computers and for developers who could use it to write programs for a broader consumer and corporate market. Like Gates and Allen, Mitch Kapor found an opportunity when he devised the Lotus program that captured the corporate market for spreadsheets. All these entrepreneurial geniuses took existing technology and anticipated new trends and needs—and thereby made their fortunes.

Looking for Trouble

Just as successful managers learn to seek out opportunities, they also must be able to go beyond solving problems to anticipating and finding them. A good problem finder must have an acute sensitivity to the environment and to the way that subtle signs of change relate to future events. When NASA decided to go ahead with the *Challenger* launch in 1987, they ignored all signs of potential trouble when they dismissed an internal report by Morton Thiokol pointing out the possibility of O-ring failure at low temperatures. The scientist who wrote that report was looking for problems whereas his bosses at Morton Thiokol and the program people at NASA courted disaster. It is hard to find specific examples of problem anticipation; they go unnoticed because the problem never arises.

Using different cognitive processes and experiential rather than componential intelligence, the problem finder employs more intuition than data. Facts are more useful in understanding the context of the situation and corroborating trends and tendencies than in serving as the basis of analytical problem solving. In one instance, when I was doing organizational research on the role of the foreman in a manufacturing plant, a problem arose. The industrial engineers had just put in new equipment on the assembly line for the fabrication of electrical cables. One of the workers, a shy, middle-aged woman, had had outstanding efficiency ratings but those ratings plummeted when the new equipment went into operation. The foreman in charge went down to observe the new assembly line before talking to the woman. He turned to me and said, "She's left-handed and the new equipment requires her to use her right hand!" He went to the industrial engineer and asked if he could rotate her machine so she could use her left hand. After it was done he went to her bench and asked how things were. She said, "Oh what a difference— I can finally do it right." By observing first-hand what was going on, without embarrassing the woman, he diagnosed the problem and then talked to her. He put all of the personal and technical information together and intuitively solved the problem with the least amount of disturbance.

Development of problem-finding skills depends largely on initiative and openness to learning new skills and to a person's opportunity to apply these skills through first-hand experience. You can learn to bake a cake by reading recipes, but you cannot make a cake without a kitchen. The much-maligned Michael Milken had researched the performance of high-risk junk bonds while at Wharton Business School, but he could not apply this knowledge until the rash of mergers and leveraged buyouts of the 1980s. The junk bond market, which he created, needed his insights and the favorable trends of that time. Nevertheless, problem-finding skills can be taught, as we will see in Chapter Eight, which deals with problem solving and conflict resolution.

Solving Problems

Problem solving, which requires a mixture of componential and experiential IQ, involves examining the facts, relating them to the current situation, classifying the problem, seeking alternative solutions, finding a solution based upon trade-off analysis, and then taking action. Academic training prepares most people for the analytical portion of the process, but not for trade-off analysis (seeing the problem in relationship to reality) and execution (taking action).

Although cognitive problem-solving skills are essential, they do not necessarily ensure a manager's effective performance. Management style and motivation also play important roles. People who score high in componential, experiential, and contextual intelligences have the native capacity to find and solve problems and to seek opportunities, but they may still fail to execute as a manager because their motivational profile (that is, what they need and want) does not fit the requirements of the managerial job. In Chapter Five, we will look at the various combinations of needs for achievement, dominance, and affiliation that are related to effective management. The most effective managers have personalities and previous experiences that fit their organization and position. In a more general sense, effective managers also have developed strong power bases and interpersonal skills.

Managerial Power: Refining Influence Skills

Successful managers are well aware of the role of power in performance. They know that achievement by itself does not make an effective manager, only a competent employee. In order to influence people to participate, to accept various roles, to build liaisons across the organization and networks for effective communication, and to get on with their jobs, managers must be able to use power effectively. Part of practical intelligence is the skillful use of a variety of power bases (that is, the sources of power such as information, rewards, expertise, authority, and so on, as we'll discuss in Chapter Six) to influence people and the environment.

For example, consider a bright, young MBA named Henry who took a position as a management trainee with a multinational company that produces microchips. For two years, he moved through the various departments in the company learning about the various operations and nuances of the organization until he was offered the job as department manager in the information process section, where he had had some experience as a trainee. He had collected notes and observations about the operations in that section, including a number of complaints about work overload, poor communications, and lack of planning. When Henry spent some time with the chief information officer talking about his goals and objectives for the department, Henry mentioned his perceptions about this section. The CFO acknowledged that he was aware of the situation and said he was firmly committed to backing up any changes that would turn the situation around. When Henry asked the CFO to come to one of his staff meetings to address the group, the staff members told Henry that it was one of the few times they had had a face-to-face encounter with upper management.

Henry then outlined his plans for achieving the short- and long-term objectives of the company to all his direct reports. He encouraged them to respond in writing with their perceptions of how they could work together more effectively and asked about their expectations just as he made clear his expectations of each of them.

In addition, Henry tackled the problem of work overload by a coordinated effort and better planning and scheduling of the work for the next three months. He involved all the staff in this endeavor. Henry instituted weekly project meetings geared specifically to problem solving. Each meeting had a definite set of goals and objectives. When the three-month period was up they all agreed that the problem was well on its way to a solution.

After six months on the job, Henry wrote a memo to the CFO, copied to all his subordinates, about the progress in the section. The CFO attended the next section staff meeting and commended everyone on their efforts and progress.

This scenario demonstrates the positive use of a number of influence skills. Henry did not implement any changes until he had researched the problem and involved everyone who would be affected. He recognized that he needed the CFO's commitment and depended on his subordinates for input and acceptance, just as his staff needed critical information and direction from him. Henry opened channels with upper and lower management, obtained information and control of information channels, established favorable working relationships, created a sense of obligation by involving all the participants, and instilled a sense of interdependency among all the participants.

As we shall see in Chapter Six, Henry was using a variety of power bases. His skill in doing so led directly to his success. That is why we devote a whole chapter to the means for developing an array of power bases.

Interpersonal Skills: Understanding Self, Others, and the Environment

In their book *Practical Intelligence*, Richard Wagner and Robert Sternberg point out that managers must be able to manage self, others, and career. Managing others and career is clearly part of the power and influence skills we have just discussed, but managing oneself is a different category. It refers to knowledge of how to manage ourselves on a daily basis to maximize productivity, including a personal assessment of the goals and objectives of the job, the priorities among tasks, knowledge of the best means of accomplishing the end result, and knowledge of what motivates ourselves. In our opening example, for instance, Stacey had excellent self-management skills when she only had herself to think of; after she was promoted, however, she was less able to handle the complexities that involved other people, politics, and the work environment. Henry, in contrast, grasped the power relationships involved in his new job and acted accordingly. Knowledge about personal motivation and other aspects of individual management style is clearly a part of practical intelligence.

Effectively managing others refers to knowledge of the work habits, strengths and weaknesses, and goal orientation of subordinates, colleagues, and superiors. It also takes into account all of the interpersonal skills needed to get people to coordinate and accomplish task activities and maximize both performance and satisfaction. For many managers, working well with their boss is a central aspect of interpersonal relationship management. Managers need to appreciate their boss's world: the personal and organizational objectives, goals, and pressures from above and below; personal strengths and weaknesses, including long suits and blind spots; preferred style of working; communication preferences (information through memos, formal meetings, or phone calls); and style of handling conflict. Without this information, managers are flying blind when dealing with their boss, and unnecessary conflicts, misunderstandings, and problems are inevitable. Table 3.1 outlines the necessary ingredients for managing your boss.

The third element of interpersonal practical intelligence—managing career—means knowing what the reward structure is, how to gain recognition, and how to establish and build a reputation in your specific organization. Each organization or career pathway has unique characteristics that may not be transferable to other organizations or careers. Therefore, knowledge about the organization's views of these factors is imperative if one is to truly develop the skills needed to manage one's career. For instance, Raymond, who was a system engineer with a high-tech company, examined his company's five-year plan and decided to transfer to the sensor division, where new R&D dollars were being spent on projects on airport security and surveillance in the Brazilian rainforests. He knew that it could be a risky move but thought it was worth the chance of getting in on the ground floor. Raymond felt that if he stayed in his present secure position, his opportunities would be limited. He built up relationships with the head of the sensor division by selling his expertise and management know-how. Raymond offered to work on projects that involved a great amount of travel to other countries that were customers for the new research projects. After two years of diligent ef-

TABLE 3.1   MANAGING THE RELATIONSHIP WITH YOUR BOSS

Make sure you understand your boss and his or her context, including:

- Goals and objectives
- The pressures on him or her
- Strengths, weaknesses, blind spots
- Preferred work style

Assess yourself and your needs, including:

- Your own strengths and weaknesses
- Your personal style
- Your predisposition toward dependence on authority figures

Develop and maintain a relationship that:

- Fits both your needs and styles
- Is characterized by mutual expectations
- Keeps your boss informed
- Is based on dependability and honesty
- Selectively uses your boss's time and resources

fort, he was rewarded with a promotion to project leader on the Brazil program. Without his foresight into the five-year plan and his accurate reading of the organizational culture, Raymond would have remained in an organizational rut without the opportunity for rapid advancement.

A final element of the interpersonal skills component of practical intelligence is managing the environment (that is, the value system, the conflict style, and the orientation to interpersonal issues within the organization). The value system defines the organization's do's and don'ts, its perception of the role it plays in the external environment and its own hierarchical structure (loose or strict), its approach to job enrichment and self-development, its view of the reward structure (monetary or other), its preferred communication channels, its view of the role of delegation, and even its dress code. All of these elements add up to a gestalt that defines the specific culture of a given organization. Without this knowledge, the most brilliant contributor can fall prey to invisible forces that hinder his or her career. Let's go back to Stacey and her failed promotion. Stacey did not take stock of the environment she worked in. The company was very interactive and depended upon cooperation and sharing of information at all levels. Conflicts were not based on win/lose dynamics but were looked upon as opportunities for joint problem solving where the participants looked for a wise solution to the conflict. Stacey did not read the culture of the company. She operated on the basis of individual effort and competitiveness. Had she mapped out the culture and modified her behavior the results would have been positive and the demotion averted.

Conclusion

The critical issue in the development of practical intelligence is knowing which skills to focus on. Because influence skills, conceptualization skills, and interpersonal skills are the three areas that distinguish superior managers from average performers, it is clear that any training or development program should include all of them. The rest of this book will develop methods for understanding and changing key components in the three areas of practical intelligence. Influence skills will be discussed in Chapters Five (needs) and Six (power bases), conceptual skills in Chapter Seven (problem solving and conflict management), and interpersonal skills in Chapters Six, Eight (values), and Nine (stress).

CHAPTER FOUR

MENTAL MODELS: HOW DO WE MAKE THE SHIFT?

When Robin flew in to Phoenix to work with Todd, who had recently transferred into her district from another sales territory, she thought it would probably just be a typical pleasant day of visiting customers and writing orders. But it did not turn out that way. Even though she had heard great things about him, Todd was withdrawn and dull, did not seem to pick up on opportunities, and had not drawn up a logical call list so that they could use their time well. Her questions to him elicited little response; Robin started to wonder whether the other district manager had "dumped" Todd on her. She found herself criticizing everything about him, his clothes, his need for a haircut, his sloppy briefcase, his way of greeting buyers he was meeting for the first time.

Robin started to feel anxious; how would she ever make her numbers with this dullard in such a key territory? Would she have to start a termination process—if so, how soon? She hated this kind of conflict; that was why she was so careful in the way she hired reps. Her team always came in first in the company in sales because she hand-picked them and nurtured their efforts. Todd had an attitude she did not like and one that, moreover, would surely keep him from making his goals. As they walked in to make their last call of the day, Robin wondered what she was going to do with this guy. He just did not seem to have "it."

How We Know What We Know

When we encounter a particular situation, our reaction to it is like the process of taking a snapshot. We scan the environment, decide what we want to focus on, and take the picture. The specific settings (lens, focus, and speed) influence the type of photo we get. Depending on the type of lens (wide angle or telephoto), breadth may be sacrificed for detail or vice versa. In addition, we highlight certain aspects at the expense of others and may distort or lose some parts of the scene as we reduce three dimensions to two. Details may be lost or blurred if we have not used the right settings; filters could further influence the image we get of the scene we are trying to capture.

As managers (and as human beings), we process information and conceptualize events and people in much the same way. Our mindset at the time determines whether we focus on the broad, the narrow, or selected portions of what we hear and observe. The first images of events and people give us data that we evaluate as being positive, neutral, or negative. It has been estimated that we evaluate 95 percent of our perceptions as positive or negative rather than neutral. In the example above, Robin had decided very early on that the experience of working together was negative. Those perceptions will color her working and personal relationship with Todd from that point forward.

The ability to be aware of our perceptions, assumptions, and feelings, and to change the way we view situations and people (and our reactions to them) is essential to the Integrated Management Style Model. The capacity to shift thinking empowers managers to make the best use of the building blocks of management style, to alter their behavior, and to affect others' behavior. In this chapter we will look first at how assumptions, perceptions, and feelings operate as part of management style, then discuss a method called *cognitive restructuring* that can be used to change the way we view ourselves, our coworkers, and our organizations.

Assumptions: What We Take for Granted

Throughout life we build up assumptions about what is and what ought to be. In broadest terms, assumptions include all the beliefs, values, and attitudes that we hold. Almost all our assumptions are based on our own or others' past perceptions and experiences. These assumptions, highly charged by emotional events and our upbringing, vary in range and depth. We have assumptions about people's motivations: they are lazy and need to be prodded into action, or they are driven by a sense of competency. We have assumptions about ourselves: I am an honest person or I am a person who has integrity. We have assumptions about causality: spare the rod and spoil the child or high levels of stress lead to high performance. Because they play such a major role in determining our needs, we must address our assumptions if we are to modify our behavior as managers.

Some assumptions are neutral. For example, I assume that the sun will rise and set every day. Because this a natural occurrence, my assumption will be right and taken for granted until the day the sun does not rise. My assumption that no one can create programming code that is as elegant and efficient as mine is not neutral; it is charged with beliefs and values that affect the way I manage the programmers who report to me. My assumption about myself and about the work to be done is fraught with imperatives of shoulds and oughts that control my perceptions of the world and people around me. It does not necessarily reflect objective reality, only my uncontested beliefs about how I should behave.

We may clearly articulate some assumptions, others may be based upon fact or doctrine that we profess. Still others, nested in the unconscious, may only be vaguely articulated in our awareness. Both overt and unconscious assumptions can drive our actions, but when assumptions are unconscious they can lead to a host of problems, especially for managers who are also confronting the assumptions of those they manage. In fact, assumptions underline the bases of all the building blocks of management style that we have already discussed. They profoundly affect how we perceive the world, handle conflict, address our needs, use power, manage stress, and prioritize our values.

There are three basic elements in assumptions: beliefs, values, and attitudes. Beliefs, the most basic of assumptions, are the relationships that we assume exist between certain facts and outcomes: $E = MC^2$, the earth revolves around the sun, disease is caused by bacteria and viruses, all men are created equal, the whole is equal to the sum of its parts, and so on. Taken together, our beliefs make up our basic underlying understanding of ourselves and our environment. Beliefs are founded on past and present experience and knowledge that has been given the stamp of approval by authorities. The electron microscope, for example, allows us to see the bacteria and viruses that we hear or read about. Some beliefs are based upon untested assumptions that can be dysfunctional—for example, that traditional IQ predicts performance in a job, or that women are the weaker sex.

Values are based on assumptions, but unlike simple beliefs, they are evaluative. Values are assumptions about what is or what ought to be that express a preference in a positive or negative way. Examples of values would include, "Experience is desirable," "People ought to be honest," "People should be free," and so on. (Chapter Eight is devoted to the explication and discussion of values.)

Attitudes, which are based on beliefs or values, are both more complex and more general. For example, some people hold the attitude that training is a waste of time and that businesses should spend more resources on assessing existing capabilities for jobs. This attitude can be thought of as an assumption based on the belief that behavior is derived completely from innate abilities. In that view, training is a negative drain on resources. The implications of this attitude, however, are more far-reaching and "loaded" than either the belief or value upon which it is based. The assumption discards all evidence that says that there are some aspects of behavior that we can change. Some may be innate, but a large number are acquired skills. Training in these areas is productive for both the individual and the organization. Unchallenged assumptions and values close out opportunities for growth and potential, especially when dealing with underprivileged and disenfranchised groups.

Everyone who manages is well aware of the importance of assumptions, but it is obviously not necessary (or possible) to be aware of everyone else's assumptions to understand them better. It is, however, crucial to sense which assumptions are salient and important in a given situation. By "salient," we mean the extent to which the person is preoccupied with that assumption, such as, "I ought to be the most technically competent person in my group." By "important," we mean the extent to which an assumption is central to other assumptions or beliefs. For example, the assumption, "I am a good manager and ought to be viewed by others as being good," is a central assumption. If this assumption is called into question, it is apt to lead to concerns about a number of other assumptions as well, such as, "I ought to be a strong leader," or "I ought to have influence within the company." Important or highly charged assumptions are usually those that are most closely related to a person's self-concept.

Because they are so much a part of us, we are often not aware of our assumptions, while at other times we recognize them clearly and specifically. The more aware we are of the assumptions we make, the better we can understand what is going on inside us. Similarly, the more we can identify other people's important assumptions, the more we will be able to understand them from their points of view. Seeking out another's assumptions often helps us become more aware of our own, just as understanding our own helps us see others' assumptions more clearly. The central skill here is being able to recognize and accept (if not approve of) the differences between our own assumptions and those of others. For example, the following list is not exhaustive but illustrates ten common assumptions that drive our behavior and relationships at work.

1. Individual self-interest fosters economic growth and harmony.
2. Competition brings out the best in people and groups.
3. Meritocracy is the only standard for rewards in society.
4. Collaboration leads to management by committee.
5. An individual is measured by his or her wealth.
6. An individual is measured by his or her personal achievements.
7. Teamwork leads to greater productivity.
8. People need to be told, shown, and trained in proper work habits.
9. People need a sense that they are believed capable of assuming responsibility.
10. People depend and expect direction from above; they do not want to think for themselves.

If you take a moment to examine these assumptions and the beliefs, values, and attitudes they engender, it is not hard to see the behavior they encourage. How well, for instance, would a matrix organization work in a corporation that assumed that competition brings out the best in people, that individuals are measured by their achievements, *and* that teamwork leads to greater productivity?

Perception: How We Interpret Experience

The process by which we take in information through our five senses and make meaning of it is all part of perception. In the chapter-opening example, when Robin came to work with Todd, she was taking in information about his appearance, his attitude, his behavior, his sales performance, and his intelligence. She put all that data together and came up with the perception that Todd was not what she had been promised and perhaps did not even belong on her staff.

In psychological types, sensing people base their perceptions on what they consider facts and details in the situation. An intuitive type of person can arrive at a perception without being aware of the concrete basis for it. Intuitive types can make leaps from the past or present to future possibilities. There are many other factors in our interpretations of situations and experiences. Given the many different ways of processing a situation, perception can vary widely from individual to individual. Scientific research on attitudes and beliefs makes us acutely aware of the role of our own perceptions in determining our behavior in a situation. By modifying our perceptions, we can alter our emotional state and our reactive behavior. Robin had a set of perceptions of Todd based on assumptions that equated casual dress and appearance with incompetence. The feeling tone was decidedly negative. If Robin could neutralize her perception and readjust her assumptions about Todd, it might be possible for the two of them to develop a more congenial and productive relationship. The technique for this neutralizing change process is known as *cognitive restructuring,* which we will look at in depth later on in the chapter.

To understand perception, it is important to realize that:

- We structure our perceptions to fit our wishes, biases, needs, and expectations. When I am hungry, I focus my attention on food and drink. A steak is more satisfying to think of having for dinner at seven o'clock rather than right after lunch.
- Emotions may influence the perceptual process, either intensifying it or interfering with it. When I am angry with a subordinate, any shortcomings I see will confirm my negative appraisal.
- We are unaware that we are distorting reality because our defenses are at work. When I project blame onto another person, it may be that I feel guilty in the situation but cannot face up to it.
- Inner factors (memory, emotion, wishes, cultural background, and psychological type) carry more weight than external factors (immediate perceptions, logical input from others). If I have been taught that minorities are less competent, I will override data where this is not confirmed.
- Previous experience with positive or negative reinforcement in similar situations generates strong biases that influence the current perception. If I have been punished for bringing up problems in the past, I will overlook and deny problems that arise in the present.
- Life experiences and traditions in our culture can influence how we process information, particularly when we interact with others from a different culture. If I have been taught to maintain a respectable distance from another person when we're in conversation (in North American culture, a foot and a half or greater), I may be put off when a South American stands much closer to me when we talk. I may retreat and focus on maintaining the appropriate distance, losing sight of what is being said.
- The human brain is systematic and selective in the way it organizes the information it receives into a perceptual whole, what German psychologists of the 1920s and 1930s called a "gestalt" (or pattern of awareness) that is based upon all sensory inputs taken in when we are awake. We are constantly combining new information with previous assumptions and perceptions in an attempt to create a consistent and coherent pattern that makes sense to us. Each thought must fit within the pattern even if it is illogical or false. Consequently, perception becomes our own construction of what constitutes reality.

- Other major factors that affect perception include regional variation, climate, population density, population variety, nationality or ethnic background and allegiance, religious beliefs, educational level, emotional maturity or immaturity, social class, professional background, and gender. A person from New York may turn off a client from Augusta, Georgia, by his accent and vice versa.

Seeing Situations in New Ways: Functional Perception

Perception plays a profound role in our organizational life: how we deal with conflict, handle gender differences, develop strategic plans for the future, implement procedures for daily operations, handle stress, motivate others, and use power. The most practical approach to dealing with the multitude of perceptions that inevitably exist in organizations is to develop "functional perception," a way of looking at how our perceptions mesh with others'. The process for developing functional perception follows these ten steps:

1. Understand your motives, beliefs, and assumptions about the world around you. Then try to understand the motives, beliefs, and assumptions of others.
2. Construct situations where hypotheses, perceptions, and concerns can be aired, tested, and confirmed or discarded.
3. Create a climate of openness for others to discuss the "undiscussable." Generate valid information, avoid premature attribution, and focus on behavior.
4. Listen to your intuitions, which are guides to your inner assumptions, beliefs, and feelings. Go beyond the surface or obvious interpretation of your assumptions. Some assumptions are layered deep in the unconscious.
5. Seek feedback from others on their assumptions, perceptions, and feelings about the situation. Give feedback to others on your response to their perspectives.
6. Take responsibility for your assumptions, perceptions, and feelings. Put your statements in the "I think," "I feel," "I believe" formats.
7. Broaden your perspective (read, listen, observe) about people, things, and events by using literature, art, politics, behavior, humanities, philosophy, ethics, and science as your springboard to a new level of awareness.
8. Accept the anxiety that goes with uncertainty. We can help others in making emotion acceptable, but must remember to separate people from the problem.
9. Do not turn the situation into a win/lose proposition. Comparing assumptions, perceptions, and feelings is not a contest or game. It is serious business, and the goal is a wise solution.
10. Recognize that as we learn we broaden our perspectives by making appropriate perceptual, conceptual, and philosophical shifts in our worldview.

As an example of a situation where functional perception could have made a difference, consider this scenario. When John Fraser, president of the elementary and high school division of Jason Publications, hired Carol Mack as sales director for his division, she came highly recommended from a rival publisher in New York. John had held Carol's job for ten years before being promoted to senior vice president of operations. His colleagues, Dick Enders (president), Mike Collins (CFO), and Mason Stuart (VP of the college division), had agreed to recruit a female for the director of sales position. Carol seemed to be the best on paper and in the interviews.

After six months on the job, Carol wondered whether John was holding onto the reins of the sales side of the elementary and high school division too much. It was natural for a period of learning to take place under John's guidance, but it appeared to her that he did not trust her ability to go it alone.

John repeatedly voiced concerns to the senior management team about his reservations of Carol. He thought she was too aggressive, she did not fit in with the Jason management style, and she did not relate well to the all-male field sales staff. John told the group that "the jury is still out on her." But he never told Carol any of this; she felt as though she was living in a vacuum when it came to feedback.

Were John's perceptions functional or were old scripts and assumptions driving his view of Carol? If he had followed the ten steps of functional perception, John could have avoided what ultimately did happen—the dismissal of a motivated and productive person. Carol's dismissal resulted in a lawsuit against Jason Publications, considerable financial damages, and John's loss of reputation.

1. What were Carol's needs and motivations? Did John understand her assumptions and beliefs about the sales director's job? How did those perceptions match his own?
2. Was Carol too aggressive? Did her style fit with Jason Publications? What was the problem with the field representatives? John needed more data than his untested perceptions about Carol.
3. John needed to discuss his perceptions with Carol in an open fashion so that both could air their perceptions and assumptions. He needed to make it possible to focus on behavior rather than on personality or hidden preconceptions.
4. What were John's underlying assumptions about women in management? Did he have preconceived attitudes and beliefs that blocked his functional perception of the situation?
5. John needed to seek information from Carol's subordinates and Jason's customers in addition to the views of the field reps.
6. John should own up to his assumptions, perceptions, and feelings and not look to reinforcement from the "in group."

7. John might try reading about the role of women in management, as well as case histories and books in this area to broaden his perspective.

8. What anxieties were underlying John's perceptions? Did Carol threaten him in some way? Did she violate his set of assumptions about how women were supposed to behave? How was Carol as a person separate from the problem John perceived?

9. John set up a win/lose situation where he was going to amass all the evidence in favor of getting rid of Carol. A win/win approach would have salvaged both Carol's and his career at Jason Publications.

10. John might have used this situation with Carol as a learning experience to profoundly change his worldview.

Checking Our Awareness of Perceptions

Perhaps the most important ingredient in functional perception is awareness of the factors that affect our response to people and situations. The key to that awareness is understanding the relatively stable set of perceptions that make up your own self-concept because, quite simply, you cannot understand other people until you understand yourself. By analyzing the perceptions that make up self-concept (what is unique about us, what distinguishes us from others, what makes us similar), we not only gain a fuller and more accurate sense of ourselves but also sharpen our ability to understand others. The following inventory is a useful way to ask the questions that will help you better understand your own self-concept.

Uniqueness. What makes you different from others? For example, think about how you are different from your boss—are you more interested in facts and details or in the big picture? What about your boss? Do you like working alone or in a team? What does your boss prefer?

Image of Others. What yardstick(s) do you use to evaluate others? For example, do you judge people by qualities such as dependability and honesty? Or other qualities? Do you judge quickly or hold off? What puts you off about other people (e.g., a confrontational approach)? What draws you to other people? What do other people do that makes you uncomfortable?

Image of Self. What do you like best about yourself? What do you like least about yourself? For example, are you well-organized? Good at follow-through? Do you tolerate ambiguity well?

Past Experiences. What are the most important past experiences that made an impression on you? When have you felt most effective at work? For instance, have you developed any new systems? What was it about that project that made it a valuable learning experience? In what settings (e.g., taskforces) have you felt least successful?

Mood. What are your mood states? Are you consistent and stable or likely to fluctuate? How do these mood states affect your perceptions? For instance, when do you become anxious and cranky? Do you have any tendencies toward depression or anxiety? What triggers those states? How do you control them? In what situations (at work and home) do you feel most comfortable and calm?

Life Experience and Learning. What are the most important things that you have learned in the past five years? How do they affect your assumptions about life? For example, what have you learned about whether a relatively structured or unstructured environment works best for you? What has been most useful in learning to deal with uncertainty? How have the things you have learned helped you find a more suitable career path?

Values. What values do you cherish? What possession—tangible or intangible—would you surrender last? List your five most important values concerning your personal and work life (e.g., family security, health, responsibility, freedom, respect, and so on).

Familiarity/Comfort Zone. In what area of activity are you most familiar and secure? For example, do you like to work completely autonomously or would you rather have a clear set of expectations and objectives, and the means to carry out your work?

Uncertainty/Discomfort Zone. In what areas do you feel insecure and anxious? For example, are you stressed when you have too many tasks to accomplish at the same time? When boundaries are unclear? When you have to face interpersonal conflict?

Wants. What one thing would you most want to do? For example, travel internationally? Study art? Become a writer?

Emotions. How do you handle your emotions? Are you more open or closed? Do you express them freely or try to modulate your emotions? What happens to your emotions under stress? What effect does the way you handle emotions have on your life at work and at home?

Focus. To what activity do you give most of your attention? For instance, do you give equal weight to job and to family? Are you able to focus on each one when you are in that situation?

Motivation. What needs drive you in life? For example, are you driven by the need for personal achievement? Wealth? Freedom? Autonomy? Control?

Completion of the Incomplete. Do you communicate the whole story? How do you communicate? For example, are you direct? Concise? Has anyone told you that you sometimes do not give all the information that is needed?

Simplification/Complication. Do you look to simple or complex explanations of people, events, and things? For example, do you enjoy detail and difficult puzzles? Or do you like to find the "common denominator"?

Feelings: How We React to Our Perceptions

Feelings—the third important component of the way that we process situations, people, and events—are our emotional reactions to our immediate perceptions. Perceptions elicit emotional responses, which become part of the "script" that determines how we will deal with a particular situation and other situations that elicit similar responses. Current feelings are based in previous experiences that we learned to see as positive or negative. We all bring our feelings to work with us, as much as we might not like to admit it. For managers, understanding the range of feelings that are apt to surface in the workplace and knowing how to respond are essential not only to shifting our own management style but also to creating a higher quality of life for everyone around us.

Our earliest emotional response, anxiety, develops out of situations where we are afraid of being deprived of food and water or comfort. Unlike fear, which is a reaction to a specific danger, anxiety is an unspecified, vague feeling of uncertainty and helplessness in the face of a perceived threat. Guilt is another feeling that develops early in our lives as the product of the "shoulds" and "oughts" that are scripted for us by the adults in our lives. We feel guilty when we perceive that we have violated some moral or legal standard as defined by figures of authority. It is important to make a distinction between guilt and shame. Shame occurs when we do not live up to what we ideally should be. Thus, a person may be guilty of a crime *and* ashamed of self. Or a person may be guilty—and know it—of violating the rules of the Security and Exchange Commission but may not be ashamed of it. That person may in fact be proud of getting around what he or she perceives as restrictive regulations.

Anxiety, guilt, and shame have positive and negative outcomes. Prolonged "untamed" anxiety leads to emotional and behavioral paralysis as the person unconsciously withdraws from situations that trigger that feeling. Sustained guilt turns an individual into a compulsive worrier or a repressed antisocial. Excessive shame forces us to restrict our actions so as not be revealed as worthless. On the positive side, anxiety can alert us to dangers or challenges that must be overcome. When we have successfully navigated through those dangers, we gain a sense of self-mastery. Dealing effectively with guilt refines our sense of responsibility and commitments to others. Controlling our feelings of shame makes us more aware of our actions towards others.

As we grow up, our feelings differentiate into pleasure, pain, hate, love, disdain, grief, hope, joy, disgust, and so on. As we continue to develop we learn to identify which feelings are attached to our perceptions. If we are punished when a red card is placed in front of us we will feel apprehension when see red in the future. We are taught basic assumptions about what is right and wrong or acceptable. In this sense our emotional state is critically linked to our immediate perceptions and our future perceptions are linked to these "scripts" about our behavior. Our feelings result from meeting the expectations of our scripted assumptions.

For example, we are taught that individual competitiveness is a worthy goal. As we go through life, we will perceive that we have won or not won the game, the sale, the desired person, or the promotion. A variety of feelings will be attached to perceptions of failure—anger at the situation, shame for not performing, incompetence, or rage at ourselves. The particular feeling depends upon our previous conditioning and the distinctive combination of assumptions, perceptions, and feelings.

Feelings often come in pairs, where one is positive and the other negative (e.g., love/hate, disgust/delight, ambiguity/clarity, panic/control). Although we tend to think that negative feelings should be avoided, there are times when they are justified. For example, you may feel indignation when someone violates your trust. The challenge is in the way you handle your indignation. Do you take a defensive position and repress your indignation? Do you lash back at the person with rage? Do you become depressed over the incident? None of these responses will help resolve the conflict. Moving from feelings of indignation in that moment toward constructive confrontation with the other person is more proactive and stress reducing. (See Chapter Eight for specific strategies for handling interpersonal conflicts.)

Assumptions, Perceptions, and Feelings at Work: A Case Study

Before Tom's recent promotion to section manager in a digital processing lab, he was a technical contributor in another section of the department. Tom was raised to be self-reliant, strong, and extremely competitive. He prided himself on his ability to solve technical problems with the greatest competence. His basic assumptions about life and work were:

- I must stand alone.
- Individuality is the highest virtue in the world.
- I must fight any intrusion.
- I will be perceived as weak if I accept help.
- I should push people away when they crowd me.

In his new position, Tom was put in charge of a group investigating technological transfer within the department that was composed of colleagues from other sections and subordinates from his section. He decided that he would make a list of the technologies that could be used in the department and present it to the group. When people questioned how he came up with the list, he became angry and resentful at what he perceived as criticism and withdrew from active participation.

Tom's perceptual filters regarded his group's questions as intrusive and aroused negative feelings. Working as a collaborator threatened his core assumptions about his self-worth. Like most autonomous people, he needed unrestricted freedom of choice, action, and expression. When he encountered this stressful situation, his reaction was to fight. Tom's assumptions conditioned him to perceive active problem solving as a personal threat rather than a challenge for the group to solve.

Tom does not have to remain stuck in this destructive cycle with his assumptions, perceptions, and feelings. He can instead choose to:

- Examine his basic assumptions.
- Accept his negative feelings as the result of these assumptions.
- Recognize that his perceptions and feelings are based on his core assumptions.
- Move toward restructuring his assumptions and changing his mind in a process that is called *cognitive restructuring*, the subject of the rest of this chapter.

Changing Your Mind Changes Everything

Becoming aware of our assumptions, perceptions, and feelings is the first step in *cognitive restructuring,* a behavioral method we can use to change how we perceive and judge the world. The advantage of cognitive restructuring is that it fully accounts not just for behavior (which has been a common way of trying to change management style) but also for thoughts and perceptions. For example, criticism from a tyrannical boss can be perceived differently by different people. If Joe has been taught that perfection is the sole goal in life, he will perceive his boss's criticism of him as a personal put-down, not just feedback on his behavior. As a result, he will suffer anxiety and fear of failure whenever he has to interact with his boss. Eventually Joe may try to avoid his boss. He may think that is a solution, but it actually compounds the problem because Joe flees in terror every time his boss is angry. Cognitive restructuring can help Joe deal with his difficulties.

The Key: How We Talk to Ourselves

One of the basic concepts of cognitive restructuring is "self-talk"—all the ways we talk to ourselves in positive or negative ways. Talking to ourselves builds up scripts for action that may be so negative that they interfere with our well-being and performance. To recognize and correct the effects of self-talk in a given situation, three elements have to be taken into consideration:

1. *Your Self-concept:* Your sense of self-worth and any corresponding negative thoughts about it that may influence your perception of the situation. If your self-concept is dominated by low self-esteem, unwarranted guilt and shame will set you up for failure.
2. *Your Instructions to Yourself:* Corrective scripts that promote new behavior. If, for example, you have a coworker who unexpectedly explodes when asked about work-related problems, you may feel angry or anxious and vow to avoid that person at all costs. The inevitable result is that small problems escalate until they reach crisis proportions. You could change your self-talk so that you tell yourself: "She feels powerless under these circumstances. She is caught off guard and her defense is to explode out of frustration. My job is to not react, let her run down, and move on to problem solving. Maybe I can identify the circumstances that trigger the explosions and avoid them by giving her a memo outlining our problems. I will try this when the next problem arises."
3. *Your Reinforcements to Yourself:* Changes in approach, even moderate ones, can be reinforced with positive self-talk. You decide, for example, to give your

coworker a memo before meetings so she can be prepared. You notice that she still explodes, but because you remain calm and in control, the outburst subsides and she moves into working on the problem. At this point, you reinforce yourself by silently congratulating yourself for taking this stance. You pat yourself on the back and say progress has been made. You did not change your coworker, but you shifted your behavior and now find that your relationship with her is moving steadily in the right direction. You also feel a lot less stress and believe that work will go more smoothly.

The Basics of Changing Your Thinking

In cognitive restructuring, three core activities are necessary for change. First, the thoughts, beliefs, and values that cause negative feelings and behavior must be identified. We must systematically bring to the surface automatic (and sometimes negative or dangerous) thoughts so that we can recognize them. Second, those thoughts, beliefs, and values must be evaluated for their validity. Finally, irrational or untenable beliefs must be countered and shifted to a more rational basis.

Step One: Identify What You're Thinking

The first task in cognitive restructuring is "thought catching." In thought catching, we become aware of automatic thoughts, images, and accompanying feelings that we have when we are stressed and that we perceive as positive or negative. For example, negative automatic thoughts might include: I will be punished for not being perfect. I will not be able to cope with my boss. The future is bleak and uncertain. There is nothing I can do to control myself. I am doomed to failure. Life has no meaning. There is no one I can turn to. I will be blamed for any failure.

Step Two: Evaluate the Impact of Thoughts

The second step is determining the consequences of the thought and whether it causes negative feelings. If we think the future is bleak and uncertain, we may very well feel despair and futility. To change these thoughts to more positive formulations, cognitive restructuring would demonstrate that:

- This reaction may not fit the reality. We may have had an irrational or distorted view of the situation.
- Continuing to hold these perceptions and beliefs will affect our present and future behavior, probably in a negative way. We will set ourselves up for failure.

Step Three: Cope With and Counter Negative Thoughts

Once we have identified the thought and evaluated the impact on our feelings and behavior, we can employ positive coping mechanisms and a technique called *countering* to change the way we handle the distressing situation.

Using Coping Mechanisms

With coping mechanisms, we learn to change distress into challenge and face problems in a calm, rational fashion. They help us abandon irrational beliefs and generate new alternatives. With countering, we develop thoughts that can be used to go against a firmly held negative belief or assumption.

For example, William works for a boss who is a micromanager. Whenever there is a problem, William's boss, Rich, comes in and wants to take over the project. William gets anxious and depressed and says to himself over and over: "The situation is futile. There is no way to cope with Rich. Everyday is doomsday at work." The presence of such thoughts is not the problem; it is that negative thoughts produce negative feelings and poor coping behaviors. A vicious cycle develops that feeds on itself if it is not interrupted. Cognitive restructuring in this case might look something like this:

Thought	Evaluation of Thought	Coping Mechanism
The situation is futile.	This can only lead to despair.	Recognize Rich is a difficult person. He feels the same frustrations and helplessness as the rest of us.
There is no way to cope with Rich.	My coworker Sharon seems to be able to deal with Rich, so I can do the same.	Follow the procedures for dealing with difficult people (see Chapter Nine).
Everyday is doomsday at work.	It will be doomsday if I continue to think this way.	I must look at work and life as a challenge.

Sarah held these beliefs about her role as staff coordinator and her boss, William: "William is the boss. I must be doing something wrong if he needles me. My role is to obey authority without questioning. We are all helpless when faced with a superior force. The boss does the problem solving, not me."

Thought	Evaluation of Thought	Coping Mechanism
My role is to obey authority without questioning.	This makes me a dependent, subservient person.	Authority has its limitations. There are no imperatives to follow. I can question, offer opinions, and still be loyal.
We are all helpless when faced with a superior force.	There are countless examples of the David's and Goliath's in the world. I can look at people who overcome superior forces, e.g., Ghandi.	I can practice role-playing with my husband. He can be the boss and I can learn to be positively assertive.
The boss does the problem solving, not me.	No one wins team games alone. Problem solving is a collaborative process.	Follow the procedures for collaborative conflict resolution.

Sarah used positive self-talk (a type of countering) when she was in difficult situations. She learned that life can be unfair and that people can be difficult, so she developed a strategy based on challenge and mastery. When William started needling her, she said to herself, "Well, here he goes again, same old William. I don't know whether he realizes what he is doing. But regardless, I can't control him, and I don't want to. I will be in charge of myself and try to work out a solution to the problem. I am not helpless and powerless. I am in control." Sarah has applied cognitive restructuring techniques to change her perceptions and reactions to a chronic situation.

Countering Negative Thoughts and Beliefs

Like coping mechanisms, countering helps to replace negative thoughts and beliefs with new assumptions and perceptions that can help to change behavior. The advantage of countering is that it is a structured process for getting at thinking that so often drives unproductive behavior. In the usual practice of cognitive restructuring, countering is used to erase noxious, irrational thoughts, but as we will see in subsequent chapters, it can also be applied to restructuring our needs, power bases, conflict styles, and stress management.

The theory behind countering is that when you repeatedly counter a negative thought, belief, or assumption, you weaken it and build up an effective charge that reduces its potency. For example, I might have an irrational belief that everyone must love me. It can be countered by: "Baloney! Fat chance in hell! Really, there are many people who are incapable of showing respect, affection, or compassion for others. When I encounter them, I must take this into consideration." The more counters you muster against an assumption or belief, the more likely you will succeed in reducing its power.

There are least three types of counters: alternative interpretations, coping statements, and countering protective beliefs.

Alternative Interpretations

These counters are designed to give us new ways to think about a situation, attitude, or person. For example, Murray, a stockbroker, believes that he must succeed in everything that he undertakes. It seems that everything in his life—family, the schools he attended, and his competitive work environment—have reinforced his high need for achievement. He is regularly anxious, tense, and depressed. If he were to develop an alternative interpretation of success, he might say to himself: "I have only so much energy to expend. If I squander it on many endeavors, I will be mediocre in all, so I'd better focus on what I really want to do." Or, he could say, "My family was a stress-ridden bunch of workaholics who never enjoyed life and were miserable for it. I should not follow their imperative." Or, "Those high-priced schools had a set of values that bred competitiveness and lack of compassion." These alternative interpretations could decrease Murray's achievement need to a manageable level, away from the driven frenzy for success.

Matthew, a middle manager, believes that if he is not in total control, all will be lost. This belief strengthens his need to dominate his subordinates, his wife, his friends, and his children. Matthew could reevaluate that assumption by developing some alternative interpretations. He could ask himself, "Now, Matthew, what would happen if you delegated the authority to Jim on the next project?"

"Well, he could fail, and my boss would come down on me."

"Do you really believe that Jim will fail and your boss would blame you? After all, Jim has followed your orders faithfully in the past. Don't you owe him the respect to prove his competence to you and himself?"

"Well, I could try a small project out with him and see what happens."

Matthew can practice this internal dialogue with all the catastrophes that he imagines would happen with his wife, his children, and his friends and even work out a worst-case scenario. If he repeatedly does this, his fear of catastrophe and need to dominate will diminish.

Coping Statements

The rationale behind the use of coping statements is that they help us anticipate problems (which we fear or dread) and devise ways of dealing with them. Coping statements are especially effective in countering negative self-fulfilling prophecies. For example, Sally believes that she cannot confront Elizabeth [her boss] on the overruns on a key project. She frets, "She'll blame me, and I'll suffer." So Sally does *not* tell Elizabeth, and the accounting system reveals the overruns at the end of the quarter. Elizabeth angrily asks Sally why she withheld the information. Sally feels guilty and depressed—another case of the negative self-fulfilling prophecy.

Instead, Sally could construct a script of coping statements so she can deal with the situation and reach a wise solution. For example, instead of thinking, "I can't face Elizabeth. She will explode when she hears the bad news. It will be kill-the-messenger time. I feel depressed. Maybe it will go away," she can try a positive coping message: "There are three reasons why the project is overrun: (1) the client added scope to the work, (2) some estimates for parts were off, and (3) Nick, a programmer, had a heart attack. These seem to be plausible reasons why we are overrun. I know this may be difficult for me to convey to Elizabeth, but I will rehearse this five times and go in and discuss this with her."

After practicing her coping routine, Sally enters Elizabeth's office: "Elizabeth, I want to update you on the project. We have encountered three significant problems, and I want your advice on how we should handle the projected overrun."

Elizabeth replies, "I'm glad you came to me before the quarter was up. Maybe we can do something about it." After the problem-solving session, Sally should give herself some positive reinforcement: "Boy, that was easy. I'm going to try this every time I have these negative thoughts."

Getting Rid of Protective Beliefs

Protective beliefs are cherished assumptions that serve as security blankets. They act as magical thoughts that maintain a strong defensive armor against change. If I don't ride hard on my subordinates, says a manager, they will goof off. The assumption behind this belief is the old saying, "Spare the rod and spoil the child." It is also tied to a need to dominate and be aggressive. The belief is so strong that the manager feels that if he or she gives it up, something will go wrong.

Protective beliefs arise because we want to maintain personal power. Putting down another person elevates us. Protective beliefs can also arise from one's social support system. If a group believes strongly in a protective belief, it is hard to stand up without fear of being ostracized. The protective belief bonds us to the group.

Protective beliefs also persist because we may feel that something disastrous will happen if we change our beliefs. In this case, the protective belief wards off unwanted anxiety. For example, someone might say, "I've been very successful in using the old purchasing system. If I try to learn the new one, I will fail. I will stick to what I know." This protective belief reduces anxiety in the short run but is self-defeating for long-run competence.

For example, Agnes, the head of the publications department in a large financial firm, uncovered her protective beliefs when she found that she was disturbed by her company's move to upgrade its hardware and software. First, she uncovered her beliefs:

1. The old word processor worked quite well. Why fix what is not broken?
2. I am an expert with twenty years experience. What do those young, wet-behind-the-ears kids know about my job?
3. My boss has praised me in the past, and he will stand by me.
4. If we change to the new system, my subordinates will think I am giving in.
5. Giving up power in any area is always dangerous.

Protective beliefs can actually be useful in helping us gain access to underlying concerns. Then we can use counters to break down the concerns. Agnes thought about what anticipated disasters those beliefs might be protecting her against:

1. I may show my incompetence if I try the new system.
2. I am getting old, and I may be slipping.
3. Maybe I am uncertain about my relationship with my boss.
4. I cannot lose control over my subordinates.
5. This is a political environment. Anyone who shows weakness will be swallowed up.

Agnes used the following counters to combat her protective beliefs:

1. I can attend the training sessions as a student. They are risk-free environments because mistakes are part of the learning process.
2. Age equals wisdom. I can use my experience with the previous system to help integrate the new one. I can act as a consultant when problems arise.
3. I will set up progress meetings with my boss to discuss the new system. He will be grateful for my positive attitude.
4. I will discuss the new system with my subordinates to get their perceptions and feelings. This will maintain my stature as a caring, receptive boss.

5. Everyone else is in the same boat—naïve and anxious. My positive attitude can lend support to others. This can lead to positive bonds and break down destructive competition.

Shifting Your Perceptions as a Manager

Most of our beliefs, attitudes, and values are positive, constructive, and reality-based, but some are based on distorted perceptions that may develop into harmful life themes. Our day-to-day perceptions may be guided by negative or traumatic experiences, or poor role models; we organize what we perceive today in the light of the past. For example, you may think, "I am helpless. My strategy to resolve this discomforting feeling is to attach myself to people who can help me." If this is a persistent pattern, you become a dependent person. You may think, "Errors are bad; I must not err. I must be constantly alert to cues that may disrupt my drive for perfection." Or, "People are potential adversaries. I organize my perceptions to be on guard against signs of competition from others. I have to be a wary person." Or, "I could be stepped on. I develop resistance strategies to cope with this perception of the world. I am uncooperative even when it is in my best interest to be a team player."

All these patterns of behavior based on previous assumptions are maladaptive if they become habitual ways of organizing our current perceptions as managers. Similarly, it is important to recognize that all manner of behaviors that we may not like in other people—egocentricity, competitiveness, exhibitionism—may be adaptive in certain situations but grossly maladaptive in others. We only have other people's behavior to indicate what is going on within them, because it is uncommon for them to reveal their thoughts, feelings, and wishes. Behavior is what we want to change, however, and in order for that to happen their perceptions of a given type of experience must first shift.

The key to perceptual shifting in the workplace is the manager's own perceptions. It starts with identifying any perceptions that have a negative effect on interpersonal relationships. For example, you might hold the belief that your boss is like someone else you know (a big brother, your mother, a teacher) who once caused you psychological harm. That past event influences your immediate perception, leading to negative feelings and judgments about your boss.

Usually an unfavorable pattern is not corrected until the faulty perception is changed and a more realistic, less damaging pattern replaces it. In other words, if earlier perceptions of an authority figure are affecting your relationship with your boss, you will have to shift your perceptions in order to remove the negative emotion you are feeling and replace it with more neutral and productive perceptions.

The centerpiece of making these perceptual shifts is completing a three-column worksheet that is divided as follows:

Column 1: List every thought or belief or assumption that causes negative effects in a particular situation. "Driving in traffic makes me crazy. I can't concentrate on anything else."

Column 2: Think of the personal negative consequences of the belief. Try to look at past experience as a guide. "When I have these thoughts I become angry, distracted, and all keyed up by the time I reach work. It is not good for me."

Column 3: Record the best argument against (that is, the counter for) the belief. Ideally, this argument will be emotionally persuasive as well as rationally sound. "No one can make me mad or stressed. I am doing this to myself. I can gain control by listening to my favorite radio station. I can use this time to go over my day's schedule in my head. I can prepare my day before I get to the office."

Plan to spend five to ten minutes a day meditating on critical past incidents that disprove the irrational belief and make sure you fill in on the worksheet those perceptions that need to be shifted because they are no longer serving you.

Cognitive Restructuring and the Elements of Management Style

The three steps of cognitive restructuring can be especially useful to modify most elements of management style. Let's look at each one individually.

Modifying Psychological Type

As an innate part of us, psychological type is not an element we want to reconstruct over the long haul. But sometimes we need to adjust to meet the requirements of the people and the task at hand. A person with a thinking (T) orientation may have to develop the opposite pole, feeling (F), in order to assess the impact of their judgments. The logical, analytical, and impersonal manner of the thinking type sometimes leaves out the human side of the equation. For example, such a person's thinking might need to shift as follows:

Assumption/Belief	Evaluation	Counters for Shifting Perception
The logic of the decision should always dictate action.	Sometimes what appears to be logical can be countered with other viewpoints.	My logic needs to be reinforced or countered by others' perceptions and concerns in the situation.
One must disregard personal feelings at all costs.	This can lead to negative impacts on others.	I must always ask, "Who is affected by this decision? In what way? Is there an alternative?"
Individual values do not count in making a decision.	Discarding personal values leads to a lack of diversity.	I must respect personal values. Only then can we reach a productive consensus on a problem.

Strengthening and Changing Motives and Needs

Our motives and needs can either be powerful forces in the service of performance or saboteurs if we let them get in the way. Cognitive restructuring can be useful in helping us identify negative needs patterns and change them for the better. For instance, Malcolm was a hard-driving aggressive investment banker who at times alienated his staff and his partners. His high need for achievement, together with his aggressiveness, dominated his managerial style. After a series of key employees left the firm, Malcolm decided he needed to modify his approach to people. He started by looking at the basic assumptions behind his achievement and aggressive drives, then outlined his assumptions, evaluated them, and developed counters.

Assumption/Belief	Evaluation	Counters for Shifting Perception
My personal goals supercede all others.	This has gotten me in trouble in the past. People see me as self-centered and aloof.	I can still fulfill my personal goals by coordinating my efforts with others in a win/win strategy.

I personally have to do the job.	I have been accused of not being a team player. Even my partners think this gets in the way of effective performance.	The firm is a team. I may be the team leader today, but someone else can lead the team tomorrow. Our goals are interrelated.
I must prove I am the best.	This assumption has created enemies for me.	I need colleagues and loyal subordinates, not competitors and enemies.

Developing Positive Power and Influence Skills

The effective use of power is a learned skill and has little to do with innate factors. Sometimes our assumptions about power get in the way of using positive influence skills. Marsha was a shy senior programmer in an educational software company who had difficulty in leading her group. It appeared that she had faulty assumptions about power that blocked her effectiveness. Three of her major assumptions are listed below.

Assumption/Belief	**Evaluation**	**Counters for Shifting Perception**
I am very low in dominance. I cannot be a powerful person.	Power is a learned skill.	Power is not dominance; it is influencing others through my behavior.
I need to be the expert at all times.	This power base has limited use. Being the expert too often turns people off.	I can use my expert power when asked for. It is like a battery charge, to be used when needed.
All power corrupts.	Some power is corrupting. Power, when used positively, gets things done.	I need to look at what is necessary to get the job done. I can influence people without hurting them. When this happens I am effective.

Practicing Effective Conflict Resolution

The way that we approach conflict management is based upon our assumptions about what causes it and how it should be dealt with. Cognitive restructuring can be particularly useful in bringing those assumptions to the surface and countering them.

Assumption/Belief	Evaluation	Counters for Shifting Perception
Conflict must be avoided at all costs.	In the long run the issue will get more serious.	Conflict is natural and can be solved by following the correct procedures.
Conflict is a contest of wills.	Conflict will degenerate into warring factions.	Conflict is not a contest. It is directing energies toward a solution.
Personalities determine how conflict is solved.	Interjecting personal attacks only exacerbates the problem.	Separate the people from the problem. Focus on perceptions, concerns, and mutual options for gain.

Managing the Irrational Beliefs Behind Stress

Stress can be caused by our irrational thoughts about the way things should be. These thoughts or beliefs can lead to internal stress that causes us misery. Sheldon, a bright but harried marketing manager, had the following irrational thoughts that needed to be restructured.

Assumption/Belief	Evaluation	Counters for Shifting Perception
My self-worth is tied to my achievements.	Failure will bring on depression or guilt.	There is more to me than my material achievements. These will change as time goes on. I must look to other avenues for self-worth.

There is a perfect and best way to do a job.	This leads to an obsessive search for the perfect way. I can be frustrated and discard one approach after another.	Some home runs go 500 feet and others just make it over the fence. A home run is a home run.
There are wicked people in the world who must be punished.	This can lead to paranoid thoughts. I will constantly be on the lookout for these people, leaving little time for anything else.	For every wicked person, there are one hundred good people. I should concentrate on being good and rewarding others for their goodness.

Coping with Organizational Culture

There are times when we face organizational changes that our beliefs can get in the way of coping with the impeding events. Jessica's company was in the throes of a merger. She uncovered four beliefs that were paralyzing her daily work patterns.

Assumption/Belief	Evaluation	Counters for Shifting Perception
The new merger will change the company.	This may happen, but the outcome is not decided.	I cannot control the macro culture. The more I focus on what I cannot change, the more futile it becomes.
The changes will have a negative impact on my group.	This thought could be a negative self-fulfilling prophecy.	I have control over myself and the micro environment in which I work.
My current or new boss will prove to be difficult.	He may be under stress or living with uncertainty as I am.	I can manage my boss by understanding his goals, needs, and style.
The uncertainty will be stressful.	Uncertainty can be managed.	I can cope by practicing stress management and relaxation techniques.

Relaxation Techniques and Cognitive Restructuring

An impressive body of scientific evidence demonstrates that the use of relaxation techniques can foster a state of readiness for changing one's assumptions, perceptions, and feelings. Relaxation can be used as a stress reduction technique, and can be combined with cognitive restructuring techniques.

Herbert Benson, a noted researcher on stress and the relaxation response, confirms that executives in a pressure-cooker environment cannot escape the realities of the situation but can counteract them with the relaxation response. Practiced every day, deep relaxation will help you attain a calmness and serenity that almost reaches a state of suspended animation. At such a high level, it allows you to suspend negative critical thinking and open up to other stress-reduction techniques to deal with your problems. In a state of deep relaxation, it is possible to reach your inner thoughts and to use them consciously. For example, you can mentally rehearse tasks and performances that will prove to be very effective when dealing with difficult employees or bosses. In a broader context, deep relaxation can help you in dealing with life's problems.

When you are ready to try deep relaxation, go to a private area and sit in a comfortable chair. Then close your eyes, take a deep breath, breathe slowly and deeply, and progressively relax your body by telling yourself to "go deeper." The following script encapsulates the key elements. Memorize this, or read it first and practice as you go along:

You are going to do three things. First, raise your eyes toward the ceiling without moving your head. Hold them like this. Now take a deep breath, exhale, and close your eyes. Take three deep breaths. Sink deeper and deeper into your chair. Let your arms go limp.

Breathe deeper and more slowly. Now focus on the muscles in your head. These muscles need to be relaxed. Feel the tension flowing out of the muscles of your forehead. Now focus on your eyes. Let the lids totally relax.

Now relax the muscles in your cheeks. Feel them go limp. Now relax the muscles around your lips and chin. Feel how your head is perfectly relaxed. Breathe more deeply and slowly.

Now relax your shoulders, your arms, and your fingers. Focus on your upper back, and let all the tension drain from these muscles. Breathe more deeply and slowly. Relax the muscles in your lower back, buttocks, and thighs. Now relax your calves, feet, and toes. Feel how deeply you have sunk into your chair.

You are floating on a cloud. Breathe deeply and slowly. Keep repeating the words "calm and serene." Stay as long as you like in this ever calmer state. When you are ready to stop, take a deep breath, exhale, slowly open your eyes, and stretch your arms.

This procedure is easily learned. You may prefer transcendental meditation or yoga. The end result is the same: lower tension, greater calm, and an open mind.

Conclusion

The key to understanding how we view the world is the APF model of assumptions, perceptions, and feelings. By focusing on these elements we can isolate and eliminate faulty views about ourselves and others. This model allows us to cognitively restucture our management style and control stress. We will be using the model throughout the book in the appropriate chapters.

PART TWO

THE ELEMENTS OF
MANAGEMENT STYLE

CHAPTER FIVE

NEEDS: THE DRIVE TOWARDS COMPETENCE

In his office in the back of the electronics plant where he was a section manager, Kevin was fretting. Several cost and schedule problems had surfaced with the new device they were building for Jetronics. He knew he should tell the plant manager, Vince, about the problems, but Vince was so touchy and demanding. He really never wanted to hear about trouble with anything at the plant, especially not about personnel issues. At the staff meeting that morning, when José (another section manager) admitted that some serious glitches were developing, Vince blew up. He called José an idiot for not identifying the problem sooner and not getting his team up to speed in solving it. Kevin knew José had been working furiously to solve the problem; he really needed Vince's advice but was intimidated by Vince's attitude. After the meeting, Kevin had seen José storm back to his section and start berating his team leaders, telling them they had better get the problem solved before the customer found out about it. Even so, there would definitely be a delay of the product release to Jetronics. So Kevin had kept quiet about the problems in his section, and now he was really worried. He scowled down at his cluttered desktop and muttered to himself, "What *are* we going to do? Jetronics could cancel the project when they find out that we're late and over budget. Then we'll all be out of a job."

The Need for Needs

We all come into the world with the challenge to maximize our talents. If we succeed in doing so, we feel competent and in charge of our destiny. Indeed, a desire for a sense of competence is part of everyone's personal development. The carpenter, the pianist, the manager, the baseball player all want the same thing: a sense of personal accomplishment. Among those whose fulfillment is blocked by physical or social barriers, this desire for competence may be even stronger.

Many psychologists have noted and described the importance of the drive for competence. Some have called it self-actualization, seeing it as the arch-motivator above all other motivations. C. G. Jung called it individuation, or the search for the total self, the full integration of our potential. By whatever name, competence is determined by our capacity to interact with the environment and to grow and flourish psychologically.

Needs are the forces that organize the perceptions, judgments, and actions that we use in our drive towards competence. They can be something we lack but seek, or something we have and wish to keep. We all have complexes of needs that we are trying one way or another to fulfill. In doing so, our needs express our personalities and affect how we function as managers. Because understanding and correctly interpreting the underlying patterns of our own and others' needs are essential to any change effort, they are a crucial building block in the Integrated Management Style Model. Vince, the plant manager, and his subordinates, Kevin and José, were all driven by patterns of need that affect more than their working relationships. Those needs also affect the plant's overall productivity and performance and the lives of everyone who works there. If any of them want to change their management style, they are going to have to look at the needs that are driving them and how those needs fit with the other elements of their management style.

There are many different categories of needs, but in this book we will focus on the fifteen that are especially relevant to management style and organizational behavior. The fifteen are organized into four groups:

1. Overall management needs (how we approach the management task)
2. Boss–subordinate needs (how we manage our relationships "up and down")
3. Interpersonal needs (the "tone" of our management style)
4. Task-related needs (the fit between organizational and individual tasks)

All of these needs are the result of a combination of nature and nurture. They are like muscles. Their mass and shape vary from person to person. We can develop them through conditioning and weight training or let them wither through inactivity. The same is true for needs. Because they are fostered by both innate drives and environmental influences, we can reshape them through mental "exercise." This chapter is devoted to helping managers understand these groups of needs, identify their own unique configuration of them, and develop some techniques for mediating those that may be problematic.

The Big Ones: Overall Management Needs

All managers have individual patterns of needs that center around exercising power (dominance), orienting themselves to tasks (achievement), and relating to their colleagues (affiliation). These needs are clearly essential not just to how the work gets done but also to how managers view their roles and themselves as leaders. Like all needs, they vary in intensity and in the extent to which they are present within each of us.

Dominance: The Need to Direct

Dominance is the need to control the environment, to be in charge, to influence or direct others' behavior. A manager with a need for dominance stresses control, influence, persuasion, or authority in supervising others. As a sole motivator of subordinates, however, dominance is an ineffective and crude kind of power (as we will see in Chapter Six). In the opening anecdote, Vince was a manager with a high need for dominance who did not want to hear about problems. His staff shielded him from any that arose and even concealed bad news about the status of the quality, cost, and schedule of an important product. When problems surfaced, Vince did what he always does: He blamed his managers for not disciplining their subordinates, who turned around and did the same to their people. In all likelihood, Vince will either have to modify his management style or be transferred to another plant, where the requirements for interdependence and open communication are not as important in getting the product out.

Achievement: The Need for Success

Achievement is the need to do our best, to be successful, to accomplish tasks that require skill and effort and that we are interested in and care about. Achievement can be satisfied in any number of ways—athletic activities, intellectual pursuits, hobbies, or professional awards, to name just a few. The need for achievement is usually an individualistic drive rather than a collaborative one. Managers with a need for achievement seek tasks that require their personal expertise, skill, and effort. More than 80 percent of successful managers are high in this need.

Most often, those with a strong need for achievement carry out tasks alone, not as part of a team, and may be unable to give up their personal involvement through delegation. A manager with an exclusive need for achievement who tries to delegate may hover, trying to do others' work for them while ignoring the big picture. Other disadvantages include isolation from those who can give productive feedback, excessive rivalry with colleagues, secrecy or redundancy in accomplishing tasks, and stress from trying to excel at all costs.

Affiliation: The Need to Be Together

Affiliation is the need to draw near to and cooperate or reciprocate with an ally, to participate in a friendly group, and to do things with people rather than alone. Those with a need for affiliation have a participative style and form strong attachments to peers, subordinates, and bosses. They like to share equally in making group decisions. Affiliative managers value teamwork and communicate well with their subordinates and colleagues. Although affiliative managers help build strong morale, they may consider tasks (achievement) to be less important than relationships.

The aim of the need for affiliation is to form mutually productive, cooperative, and reciprocal relations with others. Organizations with too many managers with low needs for affiliation have difficulty in developing cross-functional teams. Either their achievement or their dominance needs get in the way. Vince's low need for affiliation combined with his high need for dominance were at the heart of his problems as a plant manager.

More Than the Sum: Combinations of Overall Management Needs

Dominance, achievement, and affiliation may occur in managers in any of the following four combinations:

Dominance–Achievement–Affiliation

Few managers have a high level of all three overall needs, but the combination is ideal. When they are in balance, the result is a productive combination of influence, task orientation, and teamwork. The prototype for this combination of needs is General Dwight D. Eisenhower, who was supreme commander of the

Allied forces during World War II. He had the arduous job of coordinating policy, procedures, and operations among the highly independent and politically motivated allies. His ability to influence (without alienating) Winston Churchill, Joseph Stalin, and Charles de Gaulle demonstrated his needs for dominance and affiliation, while his drive to win the war in Europe showed his need for achievement. President Franklin Roosevelt picked General Eisenhower for this constellation of qualities, which he continued to use after his election as president of the United States in the post-war years, when moderation and constructive action were needed.

Dominance–Achievement

The familiar combination of dominance and achievement needs in managers results in a tendency to control and drive a task with little regard for teamwork or affiliation. Such managers give orders and delegate little responsibility. Bottom-line organizations value this type of approach, and many such domineering, achievement-oriented managers rise to the top.

Take the case of Marcia, who was placed in charge of a division in a defense-related company. The division had done well when cost-plus contracts were the vogue, but when Congress tightened funding, it had started to miss both cost and schedule targets. The managers in the division had traditionally let the engineers have great leeway with design and budget. Marcia believed this had to change and did not care who would not like it. She focused on meeting the targets at every ninety-day cycle. She began to tighten up the budget and design requirements, held weekly review meetings with all her direct reports, and demanded strict adherence to her new policies. When she heard about a problem, she left her office and went down to take care of it herself. She alienated many managers, but after six months the division turned around.

Marcia stayed on as division manager for another year until she was transferred to another division that was in trouble. After she had been there awhile, rumors started to surface that a number of key engineers were planning to leave that division. The president decided that Marcia had outlived her usefulness and asked her to leave. Marcia is the typical trouble-shooter manager who can achieve short-term results but plays havoc with morale in the long run.

Dominance–Affiliation

Dominance and affiliation together signal the need for control combined with the need for bonding and loyalty to a team. Such managers assign actual task achievement to subordinates but give them strong direction and accountability. This management style has a very political feel to it and can be effective, if it is not abused. Jack, for example, was known as a project manager who let people do their jobs without micromanaging. He saw his job as building relationships with task managers and coordinating the overall project. When it came to exercising influence, he tended to use power judiciously, acting as neither an authority figure nor as an expert. He rewarded competence and made sure the information flowed through all levels. Dominance and affiliation managers like Jack lead in a persuasive and friendly way and let others do their own work (indicating moderate to low achievement needs).

Achievement–Affiliation

In this combination, the manager emphasizes both the task and the interpersonal relationships among those who are to perform it. This highly participatory management style makes the manager part of the team and can be effective if the manager retains his or her rightful role as the head decision maker. Sheila, for instance, was manager of a design team. Her philosophy was not to dominate the group but to facilitate and to be a contributor. She wanted to be—and was—well-respected as a peer, not as a boss. In previous jobs where schedule and cost were supreme, Sheila had been less successful. Her bosses and colleagues did not seem to value her leading-by-example (low dominance) management style.

Managing Up and Down: Boss–Subordinate Needs

Within the dynamics of boss–subordinate relationships there are five needs that affect the manner in which the people in these roles interact with each other: autonomy, deference, nurturance, assistance, and abasement.

Autonomy: Just Let Me Do My Job

Autonomy is the need to make decisions independently, to feel free and not obliged to conform. Those who need autonomy wish to decide their own agenda, to work around hierarchies, and resist coercion and restriction. Autonomous people can be a great asset when they are individual contributors and do not have to work with others. They can be left alone with minimal supervision, but the downside is that unchecked autonomy can lead to off-base decisions, irresponsible behavior, and a low threshold for direction from anyone else. If the person with a high need for autonomy does not have the same goals and objectives as the organization, he or she is trouble waiting to happen.

Peggy, for example, was a marketing manager who gained recognition as a creative copy designer. She reported to Matt, a seasoned marketing director, who tended to overlook individual idiosyncrasies in favor of performance. He always said Peggy was an outspoken maverick but thought she did such a great job that he promoted her to marketing development manager. Peggy's new boss, Candace, was a strong-willed believer in respect for authority and discipline. She tended to be on top of all the projects in her group, whereas Peggy had been accustomed to more freedom of expression and had been encouraged to exercise her creative initiative. Two months after her promotion, Peggy found herself in a running battle with Candace over goals and objectives. The conflict grew out of Peggy's high need for autonomy and low need for deference (see below) and Candace's needs for dominance and deference. Peggy made the mistake of overlooking her new boss's management style and continued to behave as she always had. Neither she nor Candace understood or respected each other's style—and the results were not good for either of them or for their organization.

Deference: Let Me Find Out What You Think

Deference implies a need to respect others, to get suggestions from peers and supervisors, and to find out what others think. Because of those needs, such managers normally follow custom and respect hierarchy. Genuine deference to another generates mutual respect and is the easiest way to build a relationship, but as with other needs, it has a negative side. Extreme deference untempered by critical thinking can develop into complying with others' wishes and accepting their ideas without judgment. But too low a need for deference is a slight to others' concerns and rights. Perhaps José and Kevin in the opening anecdote were exhibiting a high need for deference, which dovetailed with Vince's need to receive deference.

Nurturance: Let Me Support You

People who need nurturance generally have positive feelings toward and empathy for others. They want to give support, affection, and respect rather than to receive them and want to give positive reinforcement when it is appropriate. Because nurturing managers consider the growth and development of subordinates, they serve well as mentors.

Organizations trying to foster better work relationships in order to build effective teams find that it is important to encourage their managers to develop a higher need for nurturance but tempered with a task orientation. Too high or too low levels of nurturance can cause problems. Cold, overly task-oriented managers alienate their subordinates; excessively nurturing managers, in contrast, can smother and hamper independence. A fair mix of nurturance and affiliation can go a long way to building the team spirit that is often cited as a necessity in American business today.

Roland, for example, was director of preventive medicine at Mercy Hospital. His staff of twenty-two health professionals had varying degrees of experience but all were competent in their specialties. Most of the departments at Mercy were run under the traditional medical model in which authority and expertise (including matters of organizational behavior) were the province of department heads. Roland decided to change his group's perspective and encouraged them to attend training seminars that would broaden their knowledge of topics such as conflict resolution, interviewing, team building, and self-awareness. He genuinely cared about his staff's professional and personal growth—and they reciprocated by working well together and respecting themselves, each other, and their patients.

Assistance: Please Support Me

Those with needs for assistance tend to want to be continually and unconditionally rewarded and supported. Such needs can cause interpersonal problems if they are too high or too low. The manager or subordinate with high assistance needs puts great pressure for time and energy on others, while the stoic who does not know how to take praise or to ask for help when he or she needs it may flounder without direction. A manager with a balanced need for assistance understands how to get support in a constructive way that is tied to performance, not to personal needs.

An example of unbalanced assistance needs would be a manager who believes that rewards have to be earned through meeting high standards for performance and is stingy with feedback to his or her subordinates but yet who constantly wants feedback from them. In such a case, the manager's nonverbal messages tell people to agree or suffer the consequences. The low need for nurturance combined with a high need for assistance places undue pressure on subordinates to give, but they get little in return.

Abasement: I'm Responsible for Everything

Those who need abasement tend to accept more responsibility than is justified. They feel guilty when things go wrong and feel liable for actions that may not even have been their responsibility. A good way to describe them is that they are hyper-responsible. This need is not common among managers, probably because people with a high need for abasement, who submit passively to external forces, tend not to make it up the organizational ladder. A low need for abasement might be equally damaging, however, as it may mean that the person takes too little responsibility for the outcomes of his or her behavior. In Japan, for example, where total quality management (TQM) originated, managers have high deference, abasement, and nurturance needs, low autonomy needs, and moderate assistance needs. In overall needs, they are high in achievement and affiliation and moderate in dominance needs. This creates a management style and organizational atmosphere where individual egos can be submerged in the team effort, where managers can readily defer to others' opinions and give positive feedback to one another. Their high degree of responsibility (i.e., abasement) stems from their desire not to lose face with their colleagues by failing.

Combinations: Boss–Subordinate Needs in Interaction

Boss–subordinate needs in combination within an individual may either complement the relationship or cause conflict within it. In a subordinate, high autonomy and low deference needs pose problems for a domineering boss, while high deference and low autonomy needs are complementary (even if it makes the subordinate seem obsequious). The need for deference may combine with the need for assistance (to follow a mentoring manager), for abasement (to humbly serve a domineering person), for nurturance (to praise in order to console), or for dominance (to be loyal to superiors and dominant with subordinates). The need for autonomy may be subsidiary to the need for achievement, such as when a person seeks to be independent in order to pursue a specific purpose. The need for deference may be subsidiary to the need for dominance (to flatter for a promotion), for affiliation (to praise in order to make friends), or for achievement (to praise others in order to obtain a goal).

A high need for abasement can work against smooth boss–subordinate relations. A stressed-out boss may play upon a subordinate's abasement needs, or an abasement-needy boss may take on a punishing number of tasks that should be delegated to others. The need for abasement fuses with the need for assistance (to humbly seek help), for deference (to be compliant), or for nurturance (to give help humbly to others). Subsidiary to abasement are the needs for autonomy (to disobey in order to be punished) and aggression (to attack in order to be humbled).

Needs for nurturance and assistance combine in a number of ways. High assistance needs and low nurturance needs are characteristic of a person who is more of a taker than a giver. A boss with this combination of needs demands that subordinates take care of everything. A subordinate with high assistance and low nurturance needs requires an inordinate amount of reassurance. High nurturance needs coupled with high abasement needs may characterize a person with a pathological need to help everyone. But in most cases, assistance and nurturance needs create a balance of give and take.

Needs for nurturance fuse with needs for affiliation (to assist friends), for dominance (to play the good parent or boss), for deference (to stroke a superior), and for abasement (to be self-sacrificing for another's sake), or for aggression (to be bluntly honest with a friend). Needs for nurturance can be a subsidiary to needs for affiliation, as in people who protect other people so as not to lose their affiliation with them. Assistance needs fuse with needs for affiliation (to have a relationship with a stronger, nurturing person), for dominance (to depend heavily on subordinates), and for abasement (to plead for aid). Assistance needs can be a subsidiary to affiliation needs (to appeal for friendly sympathy), or needs for autonomy (to plead to get one's own way), for dominance (to control another person through pity), or for nurturance (to plead on behalf of another person).

All of this talk of needs may seem like an abstract puzzle, so consider the case of Maurice, who was a middle manager in an insurance company. Labeled a loner by many of his colleagues, Maurice kept a strong grip on information flowing into and out of his department. He maintained as much distance as possible from his boss, Patrick, and repeatedly told everyone in his group that he thought Patrick could not manage his way out of a back seat.

In dealing with his subordinates, Maurice constantly complained about their lack of support for him and his strategies. When things went wrong, he was the first to blame others and refused to take responsibility for what had happened. Maurice demanded that his subordinates pay immediate attention to his problems, and if they did not, he yelled at them. Even when they gave him what he wanted, Maurice was exceptionally stingy with his thanks.

Maurice represents a manager who has high needs for autonomy and assistance and low needs for deference, nuturance, and abasement. When we understand this constellation of needs as displayed in his behavior, it explains why he is such a difficult person to work for.

Tone and Style: The Interpersonal Modifiers

The needs for introspection, exhibition, and aggression affect the quality and tenor of managers' relationships with peers, superiors, and subordinates. Called "interpersonal modifiers" because they give a unique tone or "spin" to a manager's style, they differ from boss–subordinate needs in that they may be more prominently displayed with colleagues and subordinates than with superiors. In addition, they modify the expression of other needs. For example, a manager with high needs for achievement and aggression is very different from a manager with high achievement needs who is low in need for aggression but high in need for introspection. The former will come across as domineering, impatient, and insensitive, while the latter will seem cautious, thorough, and sensitive.

Introspection: What Does It All Mean?

When someone strongly wants to analyze his or her own motives and feelings and to observe others to understand how they feel and what their behavior, motives, and feelings might be, that demonstrates a need for introspection. Managers with high introspective needs can find it to be a positive modifier when it helps them develop empathy for others. When overdone or tinged with suspicion and other negative emotions, introspection can also cause problems such as a tendency to misinterpret others' motivations or behavior.

Exhibition: Look at Me!

Exhibition is the need to be noticed, to be at "center stage" and recognized for one's personal and professional self-worth and accomplishments. Those with this need often say witty and clever things; others may become overbearing and boorish as they pursue attention. Although we all like others to quote, reinforce, recognize, and affirm us, a high need for exhibition can be disruptive. Those with exhibition needs can create conflicts in hierarchical organizations in which center stage is reserved only for those in power or in work teams where several coworkers share the need for recognition. A team overloaded with several people with high exhibition needs can become a Tower of Babel if those needs cannot be managed or counterbalanced in some way.

Aggression: Push 'em Harder

Managers with the need for aggression criticize others publicly and actively disagree by expressing open criticism, angry behavior, and frank, blunt communication. They may show anger or displeasure, or they may blame others. They like to "tell it like it is." Aggression needs bring a hard, hostile tone to a manager's style. Many organizations encourage aggression by assuming that competition among departments and individuals leads to high performance. But in such situations, people act as adversaries instead of collaborators, often with unfavorable results. Vince from our opening example was regarded as the man to get people moving. His caustic, critical style was bad enough on a daily basis, but when things went wrong, he flew into explosive rages, blaming everyone for their incompetence. Rather than face his aggression, Kevin, José, and Vince's other subordinates hid problems from him. When the submerged problems finally caught up with Jetronics, his superiors held Vince accountable. They respected his technical competence but replaced him with a manager who was noted for building teams.

Getting the Work Done: The Task Factors

An equally important part of needs patterns is the way we handle work: how we approach tasks, how we fit into a specific organizational climate, and how well we perform within various work groups. The task factors (change, order, endurance, and intensity) all dictate how managers handle the day-to-day demands of their work. For example, low change and high order needs characterize an organization that makes a simple product in a stable environment. Individuals low in these needs would feel more comfortable there than those high in these needs.

Change: The Challenge of the New

Someone with a need for change wants to do new and different things and tasks, to meet new people, and to change the daily routine. Those with this need like to experiment, to try new jobs, to shift roles and responsibilities, and to move around. Organizations with a dynamic orientation, in which tasks and priorities change frequently, are appropriate for change-hungry managers, but the same work environment would make someone with low change needs feel stressed. There is no right or wrong standard for change needs; they are determined by what feels comfortable for a particular manager in the context of a given job. A bright young college graduate, for example, with a high need for change who takes a repetitive but lucrative first job is likely to become bored and frustrated relatively quickly, a response that may well baffle coworkers with low change needs. For those with low change needs, the security and predictability of their jobs are satisfying enough.

Order: Everything in Its Place

Managers with a need for detailed, precise order and organization in their immediate environments like to work on a routine schedule with few shifts in roles or responsibilities. They want everything to be well-planned and to function smoothly and predictably. Like the need for change, there is no standard need for order that works for everyone. It is a matter of fit between the manager and the organization and the job, but this need can often cause dissension among coworkers. For example, if two people work on the same project and one is meticulous about files and documents while the other does not seem to mind working knee-deep in clutter, there are likely to be clashes, especially over things like borrowed files or software. In their boss's eyes, both may be outstanding performers—the main difference between them is their very different needs for order.

Endurance and Intensity: How the Race Is Run

The two remaining task factors—endurance and intensity—have to do with the way that we go about doing a job. Those with a need for endurance like to keep at a job until it is finished. There is a plodding quality to the need for endurance but a steadiness as well. Such managers will stick with a problem regardless of their progress, and they will put in long hours without distraction. In contrast, intensity indicates a need to work in spurts, to expend bursts of high energy for shorter periods of time. Intensity refers to how hard a person works; endurance refers to how long a person works.

Managers with needs for intensity shift from a high level of alertness and effort to periods of temporary exhaustion, followed by a gearing up to expend a new high level of energy on the same or a different task. The best job environments for those with intensity needs have some combination of dynamic and changeable tasks, daily and sudden crises, constant shifts in priorities, multiple jobs all going on at once, and highly complex tasks. Some of the jobs that fit the high-intensity profile are research and design engineers, emergency medical personnel, trial lawyers, journalists, and troubleshooters in technical or manufacturing operations.

The combination of change, order, endurance, and intensity needs can be seen clearly in the case of Seth, a task engineer with a reputation for always finishing projects. Because of his orderly work style and ability to come in on deadline, Seth was promoted to manager in a program office. After just two months on the job, however, he asked to be transferred back to his old job. When his boss asked why, Seth told him that the constant changes in specifications and priorities in his new position were causing him great stress. Seth's profile on task needs was low change and intensity and high order and endurance. Monique, who replaced Seth, loved the program office job. Her task need profile was the opposite of Seth's: high need for change and intensity coupled with low need for order and endurance.

When Needs Collide: Fusion and Crossed Signals

None of the fifteen needs we have discussed is as simple or predictable as this summary may suggest. All of them can appear in other, often problematic combinations than the ones this chapter has mentioned so far. Even though needs are only one building block of management style, understanding them fully and seeing how they combine (in both positive and negative ways) is essential for managers who want to become aware of their own behavior. That is the first step towards modifying needs patterns as part of creating a stronger and more integrated management style.

Fusion and Confusion

When two or more needs fuse, they are manifested at a high enough level that there will be negative results. Fusion may create a positive effect in some instances, but the negative combinations are more problematic. There are many fusions among needs, but the following combinations can be especially troubling:

Achievement with Dominance. In its most extreme forms, this common pattern among managers leads to too much involvement in details, high need for control, and impaired delegation skills. Achievement/dominance managers tend to micromanage tasks. Under stress, they pounce on subordinates and demand immediate results. Managers with this fusion need to stop hovering and giving orders.

Achievement with Autonomy. The achievement with autonomy fusion may create serious problems because managers focus on their accomplishments to the exclusion of others' needs. Teamwork can suffer in extreme cases, as can the manager's ability to see the big picture.

Dominance with Autonomy. The need to be dominant and at the same time autonomous creates a barrier between managers and their colleagues. Managers with this fusion of needs build a wall around their domains in order to maintain their independence and control, but have difficulty cooperating with other parts of the organization. Such managers often demand strict allegiance within their groups while at the same time preserving their own independence.

Dominance with Exhibition. The combination of dominance with exhibition leads a person to be dramatically forceful in public. The impact of this pattern depends on the circumstances. In certain corporate cultures, this kind of behavior is not tolerated; in others, it is seen as a positive statement. When bosses express these needs, only they (and nobody else) get center stage.

Dominance with Aggression. Dominance with aggression can lead to an autocratic and abusive management style. This kind of manager has a warlord mentality: "Never give an inch, and make them flinch." In certain crisis situations, such managers try to ramrod through decisions that will lead to quick fixes. But in the long run, such tactics usually lead to resentment and lowered performance.

Crossover Problems

Crossover problems occur when one need is high and another is low. For example, a high need for assistance by itself is a problem for managers who need constant reinforcement from the external environment. A low need for nurturance can cause difficulties because managers cannot give positive reinforcement to others. When high assistance and low nurturance are combined, dramatic problems result. Managers should be able to give support without looking for excessive help or sustenance in return. A manager with this particular behavioral pattern acts like a needy child rather than as a role model, behavior that is clearly inappropriate in a work environment.

Another crossover problem involves high autonomy and low deference needs, especially if the manager has a boss who has great authority. In such cases, the subordinate's needs will inevitably run up against the superior's needs. A person with this crossover pattern can survive only if he or she has invaluable skills or expertise, but the tension between manager and boss will never dissipate.

Needs and the Psychological Types

Although the psychological types we discussed in Chapter Two and the needs we have just covered are concerned with different aspects of human behavior and thus are independent of one another, the way they constantly interact is largely responsible for the enormous variety of management styles. For example, two managers typed as ENTJs—sometimes called "commandant" types—may come across very differently because of their individual needs constellations. One ENTJ may have high needs for dominance and achievement, while another may have high needs for achievement and affiliation. The first ENTJ manager will probably have a bossy, domineering leadership style, while the second will be a participatory leader.

The most significant factor in the interaction of psychological type with needs lies in the way that introverts and extroverts express the combinations of overall management needs. Regardless of needs, introverts will be more discreet, while extroverts will be more open. For example, needs for achievement and dominance create a boss-centered style. An introvert will convert this style into a strong-but-silent kind of leadership; even more specifically, an INTJ will have a forceful but autonomous management style. An extrovert, by contrast, will exert more overt guidance and direction. ESTJs or ENTJs with high achievement and dominance needs will let you know what they think about how to do a job. There will be no doubt about their criticisms or suggestions.

A combination of affiliation and achievement needs produces a participatory leadership style in people, but an introverted manager will be less participatory than an extroverted manager, who is likely to be intensely involved as a team member. When affiliation and dominance needs are combined, the result is a political leadership style. A manager's energy focuses on delegating tasks and persuading others. Introverted managers with affiliation and achievement needs will be subtle in their persuasion tactics, while extroverts will be more obvious and direct.

Because of the importance of the interaction of psychological type and needs, let us briefly survey the interaction between them across overall management needs, interpersonal needs, and task factors.

Overall Management Needs

Achievement. Perceptive types (e.g., ENTP, ISTP, etc.) often have strong achievement needs. The dominance of the sensing or the intuitive function determines which kind of data individuals feel comfortable using to meet their achievement needs. Intuitives like conceptual or abstract concepts, while sensing types want facts and details. If a particular job is not well matched with a person's perception function, he or she will feel frustrated and thwarted in satisfying achievement needs. It is rare, for example, for an INFP to be comfortable with accounting procedures or for an ISTJ to take to leading a strategic planning brainstorming session. When perception is not a dominant function, however, and when the need for achievement is low, frustration may be less severe.

For thinking types, who prefer logical and impersonal analysis, high achievement needs can mean that people issues are likely to be subjugated to the task at hand. If thinking types have dominance and aggression needs as well, they are likely to be hard-driving and impatient. Achievement needs are sometimes moderated in feeling types of people, whose concern for relationships softens their drive and ambition.

Dominance. The need for dominance in any psychological type can cause rigidity and inflexibility, depending on their perception of what they need to control. A dominant intuitive type of person may insist on taking a global, conceptual approach when more facts and details are urgently needed. In contrast, a dominant sensing type may amass too much data and miss the forest for the trees. When managers have high needs for dominance and achievement, they tend to micromanage the task and change its emphasis to suit themselves.

When combined with the thinking function, dominance needs can override a manager's concern for others so that he or she focuses on the task to the exclusion of concerns about people. High dominance needs combined with a dominant feeling–judgment function may cause managers to impose their personal values on others. They may forsake logic or insist that others abide by their opinions.

Affiliation. Affiliation needs soften the critical edge of a thinking type of person. Because they need to interact with others, the affiliative thinking person makes kinder, less impersonal judgments. Thinking types who are low in affiliation needs tend to be more critical in their judgments and take harder positions. The affiliative feeling types find satisfaction in group activities that foster the development of organizational and ethical values. Their desire for interaction and harmony makes them champions of teamwork and fair play.

Boss–Subordinate Needs

Autonomy. Introverts with high needs for autonomy find that their energy is turned even more inward and that the desire to work on their own reinforces their tendencies toward introspection and solitary debate. In an extrovert, autonomy needs may dampen the person's natural gregarious tendencies.

Deference. High deference needs tone down the impersonal side of the thinking personality type and increase the degree of feeling. Deferential feeling types will be more reluctant to reveal their values unless pressed to do so.

Nurturance. A need for nurturance causes an introvert to listen intently to others, while the same need in an extrovert will be expressed as offering others verbal support and comfort. A thinking type of person with nurturance needs will be more cautious in giving critical feedback, qualifying it with encouragement and compliments. Nurturing and feeling types will be hypersensitive to the needs of others and will avoid conflict at any cost. If they find themselves in a position where they must offer objective criticism, they will be very uncomfortable.

Assistance. A need for assistance is more apparent in an extrovert than in an introvert, who may suffer this unfulfilled need in silence. For feeling types, a need for assistance makes them sensitive to whether their own needs are being met. A feeling introvert may fret over another person's lack of responsiveness, especially if that other person is a strong thinking type who focuses on impersonal aspects of a situation. An introverted thinking type with assistance needs may brood about another person's illogical judgments.

Abasement. Extroverts who have a need for abasement export it to the outside world so that they often are the victims of manipulators. Introverts who have this need may preoccupy themselves with endless internal ruminations of guilt. Abasement needs profoundly affect all personal interactions for feeling types of people. They will feel guilty about their failures in relationships, and they will ultimately come to resent their guilty feelings. In thinking types of people, a need for abasement leads to ruminations over the circumstances that led up to a situation. Introverts will have more difficulty than extroverts in expressing and meeting this need.

Interpersonal Needs

Introspection. The need to examine oneself and understand strengths and weaknesses is an asset to all sixteen psychological types. Introspection allows us not only to understand ourselves but also to empathize with others. An introspective ISTJ is more likely to appreciate the difference of ENFP (their opposite) than an ISTJ who is low in introspection.

Exhibition. This need is paradoxical for an introvert, who may seek recognition but feel anxious behind a lectern. Writing and acting provide comfortable avenues for introverts to meet their need for exhibition. For extroverts, exhibition is a natural need because they often think and communicate best in the presence of others. The chemistry is less than perfect when the extrovert overplays this need. The overly exhibitionistic extrovert is often seen as bombastic.

Aggression. A need for aggression is amplified in an extrovert, who may publicly subject another person to criticism, barbed wit, or outbursts of temper. In introverts, aggression seeks an outlet through fantasy or erupts as modulated criticism. Among thinking and feeling types alike, aggression adds a sharp, acerbic tone to judgments. The tone is exacerbated if dominance and aggression needs are fused.

The Task Factors

Change. Change needs do not have profound effects on any single type, but they do add complexity. Every type with high change needs wants variety in their work, while those who are low in change needs will prefer a stable routine and tasks. For example, an ISTJ accountant high in change needs may want to work on tax matters one week and shift to payroll tasks the next. An ENFP ethics professor, who is low in change needs, will not mind working on cases involving versions of company fraud for weeks at a time.

Order. Although needs for order do not affect any preference in a predictable way, they can change how a type behaves. An ISTJ low in order needs can have an office that looks like a pig sty, while an ENFP high in order can maintain files that are impeccably organized. This runs counter to what we normally think of these two types. The ISTJ is assumed to be organized and neat, while the ENFP is assumed to be sloppy and loosely organized. Taking a particular type's need for order into account can help make their behavior more understandable.

Endurance/Intensity. The most significant manifestation of the need for endurance occurs when an extrovert is working with others on a task. An extrovert with high endurance needs will gain energy from the group's interaction and perform tirelessly. An introvert in the same situation will stick to the job but will probably feel sapped of energy after it is finished. The opposite outcome occurs when the task involves solitary effort. The introvert who has high endurance needs will relish the job, while the extrovert with that same level of endurance need will have to marshal inner strength to carry on. Introverts with low endurance needs find extensive group interaction very tiring. Extroverts with low endurance needs may shift from one topic to another and seem mercurial. They will not want to sit alone at their desks for long.

Modifying Needs: Shifting and Countering Perceptions

Beneath the surface of needs lie the beliefs, assumptions, and attitudes that drive each one and the behavior that accompanies it. As we discussed in Chapter Four, because our assumptions, perceptions, and feelings were learned early in life and constantly reinforce our needs, any attempt to strengthen or diminish needs must begin by shifting our perceptions. Let us analyze a case where the strength of some needs caused problems for a manager.

Muriel was the manager of the stockholder communications and relations department in an aerospace company that had both a defense and a commercial base for its business. Her job was to be in touch with Wall Street and the stockholders. It was a job that demanded skillful handling of internal accounting procedures for the Wall Street crowd, and deft handling of the reports for the stockholders. One of her major projects was the preparation of the annual report. Although Muriel was a productive worker she was looked upon as a command-and-control manager who took charge most of the time. She also liked to be front and center and receive constant recognition. Her subordinates were intimidated by her style. Muriel constantly demanded support from them regardless of what they were doing at the time. She had no respect for others' priorities. After some tough times at the office Muriel decided that she wanted to know more about her management style to pinpoint areas of strength and pitfalls.

Step 1. She took the MBTI and filled out the Need Assessment in Appendix C. Muriel was an ESTJ who had the following needs pattern:

NEEDS

Achievement	High
Dominance	High
Affiliation	Low
Autonomy	High
Deference	Low
Nurturance	Low
Assistance	High
Abasement	Low
Change	High
Intensity	Low
Endurance	High
Order	High
Introspection	High
Recognition	High
Aggression	High

Step 2. As part of her needs analysis Muriel completed the checklist for any fusion, crossover patterns, and psychological type interactions. These checklists are included in Chapter Ten. The following patterns emerged.

FUSION FACTORS

Achievement with Dominance	Yes	Command-and-control style, likely to micromanage under stress.
Achievement with Autonomy	Yes	Tendency to want to do it her way and not respect others' opinions.
Dominance with Autonomy	Yes	Likely to impose her will on others.
Dominance with Exhibition	Yes	Wants to be front and center and take most of the credit for successes.
Dominance with Aggression	No	When things go wrong she will lash out and attack others.

CROSSOVER FACTORS

High assistance and low nurturance	Yes	Demands attention and assistance without regard for others' needs.
High autonomy and low deference	Yes	Makes decisions without consulting others, disregards others' input.

Psychological Type Interactions

Low Nurturance with Thinking. Muriel is hypercritical of people and does not measure the impact of her statements on others.

Achievement with Sensing. Muriel likes to work with facts and details and tends to shy away from work that involves intuition.

Assistance and Extroversion. She openly demands help from her subordinates and peers. Muriel is likely to complain to her boss about the lack of assistance she gets.

Exhibition and Extroversion. She openly points out her brilliance to others. At times this can be overbearing.

Step 3. Identify strengths and weaknesses from the data sheets.

Strengths

- Strong task orientation and take charge style
- Adaptable to change
- Sticks to a job
- Ability to look at herself and others
- When the task calls for accurate details and organized work, Muriel is without peer

Weaknesses

- Needy type manager who seeks more assistance than she is willing to give
- A command-and-control manager who likes to get her own way
- Likes to be recognized and be front and center in groups
- Her low nurturance tends to heighten her thinking function and make her critical when she does not get her way; has been known to regret statements she made to subordinates and colleagues when she is upset
- Muriel tends to shy away from the big picture

Step 4. Identify any needs that should be modified.

- Decrease need for Dominance
- Decrease need for Assistance
- Decrease need for Recognition
- Decrease need for Autonomy
- Decrease need for Achievement (individual emphasis)

Step 5. Uncover basic assumptions behind the needs and effective counters to modify the need.

Muriel looked at the five needs that needed to be modified and came up with these assumptions and counters.

NEED: AUTONOMY

Assumptions/Beliefs	Counters
I stand alone in a world that is out of step with me.	My personal goals may be in conflict with the big picture.
I am a special person and need to be autonomous to maintain my character.	I can still be independent without building a wall around myself.

(continued)

NEED: AUTONOMY (*continued*)

Assumptions/Beliefs	Counters
The superior individual has no need for boundaries.	Some boundaries are necessary for order in the world. I am no exception.
To be a whole person you must be a nonconformist.	Some forms of nonconformity are antisocial acts.
Adherence to convention produces mediocrity.	Mediocrity has nothing to do with convention. It is a result of other factors such as: sloth, lack of practice and ability.

NEED: DOMINANCE

Assumptions/Beliefs	Counters
I must be in control to achieve my ends.	Raw dominance leads to counter-attacks by others.
My peers and subordinates would not admire me if I was not dominant.	Admiration comes from many sources, not just raw power.
There is a natural hierarchy of leaders and followers.	People can be trained to be positive leaders without oppression.
I have to be in control or everything will fall apart.	Without teamwork most projects fail.
My way is the best way.	I failed to listen to others in the past and I was wrong.

NEED: EXHIBITION

Assumptions/Beliefs	Counters
In order to be a leader, I must stand out from the crowd.	I can still be a leader without flaunting myself.
I need the recognition of others to affirm myself.	I can give myself recognition from my inner strength.

NEED: ASSISTANCE

Assumptions/Beliefs	Counters
I am the boss—people must serve me.	This is a slave mentality. It can only lead to revolt and passive-resistance.
My needs are more important than others' needs.	I must learn to respect others' needs and differences.

NEED: ACHIEVEMENT

Assumptions/Beliefs	Counters
I must prove that I can do the job by myself.	In order to achieve results I need the help and opinions of others.
My personal goals supercede all others.	This has gotten me in trouble in the past. I must guard against extreme hubris.
I am defined by my job. Therefore I must control my destiny.	I can still fufill this need by coordinating my efforts with others.

The objective of the countering exercise is to tame, not obliterate, a need. Muriel is not going to be less dominant in nature; however, she is going to develop positive ways to achieve her goals without a negative backlash.

The key to using counters to change underlying assumptions and beliefs linked to needs is repetition. If you have formed a set of needs based on nature and experience over your lifetime, a one-shot try at countering does not work. Just consider all the constant internal and external conditioning that went into what you are today. Therefore, some structured practice each day is mandatory. In addition, it is important that you produce your own counters rather than use off-the-shelf counters. Relaxation and meditation are two effective adjuncts to counters in that they enable you to become more receptive to your counter-arguments from the assumptions and beliefs underlying a need.

Conclusion

In this chapter we have looked at some of the basic needs that drive us in our pathways to become competent. These needs cannot be predicted from the psychological types and therefore have to be looked at as independent elements in our management style. We explored how various combinations of needs and psychological preference can interact to produce unique configurations of management style. The case of Muriel clearly demonstrates the interactive nature of the psychological types and need patterns. Unlike psychological types, our need patterns—because they are based on assumptions about the world—are subject to modification. The rest of the chapters will deal with the remaining elements of our integrative management style. Each component can be seen as an independent element that is shaped by our experience but interacts with the other elements to produce unique configurations.

CHAPTER SIX

POWER BASES: INFLUENCE, AUTHORITY, AND EXPERTISE

When she was promoted to chief designer of the Mercury Corporation's product brochure group, Karen was exhilarated. She was being recognized for her exceptional creativity as a graphic designer, her excellence as a manager of resources and schedules, and her collaboration skills. Now her boss, Marcia, told her that her first new project in this role would be to create and design a product brochure for an up-and-coming bathroom fixtures company, Euro-Designs. She would be working directly with Euro-Design's hands-on CEO, Bill Trebo, who had built his company into a force in the upscale world of bathroom fixtures in just five years.

When Karen met with Bill and his sales and marketing manager at their headquarters in Boston, she brought along Mark, the project manager, and Shelley, the photographer who had been assigned to the project. Bill kicked off the meeting by saying, "Karen, let me tell you something about myself. I worked my way from the bottom up. I attended engineering school at night, and I've taken courses on the history of European art. I am especially fond of the Renaissance painters and sculptors. My philosophy is that work is art, and art is work, get me? Now let's talk about Euro-Design's product brochure. I'm tired of these drab brochures that look like they were knocked off on a desktop publishing system. I want our brochure to reflect our product's elegant essence: artful bathrooms."

"I have no problem with that philosophy," Karen responded. "I try to represent the client's spirit. On my last project, we shot photos in the Brazilian rainforest for an environmentally responsible corporation. The theme was profit, yet it didn't eliminate the responsibility for respecting natural resources. It worked well with their customers."

"Great, great," Bill interrupted. "Now, I want to use Italy as the backdrop for your photos. I want Rome, Florence, and Venice as sites. I can see the Euro-Design fixtures as part of a montage of the statues in Rome, the canals and portos of Venice. Two art forms joined together. What do you think, Karen?"

"Yes, I can see connecting your products with art objects. On the other hand, I always believe that you need a human element in product photos. After all, your customers are people. I think that we can combine your idea with a living version of some of the great classic sculptures."

"Well, I don't like to mix metaphors—mix classical with Renaissance," objected Bill. "You get confused on the message. Let's stick to one period. As far as the human factor goes, maybe I can bend on that. Why don't you and your staff take what I've said and come up with some ideas that I can respond to. OK?"

The meeting ended abruptly, far short of the time Karen had expected to spend, much to her dismay. On their flight back, Karen erupted. "Every second-generation Italian wants to let you know that he loves art, opera, and pasta. As if we have no taste!"

Shelley tried to appease Karen. "Gee, I thought his idea of using Italy was quite good. I mean everywhere you look there's an interest in things Italian."

Karen glowered at Shelley. "Look, I don't need a lecture from a photographer about culture and graphic design. I can hold my own with anyone, and I've won all kinds of awards for my work." Shelley looked away and dropped her eyes. Karen continued, "Before long Bill will be telling us what type to use. We can't let him dictate our prerogatives!"

Mark, who had been silent during the flight so far, reminded her, "Well, Karen, he *is* our client."

"Yeah, right," Karen said. "Look, I got the promotion for what I know; I'm paid for being the creative genius at Mercury. Otherwise you or somebody else would be in my place."

"Hey, OK," Mark raised his hands as if to declare a truce. The rest of the flight home was spent in silence.

Late that night Karen got a call not from Marcia but from Marcia's boss, Martin Short, the CEO of Mercury. "What the hell are you trying to do, Karen? Lose the account? Bill just got off the phone after telling me that he got the perception you were criticizing his taste in art and thought he was living in the dead past! Why didn't you listen to his suggestions? I want you, Mark, Shelley, and Marcia in my office tomorrow morning at eight o'clock sharp!"

Karen got off the phone in a state of shock, wondering, "What is going on here? I'm only trying to do my job. Martin never criticized my creativity in the past. I've heard Marcia say many times that a client was being unreasonable or pigheaded. Why can't I be allowed the same latitude? Mark and Shelley didn't object. Well, I'll just have to straighten it out tomorrow."

Power: The Uses and Abuses of Influence

Karen, Bill, and Martin were all involved in a power moment, when personal forces clash over who tells each other what to do. Probably none of them was aware that each was striving to be dominant. Paradoxically, each believed that he or she was doing the right thing to get the job done well. Yet something went wrong. That "something" was all about power.

Acquiring and using power effectively is necessary for success in organizations, for managing relationships, and for individual fulfillment. As managers, our ability to use power effectively enhances (or drains) our sense of self-esteem and competence. While power operates any time or place where people are together, this chapter focuses on power as individual managers use it to influence others in achieving mutually beneficial outcomes. It will discuss how individual managers use power in social relationships within organizations and how power within groups can be used to solve problems.

Power arises from our need for dominance, but it is important to make a clear distinction between raw dominance, as seen in nature, and power that is an acquired skill and a craft. Like any craft, the use of power can be improved through practice and conscious effort; even those who have low dominance needs can improve their ability to influence others. Attending consciously to how we gain and use power is a key step in developing an effective management style. However, it is important to keep in mind that the use of power is independent of the other building blocks—it does not flow from psychological types, needs, or conflict styles. Instead, it is a learned response that depends on conscious acquisition of the necessary skills.

In organizations, the manager's power is embedded in and exercised through the networks of social interactions that are part of the work setting. In power interactions, the one who exercises power attempts to influence another. In some interactions, the attempts to influence will be reciprocal, and power flows back and forth. In a one-sided power interaction, there will be one recipient and one wielder of power. The recipient may see the interaction as negative or positive—negative if it is perceived as exploitation, manipulation, or win/lose competition, and positive when he or she benefits from it in economic, symbolic, or personal ways. In that case, both sides will feel that they have won.

The first step in developing an effective sense of power is to accept its existence. Many of us think power is crude dominance, or we make other negative assumptions that prevent us from being effective managers. Or we may be oblivious, as Karen and Bill in the opening example, seemed to be. Rollo May, in his book *Power and Innocence*, states, "As a young man, I held innocence in high esteem. I disliked power, both in theory and practice, and abhorred violence . . . I had, then, to confront my own relationship to power. No longer could I conceal behind my own innocence my envy of those who had power. This, I found, only follows the general procedure in our culture: power is widely coveted and rarely admitted. Generally, those who have power repress awareness of this fact."

The Manager's Power Bases

In general, the ability to influence other people is based in some specific form of power—the power to reward, or to coerce, or apply one's expertise, to name just a few. That is why we use the term "power base." None of the bases of power are inherent or innate; all of them can be acquired once managers understand what they are and how they work. All power bases are critical to managers in achieving the goals of the organization and to the workings of organizational life—to motivation, morale, job satisfaction, employee turnover, problem solving, and teamwork. These bases are often interdependent, overlapping, and may be used in combination with one another, as we will see in taking them up one by one.

Reward Power: Giving Something of Value

When managers give positive strokes, some form of remuneration, promotions, awards, or any symbolic gesture that is seen as a compliment, they are exercising reward power. Reward power depends on the ability to give other people something they value. It can be verbal or nonverbal, tangible (as money, a gift, or career development opportunities) or, more commonly, intangible (conditional praise for someone's behavior or unconditional praise of the person). When the praise is appropriate and genuine, it binds relationships and encourages productivity. When it is indiscriminate and hollow, it loses effectiveness.

By definition, reward power is positive, but its magnitude depends on how the recipient sees the reward. A promotion or a sizable bonus has more positive power than a complimentary letter. A manager appearing personally at the employee's work site to deliver a compliment has more positive power than a phone call.

Developing Reward Power

An effective communication style is the key to developing reward power. Some people find it hard to give positive strokes under any conditions. They are stoical individuals who believe that any amount of praise will "spoil the child." I emphasize the word *child* because that is what they are projecting onto the other person—a child–parent relationship. In most cases, the negative self-fulfilling prophecy comes true: the "child" becomes angry. The manager who holds this belief defies all the research on the power of intermittent positive reinforcement.

The ideal time to give positive reinforcement is at the completion of a defined task. If the task is a project that has taken a long time to complete, say, two years, managers can give reinforcement at various points along the way. Effective managers negotiate mutual expectations with subordinates and take time to check in on progress. Then they can give the appropriate rewards to reinforce performance.

Coercive Power: Dangerous Force

Coercive power involves physical or psychological injury. Managerial use of coercive power does not usually result in physical attack (although it can); more common forms are verbal and nonverbal putdowns, slights, or symbolic gestures of disdain. Being demoted or transferred to an undesirable department or location, or being denied resources are more extreme forms of coercive power. For obvious reasons, most rational people perceive coercive power as negative because it puts the recipient's security or safety at risk.

In practice, coercion actually works against effective performance. Studies on negative reinforcement (which is what coercion is) show that it can shut down behavior, even those actions that are necessary for productive performance. Punishing a worker for doing a bad job does not allow him or her to do a good job. The person avoids the mistake but may not do what is expected. Telling a subordinate that a report is lousy and sloppy does not tell him what are the remedial actions for a good report. The subordinate may avoid giving any reports if he or she can, or may reduce the reports to minimal and noncontroversial material.

In some cases, it may engender passive-aggressive behavior, sniping, and psychological withdrawal. If the recipient cannot be fired, as in the civil service and some unions, coercive punishment may aggravate the undesirable behavior and cause a power struggle to develop. Coercion is not a power base to develop.

If coercion is such an ineffective power base, why do managers use it? The reasons usually lie in the difficulties of confronting problems and conflict. Just as some people abhor positive strokes, others shy away from giving constructive criticism. They may be afraid of inciting conflict, worrying they will harm others. However, there are times when conflict cannot be avoided. The psychological effect of avoiding confrontation can lead to shame, guilt, anger, resentment, and retaliation. The suitable way to handle potential and actual conflict is to change one's mindset from either coercion or avoidance to positive problem solving. Chapter Seven will take up the whole subject of problem solving and conflict resolution, including methods for developing the skills to provide discipline rather than punishment.

Authority Power: Do As I Say

Managers have a legitimate right to command, just as their subordinates have an accompanying obligation to obey. That is the basis of authority power. Like some of the other bases, it has both positive and negative aspects. The increased use of authority to create standards and obligations, under the appropriate circumstances, usually results in higher motivation and loyalty. The overuse of authority power, however, can have negative consequences.

Giving constant orders like a drill sergeant does not help others to grow and become more competent. Nor does it contribute to leadership. Noel Tichy, in *The Transformational Leader*, cites six characteristics of leaders versus transactional managers: they identify themselves as change agents, they are courageous individuals, they believe in people, they are value driven, they are lifelong learners, and they have the ability to deal with complexity, ambiguity, and uncertainty. One might add to this list that they know how and when to delegate. These are in fact the positive sides of authority power. The traditional authority-based manager ignores all these principles.

Authority power is best thought of as something that managers could use rather than as something they actually do use. Always behaving as "The Boss" may be seen as negative. Managers who exercise authority power too often may buy short-term compliance at the expense of long-term commitment. Authority power can be short circuited in subtle or undetected ways. But in times of crisis or need, most people in an organization see the exercise of leadership based on authority as positive. For example, if a crucial project is beset by conflict among key managers and behind in schedule, the leader who steps in and uses his or her authority to hold weekly project meetings and to set specific goals and objectives for the teams is exercising authority power to save the day. Even if the managers resist that intervention, once they understand the gravity of the situation and the need for cooperation, they will respond to strong leadership and direction. Such a manager is exercising legitimate authority power in a crisis situation, not dictating or coercing.

Referent Power: Identifying with Those We Value

When others identify with someone because of that person's personal or professional qualities, he or she is said to have referent power. A famous rock star obviously enjoys immense amounts of referent power—her fans identify with her fame, glamour, and talent. Many managers identify with forceful and successful CEOs they read about. If the identification is based upon charismatic personal characteristics, others will envy the object of their admiration or want to be even more closely associated with the somewhat mystical powers of this intense kind of appeal. One does not build charismatic power, however; either it is there or it is not. In any case, referent power is usually seen as positive.

A more common form of referent power, one that anyone can acquire, is friendship. Through associating with others, sharing personal information, or providing something of value, managers can build on common interests, values, viewpoints, and preferences to a point that other people can get to know them. Friendship, when used with rewards and information power (which we will discuss shortly), leads to a reciprocal relationship where either person can call on the other in time of need. In effect, each has IOUs out that can be redeemed. Building referent power is necessary when dealing with peers and colleagues in an organization where the lines of authority are not clearly drawn—and that will be the organization of the future.

Developing Referent Power

Many managers, especially executives, seem unaware of and/or unskilled in the acquisition and use of referent power. Although it has the most potential, it is the least-used base of power. Organizational power is like the energy in a storage battery, which loses its charge even if it is sitting on the shelf. Acquiring referent power is one of the easiest and quickest ways for effective executives to "keep their batteries charged."

These guidelines can be helpful in building referent power with peers and colleagues:

- Get to know your colleagues. Use your knowledge about motivations, preferences, values, and interests. This insight is important in order to understand their behavior.
- Build your relationship on shared interests, motivations, and goals. Find out what they like to read, whether they are interested in sports, the theater, family life, and what matters to them about their job. Try to dovetail these with your interests. Listen actively when they talk about their interests.

- Respect different interests, goals, and values, and do not attack or disdain another person's style.
- Use reward power and positive reinforcement. Giving positive strokes, when deserved or needed, is the cheapest and easiest way to build a relationship. Remember that everyone is motivated by the need to be competent. When you affirm other people's competence, they value you.
- Invite people to influence you to show that you respect and want the perceptions, opinions, and information they have to offer.
- Give your expertise and share information, especially when you do not stand to benefit by the results of your actions.
- Minimize status concerns. Other than with charisma, referent power is based on reciprocity. People tend to relate to equals, not to superiors. You do not need to abdicate your authority or responsibility, but you should put the trappings of office in their proper place. When you have problem-solving meetings with colleagues try to hold them in small conference rooms rather than in your office. Play down formalities like last names and do not make references to powerful people you know.
- Become an expert communicator. People value straightforward and contradiction-free messages. Develop your verbal and nonverbal channels of communication.
- Get to know the informal political structure of the organization—who's the one who can get something done even though that responsibility may be outside his or her job description. The assistant to the president of the company is probably more useful in many instances than the president herself. By reading the environment and working both formal and informal channels, you will know how best to find the people who can help you, regardless of their titles.
- Get to know how people react to stress and crisis. Trying to negotiate requests when another person is under stress may doom your attempts.

Expert Power: I'm the Authority

When managers have specialized knowledge about a task, a person, or an organization that others value, they have the potential for expert power. Expert power may include communications, interpersonal skills, scientific knowledge, and so on. Such expertise is very valuable but specific to a task such as graphic design, software engineering, or commercial architecture. Information power, in contrast, is the tools (facts and data) that augment expert power, e.g., a graphic designer's knowledge of a printer's ability to run four-color jobs on a particular type of press. When the need arises or when it is solicited, expert power is usually perceived as positive. But people who offer their expert power without being asked can seem intrusive.

Expert power used by itself is a limited power base. Using it continually can put barriers between a manager and others that may be difficult to remove. Similarly, expert advice given in a condescending or authoritative manner will be seen as a putdown, while expertise that is withheld when needed can also be seen negatively. Karen and Bill in our opening scenario were both trying to exercise their expert power. But Bill was the client, and Karen tried to bulldoze him with her superior artistic knowledge.

Developing Positive Expert Power

Accumulating expert power depends on your motivation, interests, and ability to learn, but the ability to use it correctly and in conjunction with other bases determines how effective you are. Expert power comes with these cautions:

- Use expert power objectively, not to put down another person. Apply your expertise to the task, not to make someone look foolish, as Bill thought Karen was doing with him in the Euro-Design example.
- Use expert power sparingly and only when needed.
- Avoid becoming the superexpert. You will be perceived as a bore or a bombast.
- Do not get into expert-to-expert power plays.
- Pick the appropriate area(s) where you can be an expert and delve deeply. It is difficult or impossible to be an expert in everything.

Information Power: Access to the Inside Story

In his book *Intellectual Capital,* Thomas Stewart writes: "You would be hard-pressed to find a single industry, a single company, a single organization of any kind, that has not become more 'information-intensive'—dependent on knowledge as a source of what attracts customers and clients and on the information technology of running the place." He goes on to say that:

- Information is probably the most important raw material you need on the job. An evergrowing percentage of people are "knowledge workers." Information and knowledge are both the raw materials of our labor and its product.
- When the prime assets of the company are intellectual, the manager's job changes. You are measured not by the tasks you perform but by the results you achieve. The trend away from standardized mass production toward special-

ized knowledge work makes command-and-control management less necessary. You interact with teams, plan and organize, and execute many aspects of their work.

- Reversing the trend of the industrial revolution when the machine replaced humans, now the machine works for humans.

To use more of what people know, companies need to create opportunities for private knowledge to be made public and tacit knowledge to be made explicit. The converse is true; individuals can increase their information power by sharing what they know with other individuals and groups.

The information power base depends upon access to information that is not public knowledge but that is shared within the organization, especially among groups involved in similar processes. Managers and employees at all levels may have access to this information because of their position or because of connections within the organization (for example, because of friendships they have built that give them information through informal channels). In addition to access, organizations need to control the flow of information to and from the senior executive. It is entirely possible, in some closed organizations, that executives at the top have less information about what is going on than the people in the middle or even the entry levels. This happens when the CEO and his or her staff operate as a self-contained group and build a barrier between themselves and the lower levels of management.

Developing Information Power in Organizations

Opening up the lines of communications—the information flow—is everyone's responsibility. When there is too much competition for resources and power, the flow shuts down to a trickle. Building solid bases of information power is part of a mindset that begins with the assumption that the more you give the more you get. As managers and leaders, it is important to remember that when information is cut off from lower levels, rumors and gossip spread.

Information should flow upward as well as laterally and downward, and it should not be filtered or distorted. It can be disseminated formally in written bulletins, memos, newsletters, or speeches, or informally in conversation or written messages. It must always be accurate. A final caution is to avoid information overload. This can be as bad as no information at all.

As manager of your career, expanding your knowledge and trying to search for ways to gain knowledge increases both expert and information power. You grow your information power base by interaction with others. Knowledge work, like knowledge itself, is a collaborative project, the joint property of the people who do it. What we give to the team we still have, and we also have what the team makes, even though it is not solely our own doing.

The electronic age of e-mail, networks, and Web sites makes it easier to transmit information than ever before. All these Internet wonders make information power more available to managers, if they will take steps to acquire it.

Affiliative Power: It Is Who You Know

Affiliative power is gained through association with a source of authority. For example, executive secretaries and staff assistants reporting to high-level officers have affiliative power by acting as surrogates for their bosses. If they are acting according to their boss's wishes, this is a legitimate and appropriate use of power. But if it is apparent that they are acting out of self-interest, it is perceived as negative. Another example of negative affiliative power occurs when special roles in the organization are used to obstruct or block performance. For instance, when a manager interprets accounting or personnel policies rigidly, borrowing authority from his or her interpretation of rules and regulations, those on the receiving end usually do not like it.

The most common and blatant misuse of affiliative power occurs when the executive secretary to the boss uses that relationship to block or deny access to the boss. Referent power, in contrast, does not borrow from higher authorities but is based on reciprocity; people associate with each other or with groups for their own sake, not for their connection with influence or power. Because of its potential downside and misuse, affiliative power should generally be avoided.

Group Power: The Whole Is Greater

Group power involves just what it sounds like it does: a number of individuals interacting in problem solving, conflict resolution, or creative brainstorming. This power base can be considered positive only when the group's resolution of the problem or situation is greater than each of the individual contributions.

In the day-to-day operations of an organization, managers regularly and inevitably lead or participate in problem-solving groups. All too often, participants leave these groups feeling frustrated. They tend to ask themselves, "Why do we waste our time this way?" The reason for their frustration is quite simple: the manager did not understand and manage the group process. When leaderless groups are left to develop on their own, they generally end up being controlled by the most vocal and dominant individuals who may use expert or coercive power for their own ends. If the group contains members with different status levels, the high-status individuals can dominate the proceedings. On the other hand, if someone has been appointed to run the group, it can drift toward conformity.

Effective use of group power requires careful design and management of the group process, but when it works, everyone involved will feel a greater commitment to problem solving and to solutions they generate than they would have if one or two members dominate the proceedings.

Creating Conditions for Positive Group Power

To be effective, group problem solving needs to draw on positive group power. Leaders and participants can be more effective if they use the following guidelines.

1. Ensure a climate of openness to opinions, perceptions, conflicts, and possibilities.
2. Use positive reinforcement to reward everyone's contributions.
3. Ban the use of negative criticism of any group member.
4. Clarify the objectives of the meeting. Is the agenda intended to find opportunities? To solve problems? To evaluate or implement?
5. Divide the group process into six phases. These phases can take place in one session or over many meetings, depending upon the complexity of the problem.
   - Define the problem.
   - Generate opinions, perceptions, and alternatives.
   - Develop criteria for judging alternatives.
   - Apply the criteria to the alternatives and develop trade-offs.
   - Select and develop the solution.
   - Identify action steps for implementation.
6. Manage the group process by assigning major roles to individual group members:
   - The *facilitator* involves all participants in the problem-solving process, minimizes the use of premature evaluations, and brings hidden conflicts to the surface.
   - The *clarifier* restates everyone's opinions, perceptions, and attributions.
   - The *critical evaluator* analyzes and evaluates potential decisions at the end of any phase of the group.
7. Make creative use of the different management styles in the group. Identifying the range of differences in the group allows potential biases to be brought out in the open. The facilitator can use an understanding of these differences to elicit maximum contributions and to prevent conflicts over management style rather than substance. If an ESTJ participant is constantly asking for

more facts and details, the facilitator can remind that person that her sensing aspect is getting in the way of moving onto defining or conceptualizing the problem.

8. At the end of each meeting, set some time aside for the group to evaluate the process that took place at that meeting.

In groups as in other relationships, the manager who has developed referent power widely and who uses reward, expert, and information power effectively will almost certainly be able to influence others' behavior in positive ways. The other power modes—coercion, authority, affiliation, and group power—may be useful from time to time. But the manager who acquires the first four power bases and utilizes them skillfully can contribute substantially to achieving the organization's goals.

What Went Wrong in the Mercury Case?

Using this knowledge of power and what we know about assumptions, perceptions, and feelings (from Chapter Four), we can revisit the story that opened this chapter and better understand the power moments that the two main actors, Bill and Karen, experienced.

Bill's Assumptions

- About his own role: *"I see myself as the creative leader. I am the boss of the show."*
- About Marcia's role: *"I want her involvement."*
- About Karen's role: *"She will be the artistic coordinator."*
- About his power: *"I am an expert in my field and in the world of art. I have the authority and rank to command others."*

Bill's Perceptions

- *"Marcia is dumping the project onto Karen."*
- *"Karen doesn't respect my views on classical culture."*
- *"Karen is a know-it-all pseudoexpert."*
- *"My authority is being undermined."*

Bill's Feelings

- *"I am being betrayed by Marcia. She led me to believe she was going to have active involvement in the project."*

- *"I thoroughly dislike Karen's arrogance."*
- *"I am going to put my foot down; I'm paying for this!"*

Karen's Assumptions

- About her own role: *"I am the creative leader."*
- About Marcia's role: *"I have complete authority; Marcia delegated it to me."*
- About Bill's role: *"He is the client and he will respect my expertise and authority as the designer."*
- About power: *"Authority and rank turn me off. My expertise will carry the day."*

Karen's Perceptions

- *"Bill is a pompous ass. He thinks he is an expert on art. He is a pseudoexpert."*
- *"Marcia has betrayed me. She gave me ultimate authority and now she is backing down."*
- *"My own staff has turned on me. Don't they know I am the boss?"*

Karen's Feelings

- *"I feel depressed and anxious. Why did Martin overreact to Bill?"*
- *"I am right! My expertise exceeds Marcia's and Bill's."*
- *"I am going to give it to my staff for being insubordinate."*

These lists point to a number of problems in the relationships in this scenario. Both participants think that they have ultimate authority for the project: Bill because he is the CEO, Karen because she assumes Marcia gave it to her. Though we didn't examine Marcia's assumptions, she also thinks she has the authority. The root of the problem is a clash over authority power and over creative roles in the project.

Bill and Karen both believe that they are the creative force in the project. Bill perceives Karen as the artistic coordinator of his ideas, while Karen sees Bill as a meddlesome distraction. Bill sees Karen as an extension of Marcia, whom he would prefer to deal with. Marcia sees herself as an occasional consultant.

Bill undermines Karen and Marcia by going behind their backs and calling the company's CEO, Martin, whom he assumes will act on his behalf and rein Karen in. Moreover, to a degree, Bill has misrepresented Karen's attitude to Martin. Karen becomes confused and anxious after the telephone conversation with Martin. Here we have a clash over roles, authority, and lines of communication.

At this point the people involved are trapped in a power moment. Bill holds the upper hand because he controls the purse strings. Karen is caught between Bill's and Martin's anger. Martin has divided loyalties between the client and his star designer. Could this situation have been prevented? Of course!

Karen is in charge of her own destiny, but she let circumstances dictate to her. She did not analyze the situation correctly and then determine what needed to be done. Marcia has not set the stage for Karen's entry into her new position by laying out a set of expectations. Karen thinks that it is business as usual—just be a creative free spirit. She is not well versed in the pitfalls associated with dealing with idiosyncratic clients with big egos. Moreover, although Marcia has defined to herself what future roles she will play with new clients, she has not conveyed this vision to Bill or to Karen. Neither Marcia nor Karen realizes that what worked in the past—the old power bases—may be inappropriate now. The prescription for Karen is to:

- Recognize that she has no authority power with the client.
- Downplay authority and coercive power with her subordinates.
- Build referent power with Bill.
- Build a viable, explicit agreement with Marcia that defines their relationship in terms of mutual expectations.
- Build group power with her subordinates.
- Downplay her need to show her expert power—her creative bent.

A New Scenario for Karen and Bill

If the players in this story had been aware of the power issues and had learned to deal with them skillfully, the events might have unfolded quite differently. Let's review the conversation between Karen and Bill after Bill has explained his philosophy of business. He continues, "Now I want to use Italy as the backdrop for your photos, Karen. I want Rome, Florence, and Venice as sites. I can see the Euro-Designs fixtures posed in front of the statues in Rome, the canals and portos of Venice. Two art forms joined together. What do you think, Karen?"

"Sounds very interesting to me. Maybe you can expand a bit about your concept—say, how it fits with your business philosophy."

"Sure. I'm glad you had a positive feeling about my initial idea. It was just a rough start. I could expand on it if you want."

"That's what I want. If you tell me your perspective, Bill, I can build on it with my ideas. That way we collaborate, and we all win."

"Okay, Karen, let me tell you about my travels in Italy and Greece. I had some profound experiences while studying the art forms in both countries. I would like to work some of those feelings into the photos of the products that will be in the brochure. What I want to convey is that in our own way, we are artists, too."

"Now I see what you're driving at. I had the same experience when I traveled to Asia. My whole perspective on life changed. I found a new mode of expression that helped me in my work."

"Well, Karen, I see we are kindred souls."

"Bill, let me put together some of your ideas with some of mine, and I'll come back with a number of options for the first crack at the photos for the brochure. Could you send me some photos of your favorite shots in Italy and Greece?"

"Hey, that's a good idea! They won't be up to your caliber, but you'll get the idea. Right?"

"Bill, I have respect for everyone's artistic expression. I know they will be helpful."

"I will be looking forward to our next meeting, Karen. Good luck."

Karen is well on the way to building positive power with Bill. In this short scene, Karen has:

- Given affirmation to Bill's ideas (using reward power)
- Encouraged Bill to give more input to the project (building group power)
- Shared common experiences with Bill (developing referent power)
- Downplayed criticism and negative input (controlling his coercive power)
- Not assumed the role of expert unless asked (using expert power when appropriate)

The project is solidly under way, and Karen has avoided the pitfalls in the first scenario. Both Bill and Karen have power, although of different sorts. In the first scenario, both Karen and Bill exercised negative power, and both lost—Karen with her boss and Bill in gaining expert knowledge.

Understanding the way that power bases interact with other elements of management style and then applying that analysis to work settings can be challenging. It is so difficult to sort out different aspects of a situation and people's behavior that managers often do not know where to start. The following case asks you to look at a situation as though you were a manager who has to get your boss to change his mind, when he does not really want to. The extended, structured analysis will show the power of using everything you know about the elements of management style to guide the situation to a positive outcome.

Power Bases and Management Style: The Luxor Case

Imagine that you are a group manager in a computer interface department in a company that makes surface-to-air missiles. At present, five engineers report to you. Your boss is George Prince, a forty-two-year-old MIT graduate in electrical engineering. Married, with two children, ages ten and twelve, George is an avid golfer and grower of hybrid orchids. His favorite authors are Tom Clancy and Graham Greene.

George mainly uses expert, referent, and reward power. He is an ENTJ (extrovert, intuitive, thinking, judging psychological type) with the following motivational profile:

Overall Management Needs	Boss–Subordinate Needs	Interpersonal Modifiers	Task Factor Needs
Achievement: High	Deference: High	Introspection: High	Change: High
Dominance: High	Autonomy: Medium	Exhibition: High	Endurance: High
Affiliation: Medium	Nurturance: High	Aggression: Low	Intensity: High
	Assistance: Low		Order: Medium
	Abasement: High		

At the moment, the department is involved in integrating a component called "Luxor" into the radar dome of a highly sophisticated surface-to-air missile system. As group manager, you have found out that the present configuration of Luxor is faulty and has not stood up to repeated tests. George was the head of the design team that came up with the configuration, and he is obviously proud of his contribution to the project. In fact, a great deal of his ego is invested in its design. Because of the complexity of the overall program, a number of other departments are involved as well.

Because the Luxor component came out of your department and you are the lead engineer, you are responsible for its reliability and feasibility. Other department and group managers will have a say in the sign-off of the overall program, but it is your job to explain the design problem to George and to influence him to reconsider the configuration of the Luxor component.

George Prince's Management Style

George is an interesting variation on the standard ENTJ. The ENTJ prototype is a no-nonsense, take-charge manager. In George's case, however, his needs pattern changes his psychological type behavior. Because George's dominant function is thinking, he approaches issues analytically. Like most extroverted thinkers, George likes to discuss problems face-to-face before reading about them in memos or reports. Remember that the extroverted thinker embraces objective, external facts and assumptions. George's high exhibition need was undoubtedly reinforced by the success of the original Luxor design. Counterbalancing this is George's abasement need—his tendency to blame himself when things go wrong. Both of these needs might interfere with his ability to assess this situation objectively. All of these factors make it difficult for you to bring him bad news.

In George's overall management needs, his combination of high achievement and dominance needs with an average need for affiliation makes him an outspoken, dynamic boss. His extroverted thinking accentuates this style. Because George openly expresses his wishes and objectives, you have the advantage of knowing exactly what is on his mind. But as an extroverted thinker, George believes everyone else should follow the same path he does. This belief, combined with his high need for control, occasionally makes him overbearing.

Your task looks more and more intimidating, but consider the positive leverage points you can use to influence George. First, he is a deferential and nurturing person. He will listen and be supportive as long as he is not personally attacked. His high need for nurturance softens the critical impact of his thinking function. His high need for change and endurance is a second advantage because when he is convinced that problems are real and not just dumped on him, he becomes actively involved in their solution. His modest needs for affiliation and autonomy permit him to be a good team player. But these positive behaviors can be encouraged only if George perceives that his ego and his past accomplishments are not being compromised.

George's need for introspection can work either to your advantage or to your disadvantage. Because he likes to question his behavior and that of others, he may suspect you of harboring ulterior motives. Beware of seeming to have any hidden agenda with him. Because of his introspection, George will not make any impulsive or premature decisions. He will want ample time to digest the information and assess the full impact of the situation.

It will be essential for you to consider the kinds of power George uses. His reliance on expert power means that you must do your homework and be knowledgeable enough to present your case with assurance. If he suspects that you do not know the subject well, he will try to overpower you with his superior expert knowledge. Because George was instrumental in the Luxor design phase, he will resist changes that question his expertise. George's referent power can be the basis on which you can build your relationship with him.

Your Approach to George

Step 1. Set up a meeting with George. Schedule a time when there will be no distractions and be sure to allow enough time for genuine dialogue to develop. It would be wise to warn him in advance that there are some system problems that need his attention. You might request the meeting by saying: "George, I'd like to talk about the current status of the Luxor program. You were one of the key players in the conception of the design. I need your help to work out a few details that have arisen in the past month. I know you want to be apprised of current developments. Can you set aside some time to analyze the situation?" Note that you are asking for his help, not dumping the problem on him. You are appealing to his nurturance and exhibition needs. By emphasizing an analytical approach, you address his dominant thinking function. Reminding him of his desire to be kept up to date is a way of making him feel on top of the task, so his dominance and achievement needs will still be met. This approach also allows him to exercise his expert power.

Step 2. At the meeting, be careful not to openly attack the original design because that would put George on the defensive. You want to neutralize and depersonalize the problem. You might phrase an opening question this way: "Could you review for me the reason for including the Zeta switch in the control module? It seems like a very sophisticated mechanism. Let's look at how it interfaces with the other software." This question asks for his response before giving him the actual data on the malfunction. He is still in charge of the input and the rationale behind the design. You also credit him for coming up with a very sophisticated design. So far, all your statements have been positive unconditional strokes for George with a conditional emphasis on the interface problem.

Step 3. Once you have established a rapport with George, use the objective principles of logic and analysis as the basis for discussion. You might suggest the following: "That point about the switching component appears to be the key problem. I wonder if there might be an alternative principle that would ease the interface." Keep the discussion objective and focused. You want George to see the potential problem for himself. It is highly probable that at this point George will ask for more information. If he does, you can present it and the possible solutions in an objective and participatory way.

Step 4. If you have gotten this far and George sees and accepts the problem, involve him in the solution. If he has no time, offer to come up with some alternative solutions that he can discuss with you in a future meeting. By doing this, you allow him to retain some control over future developments and to maintain his original ego involvement in Luxor. You could say, "George, you were intimately involved in the Luxor design, and the concept is totally acceptable. However, I need your help in the current interface with the XYZ components. How do you see us attacking this isolated problem?" You are now positively stroking George for past efforts and appealing to his nurturance need for help.

Step 5. Get a commitment to the next steps by outlining your own involvement and his in a psychological contract. If he wants to be the honcho, let him. If he is willing to delegate some authority to you, then make sure that you and your co-workers understand exactly what that authority includes. You might say: "Well, we agree that some changes need to be made. As I see it, you are willing to critique our proposals and trade-off analyses. I will go ahead and prepare the redesign, get some feedback from the tests, and check in with you in two weeks. Is that acceptable?" These statements clarify his involvement and yours and respect his high need for deference.

Step 6. Maintain feedback with George to ensure that he is aware of the progress on the program. For example, you might say, "We made some preliminary changes, George. I'd like to go over the rationale for those changes with you. We need your analysis. There seem to be six areas that need to be tweaked in order for a positive interface to take place." This statement appeals to his dominant thinking function.

The analysis of this case integrates all the information you have about George's management style. It illustrates the importance of knowing more about an individual than only his or her psychological type, because George is not a stereotypical ENTJ. The exercise is not an attempt to change George. It accepts him as he is but assumes that you, the group manager, can respond to him more effectively by recognizing and adjusting to nuances in his behavior. Nor is the exercise an attempt to manipulate George. Manipulation implies acting in one's self-interest to injure another party. The objective here is to get a job done to everyone's satisfaction.

To influence George Prince, you must also have a good sense of your own management style and be able to adjust your behavior. Self-knowledge and flexibility are your two most powerful tools. If you, like George, also have high achievement and dominance needs, or if you are high in autonomy and low in deference needs, you might find it difficult to adjust your style to his. Similarly, any defensiveness or aggressiveness on your part will make it impossible for you to establish a dialogue with him. By placing your task and objectives in the forefront and by recognizing and accepting the differences between you and George, your odds of success increase dramatically.

Points of Influence: A Quick Review

When considering how best to influence another person, the cardinal rule is to focus on the dominant function of their psychological type, whether it be a perceptive function (sensing or intuition) or a judgment function (thinking or feeling).

To review, there are eight patterns: introverted intuitive, extroverted intuitive, introverted sensing, extroverted sensing, introverted thinking, extroverted thinking, introverted feeling, and extroverted feeling. Here is the best way to approach each of the four dominant functions.

Influencing Sensing Types

Use facts, concrete examples, detailed outlines, and written reports for introverts, and verbal reports (with backup) for extroverts. If you are an intuitive type, you will have to use your inferior (sensing) function. Avoid making blue-sky proposals or anything that cannot be supported by the five senses. Brainstorming is a difficult activity for sensing types. When put on the defensive, they can amass huge quantities of data to support their positions, so avoid getting into fact warfare with them.

Extroverted sensing types excel as realists. They measure their lives by actual experiences and concrete data and objects. Remember this, and try to use it to your advantage. Introverted sensing types measure life by subjective impressions, some based on the outer world and some based on their inner world. To deal effectively with them, you must understand where they are coming from.

Influencing Intuitive Types

Discuss opportunities for the future and the implications of various plans. Look at the concepts behind an idea or problem. Use details to support arguments, but do not let details detract from the argument. Intuitives can live with ambiguity, and they love wild excursions into problem solving. Ask: "What if?" "Let's imagine." "Are there other possibilities?"

Be enthusiastic with an extroverted intuitive, and be subtle with an introverted intuitive. The best strategy with introverted intuitives is to get them to verbalize their inner visions and dreams. Once their thoughts emerge, a river of insights begins to flow. Go with the flow. Ask questions to show introverted intuitives that you understand their insights. Point out other relevant factors. Give them time to reflect on those factors or to seek clarification. Move slowly but with deliberate determination to understand their position and to let them grasp your side of the story.

Influencing Thinking Types

Use logical analysis and be objective. Suggest rational, logical approaches. Avoid personal opinions or value-laden arguments. Place emphasis on the principles involved. Thinking types hate a half-baked solution or a weak proposal, so do your homework. Trade-off analyses are very effective with thinking types.

Thinking types (especially introverted thinking types) are sometimes oblivious to their environment. They focus mainly on the rational aspects of the situation, sometimes without regard for the effect they have on others. Tact is not their best attribute, except when needs such as nurturance and affiliation modify their thinking function. Do not allow yourself to feel hurt by a thinking type's tactlessness, especially if you are a feeling type.

Influencing Feeling Types

Appeal to the individual's personal involvement, emphasizing positive contributions. Avoid blaming the person and focus instead on conditional factors that need changing. Do not try overtly to influence a feeling type. Because they require time to tune into an atmosphere, they may slow you down. If the atmosphere is not to their liking, they may subtly impose their own. Ideas and facts are not enough for them. They must evaluate and relate to things. Because they are tuned in to the environment and other people's emotional states, feeling types can be either tactful or cutting. A hurt feeling type may recognize and take advantage of another person's vulnerability.

Tuning in to the Needs Profiles

Most needs potentially have both positive and negative dimensions. For example, a high need for achievement is an advantage when a job requires a strong individual contribution, but it is a disadvantage when a team effort is required. A need for dominance inspires coworkers when a situation demands leadership and authority, but otherwise it is self-serving and rigid, harmful to both the dominant person and the other people involved. Because needs modify a person's psychological type, your skill at influencing others depends upon tuning into their motivational profile.

The first step is to determine a person's overall needs profile (achievement, dominance, and affiliation). Influencing an affiliative extroverted thinking type is very different from influencing an achievement-oriented introverted intuitive type. You can bond with an affiliative extroverted thinking type by using teamwork and collaboration and by emphasizing logic and reason. Achievement-oriented introverted intuitives are the most individualistic and circumscribed of problem solvers. Getting them to express their ideas is the best way to influence their solutions. Always keep in mind the inward-looking tendencies of the introverted intuitive. They will look at you and appear to be attentive but they may be actually scanning their ideas and cataloging them. At this point it would be good to ask what they are thinking about and whether they are willing share it with you.

You will be pleasantly surprised when the introverted intuitive replies with a well-articulated statement of what he or she was thinking. It will be logical and conceptually sound.

You will also need to cue into boss–subordinate relations (needs for deference, autonomy, nurturance, assistance, and abasement). Individuals with high autonomy needs can be difficult to work with if they sense you are violating their personal space. Because George Prince, for example, has only a moderate need for autonomy, he will not consider you to be a threat. High deference types usually expect the same treatment from others. Low deference types fall into one of two categories: those who expect deference from underlings and those who do not care about it. You must be the judge. Because George is high in his need for deference, this should work in your favor. He is likely to be willing to listen to you with a degree of respect, as long as you show the same respect to him in return. Nurturing types like to feel that their ideas and actions are appreciated; otherwise they feel neglected or rejected. George's high nurturance needs will probably moderate his domineering attitude, making him paternalistic. If you address the side of him that wants to be a helpful coach and mentor, he will be very approachable.

Individuals with high assistance needs demand a lot of attention and support from trusted friends and associates. When a need for assistance is intense, it is a burden on relationships. George's low needs in this area would not interfere with your ability to influence him.

Abasement needs are a problem, whether they are extremely high or extremely low. For people high in abasement needs, criticism causes resentment, anxiety, and depression. In an abasement-needy boss, criticism can touch off retaliatory behavior. People who are extremely low on abasement needs may be either totally without guilt and responsibility, or they may deny that they have this need. George Prince has high abasement needs. He is the take-charge boss who feels guilty or super-responsible if things go wrong. Because the Luxor component was George's achievement, you must be very careful not to make him think that you are pinning responsibility on him.

Among the interpersonal modifiers (introspection, exhibition, and aggression), introspection needs are positive when they make people empathetic. Because George is high in his need for introspection, he will probably understand the bind you are in, as long as he does not feel that you are blaming him or undercutting his previous efforts. George also has high needs for exhibition, undoubtedly reinforced by his original design concept. Keeping this need in mind, you might suggest to him future opportunities for recognition.

As an extroverted thinker, George is fortunate in being low in his need for aggression, as otherwise his manner might be quite sharp. His thinking function is further softened by his high need for nurturing. You should be able to have a reasonable conversation with him. Imagine confronting the bombast of an extroverted thinker high in aggression and autonomy needs and low in nurturance needs!

The last step in tuning into another's needs profile is to integrate their task factor needs (for change, endurance, intensity, and order). George's high need for change will work in your favor if you present the problem as a challenge and a chance for improvement. If he were low in a need for change, he might maintain a rigid and inflexible position. George's high need for endurance was an obvious advantage for him when he was generating the Luxor program, but it probably has little bearing on this situation. Nor are his moderate needs for order and routine significant in the current situation. If he had an extremely high need for order, you would have to proceed cautiously, arming yourself with information for every discussion.

Conclusion

Managers at all levels, regardless of position or status, can build power bases and enhance their ability to influence others by developing skills to fit the specific situation and job. The key to the effective use of power is determining who and what you are trying to influence. Knowing when to use reward, group, or expert power, for instance, depends on the circumstances. As you can see from the analysis of George Prince in the Luxor case, understanding someone's use of power bases is best accomplished through a fairly structured process. Shooting from the hip or assuming that someone else is like you is a good way to exacerbate a difficult situation or cause all kinds of problems in communication and working relationships. Besides, it is highly likely that you will not get what you want if you have not taken the time to truly understand the situation and the players involved. If you use methods in this chapter for looking at the ingredients of your own and others' management style, you will get more of the results you want.

So far we have looked at three of the building blocks of management style: psychological type, needs, and power. The next chapter focuses on an equally important aspect of management style—the ability to solve problems and to resolve conflict productively. For most managers, conflict is an ongoing and particularly troublesome part of life in organizations. If you have a tendency to avoid conflict or feel frustrated in your ability to find win/win solutions, the next chapter will help you understand your own approach and develop new ways to this important part of learning to be a good manager.

CHAPTER SEVEN

PROBLEM SOLVING AND CONFLICT MANAGEMENT: CATALYSTS FOR CHANGE

Max Stanford, the marketing and sales manager at Coopersmith & Gordon, was pumped. He had just gotten the word from the research and development group that ExtremeAscent, the new mountain bike prototype they had been testing, had been released to manufacturing and would be ready in three months. Max could not wait to get the new bikes out to dealers. This was going to be their hottest product ever.

All through its development and their market research, despite occasional discussions about whether they really needed another bike with a profile like the eight other models they had, they had maintained their incredible esprit de corps. The only naysayer had been the western regional sales manager, now the ex-western regional sales manager, Vicki Austin. Vicki had been a bummer, Max thought, always bringing up objections, trying to put the damper on their ideas. Coopersmith & Gordon had always made the best bikes, stayed way ahead of the curve in technology and design, and Max and the rest of the team knew they could not lose, not with this bike or any of the others they had coming. So what if there were some new players in the market, coming in from Europe and Asia? Or so what if the last bike they had introduced had not quite sold at the level they had expected? Everyone agreed that it was just a blip in the market. Except Vicki, who kept harping on problems until everyone just wanted to scream. They tried to reason with her; she was the only one who had so many doubts. But finally she just quit and took her bad attitude with her. Good riddance, Max thought. Her replacement, Philip Frohman, was a much better team member, had sold bikes for Matsu, and had even raced professionally—he really knew bikes.

Six months later, though, Max and the rest of the staff at Coopersmith & Gordon were dismayed. How could it be that ExtremeAscent had been met with so little enthusiasm among dealers and consumers alike? There had been a number of very hot new bikes from their competitors that had come out at the same time, but Max could not see how dealers would be so indifferent to this new C & G model. The press on it in the magazines had not been that great either; the reviewers said it was the same old thing, just another knock-off, not exciting, just different colors and slight changes to the design. This was not true, not really. Nobody else at C & G could quite figure out what had happened either, and the failure had left them all feeling confused and upset. For the first time in a long time, there was a lot of arguing, complaining, and finger-pointing. Max was stumped. He hated the atmosphere in the office. What, he thought, are we going to do to get past this failure and recover our team spirit?

Conflict: Necessary Evil or Just Necessary?

Human beings have forever disagreed about one thing or another. When early humans were threatened over their rights to a water hole or an animal carcass, they had only two options—fight or flight. They could battle against the threat or withdraw. The Latin root of conflict is *fligere*, meaning "to strike," and for the Romans a conflict was a clash of arms, a dashing together of bodies, a prolonged struggle to the death. By the fifteenth century, the meaning of the word "conflict" had expanded to include disagreement over ideas, although it retained the connotation of a battle, as it does today. We still think of conflicting interests as incompatible, and we conceive of conflict as having winners and losers. In the ExtremeAscent example, the dynamics of conflict surfaced in a number of forms: in the way the management group made its decisions (and ostracized the one lone dissenter) and in the aftermath of product failure as they tried to get back on course and instead fell into blaming each other and arguing about what should have been done.

Conflict does not have to be seen exclusively as a negative force, however. Some people seem to view it as neither positive nor negative but as something that just is, as a gift of energy or a catalyst for positive change and new direction. In this more optimistic view, neither side in a conflict loses. The truth is that conflict can be both negative and constructive. It incorporates both undesirable and aggressive aspects of behavior as well as more benign and graceful tendencies to seek peace and harmony. Conflict is a fact of life, but we can learn to move beyond the fight-or-flight response, depending on our willingness to remold our archaic responses and to re-educate ourselves about alternatives.

We all learn how to handle conflict early in life. We watch the way our parents deal with conflict—anything from avoidance to confrontation to collaboration. A child raised in a Quaker household will tend to turn the other cheek when conflict arises. If your family believes in an eye-for-an-eye set of values, they are likely to respond to conflict with confrontation and hostility. Whatever approach to conflict you learn early on, it is not fixed, nor is it necessarily related to your psychological type. One extroverted type of person may avoid conflict, while another confronts it; each one's behavior will be quite different. Regardless of your current style of handling conflict, you can modify it to make it more effective, mainly through understanding your assumptions and using the techniques we discussed in Chapter Four to shift them. Whatever you can learn you can unlearn—even something as fundamental as conflict management.

Sources of Conflict in Organizations

Although conflict is common in all organizations, the reasons for clashes are generally based in five main sources: goals, roles, interpersonal styles, procedures, and structure (indicated by the convenient acronym GRIPS). Whatever the nature of the organization, any strategy for handling and resolving conflict has to start with identifying its origins.

Goal Conflicts: What Are We Doing?

Conflicts about an organization's mission and goals may arise for all kinds of reasons. If goals have not been clearly defined, misinterpretations of them can lead to conflict. For example, in command-and-control, top-down organizations, departments and functions are relatively isolated from one another. Mutual objectives are poorly coordinated, managers tend not to delegate, and people are not encouraged to make decisions or question what is going on. The leaders at the top know the goals, but people below them may not be aware of or understand them. Even if goals are clearly defined, conflict over them may arise, either because of genuine differences of opinion or because people are behaving in self-serving ways.

A good example of this kind of conflict is the case of IBM's entrance into the personal computer market in the 1980s. One group of high-level executives, who disputed the viability of the goal of entering this new market, gave the effort only token commitment. The result was disastrous. IBM abdicated whatever market share they had to PC clone manufacturers and squandered an excellent opportunity. The conglomerate mergers of the 1970s also represent good examples of goal conflicts. Companies with different cultures, products, and management styles were cobbled together without much forethought about the consequences. Many failed. Because of their impact on an organization's overall strategy, conflicts over goals not only can be the most intense but can also have the most severe consequences.

Role Conflicts: Who Is Doing What?

Role conflicts arise when there is disagreement about who is performing what functions, in what manner, and with what other members of an organization. Every organization, even those structured around work teams, has to specify how work will be done—who has authority, what is the appropriate amount or type of work for a group to take on, what exactly is a group supposed to do to contribute to the overall effort, how that contribution is to be integrated with others' efforts, how resources are to be divided up. Conflicts with roles generally stem from four problems: overload, ambiguity, overlap, and competition.

Role overload results when a particular assignment demands too much work from one person. The conflict lies between the overloaded worker and whoever defined what that person was supposed to do. It may also occur when the work is too difficult, indicating that the work process should be restructured or that more training is needed. If, for example, someone is handling several projects and has his or her workload doubled as part of a "reorganization" under a new manager, that person will be severely overloaded and is likely to complain or become involved in disagreements with coworkers about the equity of the situation.

Role ambiguity arises when a role is not clearly defined, or when someone is uncertain about what his or her role entails. A recently hired MBA, for instance, may find herself reporting to a boss who has an intuitive free-wheeling style and solves problems as they occur with a minimum of formal meetings. The new employee, who is used to more structure and prefers a more factual approach to the work, decides to write extensive memos about problems as they arise, sending them to her boss and the other managers. She may be shocked when she gets a six-month review that gives her a low performance rating, citing lack of initiative and indecisiveness. The role ambiguity in this case is that the boss expected the new MBA to be an on-line trouble-shooter like all of his other managers while she was operating as a cautious and (she thought) responsible manager. That it created a perceptual vacuum frustrated her and led to conflict within the group.

Most organizations today depend upon many individuals, each of whom has a distinct role in creating the final product. The manufacturing people are responsible for fabrication; the quality control people are responsible for quality; production control is responsible for the schedule; testing is responsible for reliability; and so on. At critical points along the way, all the departments contribute to the final result. But instead of recognizing their mutual interdependence, it often happens that one group will see another as duplicating or in some way interfering with what it is supposed to be doing. The conflict that results is about role overlap. It is common, for example, for quality control and production to experience role overlap. The people in quality control may pride themselves on their exacting standards and adherence to specifications. Their colleagues in production want to meet those standards too, but are also responsible for getting the product out the door. If the quality control people insist on their way, they may sometimes demand such exacting changes or revisions that schedules may be delayed and costs increased. In such cases, quality control sees its role as overlapping with and superseding that of the production people. There might be other solutions to the problems, but they will never be found if both sides continue to struggle for control of their overlapping roles.

Role competition adds an element of nastiness to role overlap conflicts. Groups come to see themselves in competition with each other and no longer believe there is a solution to their conflict. They are ready to fight, to beat the other guy, or seek revenge for past insults. They fight out in the open or use underground guerrilla tactics. In the quality control versus production situation just mentioned, suppose that a manager held a monthly contest between the quality control and production people to see who could outperform the other group. Quality control would win if they could prove that production was at fault, and production would win if they could prove quality control imposed arbitrary standards. The winning group was feted at the end of the month with a victor's trophy, while the losing side received a dunce cap to be displayed in their department. You can imagine what all of that did for cooperation and collaboration on mutual goals. They probably did not believe they had *any* mutual goals.

Interpersonal Style Conflicts: Whose Quirks Are at Work Here?

Among managers, interpersonal style is the most human, fascinating, and important aspect of any organization. Managers' individual quirks, strengths, weaknesses, and peculiarities profoundly affect all goals, roles, and decisions. We have only to look at the impact of leaders on their organizations to see how it reflects their interpersonal styles in hundreds of ways, no matter how large that organization grows. The biggest conflict in organizations is between what management guru Peter Drucker calls the administrators and the lunatics (*The Effective Executive*, 1968). Administrators are sensing types who like to make things happen on time, budget, and schedule, according to the rules. Lunatics are the intuitives who do not want to play by any rules—they just want to play the game for the thrill of it. Another common clash is between a participatory management style (high achievement and affiliation) and a command-and-control style (high dominance and high achievement). Resolving conflicts that arise from interpersonal style depends on how well you understand your own and others' styles. When you understand those styles, you can work on adjusting your behavior to work more effectively with others.

Procedural Conflicts: How Are We Doing It?

Depending upon the type of organization and the products it generates, procedures affect everything from accounting to management information systems to personnel to technical issues and manufacturing. But procedures are not as cut and dried as we might like them to be; conflicts arise when people disagree about exactly which ones will get the job done best. For example, if a company knows that it needs to get a new series of computers, top information systems people may be asked to come up with recommendations. One manager might argue for a Windows-based system because it has the greatest number of software applications, while another thinks the Macintosh system would be better for handling graphic design projects. In such a case, the discussion can degenerate into squabbles over the merits of Macs versus Windows. The managers have lost sight of the task, which is what should dictate the choice. Unless the people are separated from the problem, the group may choose the wrong procedures or tools.

Structural Conflicts: What Keeps Us Apart?

Sometimes conflict arises because of the way an organization is structured, including people, departments, functions, and overarching management attitudes and messages. No one individual controls these structural sources of conflict; they are the shared responsibility of the organization and of various cultural and social factors that shape it. If the CEO, COO, and the board of directors of a company believe that internal competition brings out the best in people and that cream rises to the top, these assumptions will shape the organizational climate. Alone or combined, they encourage internal competition rather than cooperation.

Structural conflicts may arise from any of five negative elements including:

1. *Dependence on blind trust.* People have no opportunity to verify the truth of statements about what is right, best, or appropriate or about what is going on.
2. *Unclear goals and objectives.* Groups may operate according to an assumption that they should be maximizing short-term results and disregard long-term consequences. Making a big profit from a customer may look good on the

ninety-day profit sheet but it also may come back to haunt you when you want repeat business.

3. *Psychological distance between groups.* The manager who pits quality control against production creates psychological distance between them that can lead to conflict.

4. *Physical distance between groups.* Many organizations believe that isolating one function from another allows the group to maximize its potential without outside interference. Putting an R&D group in the woods thirty miles from the manufacturing plant may be good morale for the research scientists but it works against integration and implementation on a practical level when projects get to the production phases. Companies have come to recognize that mixed function teams work well when they are in close proximity and meet regularly to solve problems.

5. *Decrease in communications or communication only through memos or e-mail.* Although written communication is essential, it is not sufficient. Face-to-face interaction through meetings or teleconferencing is just as important because it gives people more of a sense of the feelings and tone. It also gives everyone a chance to ask questions and make comments, thus lessening the limitations of one-way communications.

Now that we have surveyed the sources of conflict we can turn to the ways that people tend to handle disagreements and disputes once they arise. Through education, work experiences, family, friends, and colleagues, you have probably developed your own patterns and styles of conflict resolution. Those "natural" styles may or may not be working for you; in any case, a greater awareness of your and others' conflict management styles will be helpful in enhancing your effectiveness as a manager.

Styles of Managing Conflict

Management research and literature have defined a number of ways that individuals handle conflict. Keep in mind that each of these styles is based upon your (and your colleagues' or opponents') assumptions, perceptions, and feelings, which have to be uncovered as a first step in finding a solution. Then you can use the cognitive restructuring techniques we talked about in Chapter Four to modify your behavior and move toward more effective ways of handling the conflict. The seven styles of conflict management are: the win/lose style, the lose/yield style, the lose/leave style, the compromise style, the win/win style, the contextual style, and the paradoxical style (which is actually no consistent style at all).

The Win/Lose Style

The win/lose style has maximum concern for personal goals and minimal concern for relationship. It is the ultimate competitive stance. This is the style that Roger Fisher, author of *Getting to Yes* (1981), calls the "hard" position because it disregards people and their interests and concerns. The result is an aggressive insistence on your position. People with the win/lose style of handling conflict assume that:

- The others in the conflict are adversaries
- We must seek victory and demand concessions
- We must be tough on people
- We distrust others
- We must dig into a rigid position
- We must make threats
- Others must be misled about our bottom line
- We must get what we want at their expense
- We will search for the single solution we want
- We insist on our position
- Negotiations are a contest
- We must apply pressure

People with the win/lose style assume that winning is not simply the important thing but the only thing. They see conflicts and differences as natural and inevitable, and they believe that some people have the skills to win and others do not. Because right will ultimately prevail, whoever is right must defend that right and any means is justified. In this Darwinian worldview, only the strong survive.

For example, a manager who maintains tight control over information, who lets no one question his judgment or decisions, who pushes his group, and who likes the feeling of keeping them "on their toes" frequently finds that he lives in a world of almost constant conflict of one kind or another. He sees any encounter as a competition and looks at every confrontation as a chance to get his way—after all, everybody else is a fool anyway. It is almost impossible for his opponents to feel anything but vanquished when he is done with them. Such a manager usually has high turnover, but because this style embodies American values of individualism, strength, and competition, he is often tolerated and even encouraged.

The Lose/Yield Style

In this style of handling conflict, there is maximum concern for relationship and minimal attention to personal goals. Roger Fisher calls this the "soft" or "let's be friends" position. The lose/yield style assumes that:

- We can be friends with others
- We must strive toward agreement and harmony
- We will readily give concessions
- We must be soft on people and the task
- We can trust others without verifying the truth of statements
- We can change positions easily
- We must make an offer to appease the others
- We can disclose our bottom line
- We will accept personal losses
- We must insist on agreement
- We must avoid a contest
- We will yield to pressure

The underlying psychology of the lose/yield style is that differences drive people apart. But this psychology fails to recognize the fact that automatic deference to others is a form of rejection. Walking away from conflict signals an unwillingness to engage in dialogue or to resolve differences. As Fisher says, "Being nice is no answer." Two "soft" participants may try so hard to outdo one another in being kind and gentle that they lose sight of the problem. Like the win/lose style, the lose/yield style rarely produces a beneficial decision for either party. Some managers, for example, approach every conflict as a way of making friends. They tell jokes at the opening of staff problem-solving meetings to the point that the boss usually has to interrupt and ask that they get down to business. They will answer inquiries about progress on tasks by telling everyone not to worry, that it is under control. When pressed on this point, they will apologize profusely and accept blame and promise it will not happen again. They are always trying to get others to agree with them and regularly suggest that everybody go out and socialize together. Underneath all the smiles and friendliness, however, such managers are constantly tense about the conflicts that never seem to get resolved, about their own personal goals that seem to be ignored.

The Lose/Leave Style

Those with the lose/leave style avoid all conflict, including any issue that seems divisive. They physically distance themselves. They clam up. They tell jokes. They do anything to divert attention away from the problem. The lose/leave style assumes that:

- Conflict is irrational
- Conflict can be ignored

- Avoidance is acceptable
- They can observe the conflict without participating in it
- The goal is compliance without commitment

Driven by their belief that all conflict is irrational, this style argues that it is best not to confront a senseless struggle. It is the least effective conflict style of all, and it leaves all parties feeling frustrated and thwarted.

The Compromise Style

In some ways, the compromise style is a variant of the win/lose style. Compromisers are willing to concede something in order to gain something or to move the bargaining forward. The best example of this style is the American political system. The compromise position assumes that:

- Conflict will submit to bargaining
- The participants must follow the rules
- The participants must show goodwill by exchanging concessions
- The participants can exaggerate their demands, knowing that they must eventually make concessions
- The participants must be tough
- Rhetorical appeals to justice and the common good are effective and expected
- The goal is compromise
- Leave a little on the table so you can come back tomorrow to win

Compromisers believe that progress and the common good are at stake in a conflict, so everyone should be willing to give a little in order to take a little. The compromiser's underlying psychology is to limit the losses and emphasize the gains. After all, half a loaf of bread is still bread. (Peter Drucker, in *The Effective Executive* [1968], countered this view by pointing to what may be at stake: "A half a baby is a dead baby.") Many compromises only make the problem worse, leaving the participants somewhat dissatisfied. Because of the high degree of interdependence within most organizations, many win/lose styles of conflict become tempered into a compromise approach.

A poignant example of the downside of the compromise style is the typical budgeting process in organizations. Many managers build cushions into their estimates, knowing that some percentage of what they propose will be cut. And they may include a number of throwaway items they are willing to concede. All of this maneuvering is designed to get their budget approved—period. They have perfected the compromise style, but everyone knows exactly what they are doing. The game is played over and over. If the rules of the game change—for example, a new boss requires zero-based budgets for each department—these managers will have a hard time coming up with a substantive plan that justifies what they are asking for.

The Win/Win Style

In this collaborative approach (also known as principled bargaining), the participants see themselves as problem solvers trying to arrive at a wise decision. They emphasize the interests of all the participants. The win/win position assumes that:

- The participants act as mutual problem solvers
- The goal is a wise outcome
- We must separate the people from the problem
- We must be soft on people: Give reinforcement to others for honest attempts at problem solving; encourage open communications; empathize with the other side
- We must be hard on the problem: You can be just as hard in talking about your interests and encouraging the other side to do the same; you are addressing mutual concerns and it advisable to be as committed as you can
- We proceed without blind trust by setting up procedures to verify the truth of any statements
- We focus on interests and concerns, not positions
- We explore interests and concerns in depth
- We avoid having a bottom line
- We search for alternatives for mutual gain
- We develop objective criteria to evaluate the options for mutual gain
- We are open to reasonable suggestions and solutions; we can adjust our criteria if others are more sound
- We yield to principle not pressure: Principles are the basis for arriving at a wise solution; focusing on interests and concerns, exploring options, and using objective criteria, we can yield on any of these principles if they have merit

The win/win style examines the participants' intense interests, knowing that understanding those interests will shed light on the problem and that satisfying them must be part of the solution. The focus is not on coercion or persuasion but on problem solving. The win/win style pools the intellectual resources of all the participants to generate a variety of mutually beneficial options that emerge as part of the process. A wise decision is the happy outcome, and all the parties feel that they have benefitted from the process and the result. There is no sacrifice of either goals or relationships as there are with the other styles.

Unfortunately, the wisdom to carry out this approach does not come naturally. The win/win style must be taught and then reinforced through practice. All participants must acknowledge and accept the set of assumptions, listed above, for the win/win style to work.

The Contextual Style

All five of the positions we have just discussed presuppose that the participants in a conflict have a well-established, consistent style of managing conflict. But what about individuals who vacillate? They may use all five techniques at various times or in various conflicts. For example, a manager who needs to be deferential may adopt a lose/yield position in a conflict with his or her boss. But when encountering a conflict with a subordinate, this same manager may resort to a win/lose approach or a compromise style. If the stakes are high, he or she might use the lose/leave strategy. In most organizations, this chameleon-like, contextual conflict resolution style is the most common. That is not necessarily bad, either for the manager or the organization. If you understand the variations of conflict resolution styles, you can adopt whatever seems best for a particular situation or whatever has worked in the past.

The Paradoxical Style

In this conflict management style, which is a variation on the contextual style, a manager may use two opposite patterns simultaneously or sequentially. For example, a person using a win/win style might shift to a win/lose approach, either gradually or abruptly. No matter how it takes place, the change jolts the process and confuses the participants. People who constantly use the paradoxical style usually have competing assumptions about conflict that are internally inconsistent. If, for example, a manager knows that she has to cooperate with her colleagues to achieve her goals but has always been a tough competitor in debating and in her work as a sales rep, she may combine those styles in negotiating a conflict. The result may be confusion, not to mention prolonged conflict.

What's Your Conflict Management Style?

As was true for the process of shifting needs and power bases, one of the first steps in modifying conflict management style is to identify what it is. The Conflict Style Survey in Appendix E can be used to help you determine yours. Once you have identified your style, you can then use cognitive restructuring techniques (see Chapter Four) to change your basic assumptions, preferably to a win/win style, which is most productive for managers in the variety of situations they face. In fact, when you are involved in a conflict resolution session, it is good practice to write your win/win assumptions on a whiteboard or flip chart so that the group can refer to them at critical points in the discussion. The group must buy into these assumptions before the process starts. If anyone in the group feels that an assumption has shifted to one of the other styles, having the win/win assumptions listed where everyone can see them makes it possible to reevaluate what has happened and shift back to the win/win style.

Beware of Groupthink

One of the major pitfalls in conflict resolution is groupthink, meaning that a group can be so intent on agreeing with each other that they can no longer realistically appraise alternative courses of action. The concept arose from psychologist Irving Janis's observations in his research on high-level governmental decision making in the 1970s (*Victims of Groupthink*, 1972). Janis noted that groupthink was more prevalent in cohesive groups where the drive to reach agreement hindered the group's capacity to evaluate the impact of their decision. Group pressure transforms minority opinions so that they conform to what the majority of the group believes. Group leaders are especially important in shaping the group's beliefs, but everyone participates—verbally and nonverbally—in enforcing them. The enhancement of the "we feeling" of cohesion becomes the dominant force. As Janis states, "The more amiability and esprit de corps there is among the members of a policy-making group, the greater the danger that independent critical thinking will be replaced by groupthink, which is likely to result in irrational and dehumanizing actions directed against outgroups." In Janis's view, the members affected by groupthink are victims who are unaware that their decisions eventually will come back to haunt them, as we saw in the opening story about the bicycle company. Max and his other managers loved their closeness and valued their shared vision so much that they persecuted their sales manager, Vicki. They were so convinced that what they were doing was right, that their product could not fail, that they lost their objectivity—and the ability to listen to anyone who contradicted them.

Symptoms of groupthink to watch out for include:

1. *A sense of invulnerability.* Most or all the members of the ingroup share an illusion of invulnerability that reassures them about obvious dangers and leads them to become over-optimistic and willing to take extraordinary risks. It also causes them to fail to respond to clear warnings of trouble or danger.
2. *Rationalization.* Victims of groupthink collectively construct rationalizations to discount warnings and other forms of negative feedback that, taken seriously, might lead members to reconsider their assumptions each time they commit themselves to a position.
3. *Morality.* The group members believe unquestioningly in the inherent morality of their position. Members are inclined to ignore the ethical or moral consequences of their decisions. Evidence that may question their stance is summarily dismissed.
4. *Stereotypes.* The group develops stereotyped views of outside groups. Outsiders are perceived as enemies or incompetent and therefore can be ignored. The stereotypes become hardened and difficult to change. Using these stereotypes as characterizations of others gives the ingroup a sense of superiority.
5. *Pressure.* Certain participants in the group apply direct pressure to any individual in the group who expresses doubts about any of the group's shared illusions or who questions the validity of what the majority wants to do. The deviant is forced back into the group mold or out of the group.
6. *Self-censorship.* The group avoids deviating from what appears to be group consensus; all members keep silent about their misgivings and even minimize their own doubts.
7. *Unanimity.* Victims of groupthink share an illusion of unanimity concerning almost all judgments expressed by members who speak in favor of the majority view. The group becomes self-reinforcing and believes in its infallibility.
8. *Mindguards.* Selected members of the group appoint themselves as "mindguards" to protect the leader and fellow members from adverse information that might break the solidarity of their position.

The consequences of groupthink are not hard to imagine, especially for rational decision making. A group that has fallen into groupthink limits the range of possible alternatives and limits or dismisses information from outside sources. They may make premature judgments on this limited course of action and commit the organization's resources to a path that may be disastrous. At Coopersmith & Gordon, Max and his colleagues went right on producing a bicycle that probably had limited possibilities for success and cast out the one person who might have pulled them out of groupthink. The consequences were not just lost sales but broken morale, confusion, and lost sense of purpose.

What It Takes to Handle the Tasks of Conflict Resolution

The ingredients in every conflict include:

- The people who generate the conflict
- The interests that lie beneath their positions
- The possible options open to all parties
- The criteria used to judge the worthiness of the options for mutual gain

Each of these four elements requires that certain tasks be performed in order to resolve the conflict effectively for mutual gain. The following table summarizes the tasks associated with each element, after which we will take up each one of them and, using examples, show how the tasks can be accomplished.

Elements	The Task
People	Separate the people from the problem
Interests	Focus on interests, not positions
Options	Generate a variety of possibilities before deciding what to do
Criteria	Insist that the result be based on some objective criteria

First: Separate the People from the Problem

Susan, a manager, confronts a subordinate, Beth, the day before Susan is going to going to make a presentation to an important client. "Why didn't you tell me that you were including this material in section two of the presentation? I want it revised or taken out."

Beth reminds her, "I showed you this material two weeks ago and you approved it."

Susan snapped. "I don't care what you say, do what I tell you."

Beth hurriedly revises the section and shows it to Susan, who rejects the changes. Beth shouts at Susan, "I quit!"

Susan, taken aback, cries out, "Don't do that! I need you for tomorrow." In this situation both Susan and Beth could not handle the problem without getting upset and angry. Susan, in the first place, lost sight of the fact that in dealing with the task—a presentation to a client—she forgot that she was dealing with a human being who has feelings, emotions, and her own points of view. In her anxiousness to put the company's best foot forward, Susan focused on the task and left out Beth. In the heat of the moment, both lost their cool, and the conflict escalated.

Before coming down hard on a problem like Susan did, ask yourself, "Have I looked at the impact of my decision on the people involved?" In this case, Susan had a stake in a long-term relationship with Beth. She realized this, all too late, when she heard Beth's reaction to her hard attitude. The conflict over that one section was far less important than maintaining Susan and Beth's productive working relationship.

Doing your job and maintaining a good working relationship need not be at odds with each other. The key point is to separate the people from the problem. Many times these two get intertwined with each other. We think we are dealing with the task, but the other person is taking the situation personally because of his or her own (often inaccurate) perceptions or because of poor communications. In any case, what you thought was simple task-oriented criticism turns into a human relations problem. Dealing with the people in a conflict situation involves addressing the role of three key ingredients: perceptions, emotions, and the communication between you.

Perceptions. In any conflict there will be very different perceptions; otherwise, there probably would not be a disagreement. Each side may see only the merits of its case and only the faults of the other side's. It is important to take into account and respect each other's perceptions and to make them part of the problem-solving process. We begin to do that by listing the perceptions of everyone who is involved, then discussing those perceptions in-depth to get at the underlying reasons for the conflict. By letting people share their perceptions and discuss them, they feel that they are being taken seriously. Keep in mind that all participants must reveal their perceptions; there cannot be any silent voices in the group. Everyone should state how he or she sees the problem. If you are a manager in charge of this process, it is essential to stay neutral. Do not look for faults in their perceptions. Try to see the situation and their point of view as they see them.

Emotions. Feelings and emotions are an equally potent part of a conflict situation that need to be acknowledged. Ask yourself, how are you feeling about the situation? Are you angry, tense, intimidated, or anxious? All of these emotional states affect how you deal with the other side. How do they feel? If you are emotionally involved in the situation, it is highly likely that they are feeling the same way. The more you try to brush aside emotions the more they resurface and cause more problems than if they had been handled in the open. Discussing how you feel makes emotions legitimate and controllable.

In fact, you may want to set up rules for handling emotions in your negotiation. For example, you may want to set aside a period of time where feelings can be expressed. An important rule could be that only one person at a time can express his or her feelings as you go around the table. There may be times when an emotional outburst will occur, but the worst thing you could do would be to counterattack and escalate the emotional intensity. Remember that the outburst was probably prompted by that person feeling powerless or threatened by what was happening. Rarely do people stage emotional outbursts for effect. By controlling your reaction, you allow the other person to let off steam. You can say that you understand their concerns and that sometimes you feel the same way. By admitting that everyone is in the same boat, you can bring the focus back to acting as mutual problem solvers and move on. Accepting an apology or giving one shows a great deal of empathy for the other person and costs very little.

Communication. If the conflict-resolution process is based on talking, not on any forms of violence, and is predominantly cooperative and not competitive, antagonistic, or coercive, the outcome will be acceptable to all participants because it addresses their concerns. Susan Heitler, a psychologist, lists the following communication processes that need attention in conflict resolution:

- *Saying:* Verbalizations need to be explicit, non-threatening, and focused on data. "I would like you to be at your desk ready for work at 9:00 a.m." is better than saying "I want you to be on time." "The shipments on November 7 and December 11 were late" is better than "You are always late with your shipments."
- *Listening:* The listener has to be focused on what the other person is saying. That means holding back on judgment, rebuttal, or distractions. You can show that you are willing to listen by: having a relaxed posture, showing varied eye contact, making appropriate gestures, leaning forward, maintaining a suitable seating distance (not too far or too close), and facing squarely toward the other person.
- *Creating symmetry:* Equal strokes for equal folks. One person should not do all the talking while the other does all the listening. A facilitator should monitor the process and draw out the silent ones. As a communicator you can encourage the other person to respond to your points by saying, "I have finished on that point. Now it is your turn to respond."
- *Summarizing:* Each participant should paraphrase what he or she thinks the other person has conveyed. A summary of the points of agreement and both sides' concerns helps move the process toward a final solution. In addition,

an integrated summary of the problem states the essential concerns of both sides. For example, "We are both concerned with quality and cost." If both sides agree to that summary, they will feel less like antagonists and more like teammates working together to resolve a shared problem.

Another important ingredient in communication is showing respect for the other person's viewpoint. That does not mean accepting or not accepting the other's viewpoint; it is simply a matter of avoiding evaluation, making positive statements about the other person, reviewing options, and using the other's name as a way of maintaining the personal connection.

Second: Focus on Interests and/or Concerns, Not Positions

In the win/lose style of conflict management, the opponent's interests are ignored or defeated. In a win/win style, in contrast, participants in a conflict explore their concerns at deeper levels in order to find mutually compatible solutions. In this process, the two sides move from initial proposals (positions) to concerns and then to new solutions that address their mutual concerns.

Behind every position is a set of underlying concerns. If one manager wants to reorganize the R&D department one way and another manager thinks it should be done a different way, they have positions that appear at odds with each other. If they stopped at this point to try to reconcile their positions, neither would probably be willing to change. By bargaining from their positions, the outcome would probably be a win/lose, lose/lose (depending on who won), or a compromise solution. The best way to resolve this conflict is to get at each person's underlying concerns. Why does one manager want to reorganize the department in this way and the other manager in a different way? If they go on to explore underlying concerns further, they may hit on a plan that satisfies both their concerns. One manager's plan has certain benefits, but so does the other's. Behind their initial positions are needs, desires, concerns, and fears. Uncovering and reconciling their interests and concerns is better than focusing on positions themselves (i.e., their individual, specific plans for the department) because beneath each position lie many more interests than those that are directly in conflict.

The next step for these two managers is to make a list of their interests and concerns without judging the legitimacy of each other's concerns. This would end up being a win/lose situation that could fracture the process. At this stage, both of them need to put the problem before the solution. They must uncover and explore the concerns before inventing options for mutual gain. One temptation to be avoided is to drag up a similar situation from the past, as in, "Your plan last year for changing the way work is assigned didn't work out." That does not help the two of them reach a solution. In fact, it will probably escalate the conflict. Forget the past and concentrate on the present (concerns) and the future (options). When both of them admit that they have concerns about reorganizing the R&D department and are willing to explore the situation, they are being hard on the problem not on each other. By acknowledging that each has valid concerns, they are being soft on people. Once they have exhausted their list of concerns they are ready for the next step: the search for options for mutual gain.

Third: Search for Options for Mutual Gain

Once you have separated the people from the problem and looked at mutual concerns, it is time to look for options for mutual gain. This process does not mean looking for a compromise that requires sacrifices, but making a legitimate attempt to find solutions that meet all parties' interests. At this stage, it is important to make sure that the group avoids premature judgment, does not limit the options, and makes sure that everyone feels they share the problem.

Avoiding premature judgments. As problem solvers, we tend to be reactive rather than reflective. We want to rush to solve the problem before we have given adequate thought to the various options open to us. In crisis situations, quick reactions are necessary and valuable (when they prove to be correct). In complex cases where the conflict is long-standing, leaping to conclusions can lead to frustration and error. Brainstorming and a more structured approach to analyzing options are effective tools for preventing premature solutions.

Brainstorming is particularly useful in generating options, possible causes for the problem, and alternative approaches. Because lots of activities may be called "brainstorming" but are not, true brainstorming follows several ground rules:

Before: Define the objective of the session, i.e., to uncover participants' underlying interests or to search for options for mutual gain. Limit the group to between five and nine participants; with more than nine people, the group may break apart, but fewer than five limits the amount of input. Hold the meeting offsite to change the mindset and keep the atmosphere informal (no dress codes, no formal hierarchy, etc.) The participants should all be knowledgeable in the area and skilled in interpersonal interaction. Choose a facilitator who will keep the process on track.

During: Seat participants side by side facing a written statement of the problem on a flip chart or board. Clarify the ground rules: no premature closure on defining the problem and no evaluation or criticism of others' ideas during the session. Encourage wild ideas and lots of them, and foster an atmosphere where everyone can build on and modify each other's contributions. Give positive reinforcement for all attempts. Record everyone's ideas in full view of the group.

After: Put a star next to the ideas that the whole group agrees are most promising. Build on the other ideas and set up a time after the brainstorming session to evaluate ideas and decisions. Decisions and evaluations should not be made during the initial brainstorming session.

One way of ensuring that you do not make premature decisions or limit your options is to use a more structured approach to problem solving called the Four-Quadrant Method. (See Table 7.1.) It is helpful to draw the quadrants on a wall in front of all participants.

The Four-Quadrant Method is a general problem-solving procedure used to promote systematic thinking. The group starts with Quadrant I and moves through the other three, which prevents skipping or short-circuiting any of the steps. Leaping to Quadrant III without going through Quadrants I and II leads to premature closure because the group has not adequately recognized the problem or diagnosed the cause. Lingering too long on Quadrants I and II leaves out the

TABLE 7.1   THE FOUR-QUADRANT APPROACH

Evaluation ↓	Diagnosis ↓	
Quadrant IV *What should we do?* Ideas about what to do and who might do it to take action on a general approach.	Quadrant I *What is wrong?* Identify perceptions of: • what we dislike (symptoms of the problem) • a preferred solution Identify the differences between the above.	**In the Real World** ←
Quadrant III *What are our options?* Possible strategies for overcoming the causes of the problems that have been identified.	Quadrant II *What is causing the problem?* Possible reasons that the problem has not been resolved or the conflict settled. Possible causes that you could address to solve the differences in Quadrant I.	**In Theory** ←
Action ↑	**Reflection ↑**	

action steps. The Four-Quadrant Method can also be used as a diagnostic tool. The group can use it to ask questions such as, "Where are we in the four quadrants? Have we examined all the factors in each quadrant? Are we ready to go on to the next stage?" By keeping the model in front of the group, you can determine what quadrant you want to be in or which one you are in. A group may go backwards and forwards in the quadrants to clarify points. Appendix F offers the Four-Quadrant Problem-Solving Preference Assessment, a tool to help you determine which quadrant you prefer to operate in so that you can identify your biases in problem solving.

Fourth: Use Objective Criteria

After the hard work of exploring interests and coming up with options for mutual gain, the group still faces the problem of deciding which option(s) to choose. As Roger Fisher states in his book *Getting to Yes* (1981), "The more you bring standards of fairness, efficiency, or scientific merit to bear on your particular problem, the more likely you are to produce a final package that is wise and fair. The more you and the other side refer to precedent and community practice, the greater your chance of benefiting from past experience."

The actual criteria the group uses will depend upon the particular situation, but it is best to make sure that all parties agree to the ones that are chosen. Table 7.2 shows a set of fair standards that could be used as the basis for determining the unique standards by which the outcomes of a successful negotiation could be judged. In some cases you may apply multiple criteria in judging options for mutual gain. Multiple criteria such as quality, cost, and schedule (used frequently in manufacturing decisions) can be equally weighted or given differential weights, depending upon the circumstances. In discussing objective criteria with the other side, each issue should be framed as a joint search for the fair standard to be used. You can ask participants to explain the theory behind a criterion. If

TABLE 7.2   EXAMPLES OF FAIR STANDARDS

Market value	Legal precedence
Precedent	Moral standards
Scientific	Equal treatment
Professional	Tradition
Efficiency	Reciprocity
Costs	Quality
Schedule	Customer requirements

one group says that cost is the most important criterion, you could ask, "On what basis is this true?" If the answer is that there has been a precedent in the past for this criterion, you can ask whether or how it is appropriate to the problem at hand. In searching for objective criteria, it is necessary to be reasonable and open to suggestions. Make sure, too, that the group(s) agrees on objective criteria based on principles, not pressure.

Problem Solving at Overland Services: A Case in Point

The purchasing department at Overland Services Company has decided to implement a new billing and requirements computer system for customer service because the present system is slow, inadequate, and limited. The program office, which has the direct contact with the customer, does not want the purchasing department to make any unilateral decisions about choosing the new system.

When the problem is diagnosed, it is apparent that a win/lose process of imposing a new system on the program office will breed resentment and obstructionism during implementation. The customer's requirements can only be met if purchasing and the program office collaborate.

Each group is asked to come up with three or four major concerns related to the performance of the purchasing system. Purchasing says that they are most concerned that the new system be fast, compatible with other purchasing requirements, and cost efficient. The program office wants it to be specific to the customer's requirements, easy to comprehend, and reliable.

Based on these concerns, the groups isolated three hardware systems and four sets of software as possible choices. After a number of joint sessions, they agreed on the following criteria for judging the system:

- Efficiency (the ability to obtain data and output quickly)
- Quality of the output (the program office and the customer can understand it)
- Satisfaction of customer requirements based on survey and interview data
- Professional standards of performance for the hardware and software (according to the purchasing department's goals)
- Cost (an important but not over-riding consideration).

At this point, the two groups construct a problem-solving matrix to evaluate the alternatives. When the criteria are applied to the three systems, they select one option. Because both groups had reached a mutual agreement on the concerns and the criteria for judging the options, everyone is satisfied with the outcome.

Conclusion

In summary, we can state that conflict is natural, normal, and cannot be ignored. There are functional and dysfunctional strategies for handling conflict. Most important, conflict is not a contest or test of wills. By the clarification of perceptions, interests, and concerns, we can move toward the search for options for mutual gain. In the search for wise solutions to our problems, effective communication is one of the cornerstones of the process. As we saw in Chapter Four, our assumptions drive our behavior. It is necessary to adapt a functional approach to conflict resolution by striving toward win/win solutions. The important point is that effective conflict resolution strategies are a learned response. By identifying underlying assumptions we can relearn new assumptions that lead to effectiveness. Like the prescriptions for developing power, we have the ability to modify our behavior. In the next chapter, we shall address the issues of values. They are closely linked to conflict styles in that they are learned and are the basis for some of the deep-rooted conflicts among people, cultures, and nations.

CHAPTER EIGHT

VALUES: CLARIFYING WHAT YOU STAND FOR

Charlie Marsten was complaining, "Why are we having this ethics and values meeting? I've got to plan my meeting with the advertising group on the new fall lines. What do values and ethics have to do with business?"

Joe Borland agreed, "As far as I'm concerned, values and ethics are a person's own responsibility. The company is guided by the market, not the individual."

"Yeah," said Harry Wheatley. "What happened to good old-fashioned capitalism? Caveat emptor—the invisible hand of the market and all that good stuff? Survival of the fittest . . . that's what free competition is all about. You can't let personal feelings or values get in the way."

"Right," Michele Bolton put in. "We're a profit-driven company that is responsible to its stockholders. Don't ever forget that."

Anna Weinberg summed it up: "I was taught at business school that business is amoral, not immoral. We all know there is a difference between the two."

Tom Woods, president of BGL, a clothing and uniform manufacturer, listened to his staff express their views about the company's new Ethics and Values Committee. The government had audited the company over the pricing of a clothing contract and was going to take action, claiming that BGL had overcharged them. Tom was appalled that this had happened. He believed he was fair, honest, and equitable, and he expected his staff to follow suit. But he later found out that one of his most trusted employees was responsible for setting a higher price for the government contract market.

Some time after the incident, Tom had gone to a seminar on the role of values in the organization and had come back with a proposal for an oversight group called the Ethics and Values Committee. At this first meeting, he wondered how he would respond to his management group's grudging attitude and resistance to the whole idea of ethics and values.

What's All This Fuss About Values?

BGL's story is not unusual in the current business climate. For one reason or another, the role of ethics and values has become increasingly important in many organizations, despite recent past history that has tried to deny both. "Rules? There are no rules," Aristotle Onassis is credited with having said of his view of world business. That buccaneering style of management did not garner him a favorable response from the world powers when he tried to gain a monopoly on Middle Eastern oil in the late 1950s. Vice President Richard Nixon reputedly told a CIA agent, "If you have to kill him, don't do it on U.S. soil."

What do we mean by values and ethics, and why should business concern itself with them? In our society government grants business organizations the privileges and support they need in order to operate. That relationship has helped to produce the Federal Reserve, satellites, Silicon Valley, the interstate highway system, and any number of other forms of assistance to business (such as the corporate bailouts extended to Chrysler in the 1980s). In our democracy, business and national authority are allies, not enemies. Even so, there are rules of the game that everyone—including business organizations—has to follow. Knowing what those rules are—the values and ethics of how we operate—is important both for managers and their organizations. Values are clearly rooted in our upbringing and life experiences, our religious beliefs, our peers; we are not born with an innate sense of what is right, just, or good. Values determine how we act out our needs, how we use power, and how we handle conflict. Like the other aspects of management style that are learned, values can be modified or, more explicitly, clarified so they are consistent.

There is no strict formula for the right set of values as long as they are positive. This chapter will not discuss negative values like greed, avarice, or racist domination; rather, it will present an array of positive values that can form unique constellations that will serve you as a manager. The task is to understand our values and how they fit into the context of our lives, both organizationally and personally.

Information theorist Thomas Stewart states: "If 'values' and 'vision' and 'empowerment' and 'teamwork' and 'facilitating' and 'coaching' sometimes sound like so much mushmouthed mishmash—which they sometimes are—that's a reflection of the fact that managers are groping toward a language and a means for managing knowledge, knowledge work, and knowledge-intensive companies" (*Intellectual Capital*, 1997). Values are part of the manager's language that need to be defined, clarified, and integrated into the woof and warp of the organization's everyday activities. In this day and age, when companies are forced to comply with government regulations and face so many external challenges, organizational values are bantered about without much thought to their meaning and depth. We need to address the issue of what subset of societal values is necessary and sufficient for a values-oriented company. Our assumptions about society and individual values cannot be separated from our business lives; because they are intimately intertwined, we must be consciously aware of them both.

The Importance of Organizational Integrity

Lynn Sharp Paine, in a 1994 article in the *Harvard Business Review* called "Managing for Organizational Integrity," points out that managers must acknowledge their role in shaping organizational ethics. If they do not, the legal and marketplace implications can be serious. She cites four cases that represent positive and negative outcomes of value-related incidents.

Negative

Sears Roebuck misled customers and sold them unnecessary parts and services.
Outcome: Loss of sales and reputation.

BeechNut misrepresented apple juice as 100 percent pure when it actually contained only water and chemicals.
Outcome: Loss of market share and consumer confidence.

Positive

Johnson & Johnson handled the Tylenol crisis by recalling Tylenol capsules.
Outcome: Public acceptance and maintenance of market share.

Inspeech (now Novacare) tackled the mistrust and value clashes between financial managers and therapists in their health care system.
Outcome: Research and corporate soul-searching resulted in a mission statement that reoriented the company.

Paine believes a corporate strategy based on integrity holds organizations to a more robust standard of behavior than those designed to merely comply with governmental regulations. While legal compliance is rooted in avoiding liability, organizational integrity is based on the concept of self-governance in accordance with a set of guiding values or principles. The task of ethics management is to define and give life to an organization's guiding values.

Organizations that want to develop an integrity-based strategy and mission statement need to understand that integrity is broader, deeper, and more demanding than legal compliance. It cuts right to the organization's guiding beliefs (and its members' beliefs as well). Integrity requires an active effort to define the responsibilities and aspirations that direct the company in its ethical path. As Paine points out, "Executives who ignore ethics run the risk of personal and corporate liability in today's increasingly tough legal environment." Corporations need to do more than comply with the law; they must accept the fact that business is a morally bound institution and that they are held responsible for their members' unethical behavior. No longer are there isolated fallguys for the corporation. The implementation of an integrity-based strategy for a company involves defining its values and aspirations and its social obligations, including compliance with the law.

This "values thing" is not some passing fancy that will eventually go away. If you scan the business and op-ed pages of newspapers, you see hundreds of inches of type devoted to the topic. The reason is simple. Business is a part of life and values are a part of both. As globalization and corporate mergers increase, we will be faced with many more moral dilemmas concerning treatment of workers, unequal pay scales, bribery, toxic imports, and greed, to name just a few of the issues. The way they will be handled depends upon the values of those who have to deal with them.

What Are Values?

When we talk about values, we are talking about a preference for things to be one way rather than another. Values are a mixture of feelings and beliefs and our responses to the world around us. Explicitly or implicitly, we constantly value things, people, events, and ideas as good or bad, pleasant or unpleasant, beautiful or ugly, appropriate or inappropriate, true or false, virtuous or immoral. Our ideas about life and how it should be lived define our values.

The ultimate function for human values is to give us a set of standards that satisfy our needs and at the same time maintain and enhance our self-esteem. Adhering to a set of values makes it possible to regard ourselves and to be regarded by others as having met societal and institutional standards of morality and competence. In essence, human values consist of a relatively small number of core ideas or beliefs that represent what is desirable. Different people may set priorities among those basic values in a variety of ways. For example, take the basic values of freedom and equality. If we value freedom over equality, that gives priority to hierarchy and privilege. If they both are weighted equally, that produces a more participatory and democratic orientation. If freedom and equality are both devalued, that results in totalitarianism.

If the words that represent these core values were eliminated, children growing up in such a society would have no reference points to live by and no language with which to rationalize their behavior. They would not have any rules to guide them in meeting societal demands about how to behave competently or morally. Without adults and a firmly established set of values, the group of shipwrecked schoolboys in William Golding's *Lord of the Flies* degenerated into primitive, destructive human beings. Their behavior was guided by base instinct and undeveloped moral character.

When organized into a cohesive pattern or system, values are reflected in our choices and actions, in the way we resolve conflicts and satisfy our needs. If your values involve brotherly love and charity, for example, they will affect the way you handle conflict at work. It is likely that you will adopt the lose/yield style where you do anything to maintain the relationship, even if it means you do not achieve your personal goals. Similarly, if you believe in fairness, equality, and honesty, you will probably opt for the collaborative strategy for resolving the conflict. (See Chapter Seven for a full discussion of conflict-resolution styles.)

Where Do Values Come From?

We know that values are learned through experience and are incorporated into our thinking early in life. Research on the development of values suggests that the link between values and overt behavior strengthens as we mature because we learn more values and internalize them into an integrated package. The paradox is that as we grow older, our values are under more pressure as we interact with other groups and institutions that affect our value orientations.

In business, for example, values drive all kinds of trends and strategy. In today's world, there seems to be general agreement that bigger is better. The string of mergers and acquisitions in all sorts of industries from publishing to espresso bars to automobiles and oil have been broadly applauded by investors and business analysts. The mergers have been accompanied by another trend: the rapid development of national chain retailers. Driving these trends are values that have to do with efficiency and the importance of stock market valuations. Bottom-line business decisions and strategy are more highly valued than the effect on local communities, employees, and customers, factors that tend to be considered after the fact. It is not possible to tell whether the creation of all these conglomerates is "good" or "bad." What is significant are the values that stand behind and drive the business decisions.

Some values are explicit and appear to us as clear and coherent. We can state the value, show how we use it in making judgments, and identify its limits. For instance, a devout believer understands a highly articulated set of beliefs based on theology and dogma. A priest with many years of training will have a high degree of cohesion in those values, whereas a lapsed believer will have a much looser sense of them. Other values are more implicit and may even resist becoming explicit. Implicit value structures can lead to moral inconsistency when there are conflicts among them. For example, being the head of a company's fair practices committee and holding deep-seated prejudices against certain ethic and racial groups may lead to professing fairness but practicing discrimination.

As we saw in Chapter Seven, explicating values and assumptions is important in conflict resolution and problem solving; unless they are articulated, they cannot be addressed. For instance, the implicit belief that competition produces excellence may drive entrepreneurs to superb innovations. At the same time, an organization may have an implicit belief that cooperation is needed to coordinate research and development with production. If these two competing values are not integrated, employees may get conflicting messages. While competition with another company is acceptable in a free market, competition within the organization leads to unresolved conflict and wasted effort.

As we learn and grow, we begin to set priorities and give patterns to our values. Differences among individuals may not lie so much in the presence or absence of particular values but in the way each person arranges them in hierarchies or priorities. For example, there is supposedly a shift in the importance of family security (a personal value) versus the time organizations demand of their employees. The organization's priorities are clearly in conflict with employees who have a different value orientation. This can have serious consequences for organizations that do not read the shift in values. Some highly qualified people will be disenfranchised and the organization may suffer.

Managers' Primary Values: Are They Enough?

When managers are asked to list their most cherished values, they name honesty, family security, and being a responsible person as the top three (with honesty and family security cited far more often than responsibility). Stephen Carter, a professor of law at Yale University, has made the case that honesty by itself is insufficient as a primary value ("The Insufficiency of Honesty," 1997). Being brutally honest with a handicapped worker over his or her inability to lift heavy objects is not virtuous behavior, even if it is totally true. Telling a colleague that he is not smart enough to do a job serves no purpose but to prove that you are callous and unfeeling. Far more important is integrity, an entirely different value. According to Carter, acting with integrity requires three elements:

1. Discerning what is right and what is wrong. This means ascertaining the truthfulness of our beliefs based on solid evidence.
2. Acting on what you have discerned, even at personal cost.
3. Saying openly that you are acting on your understanding of right and wrong.

Carter advocates testing and examining the integrity of our assumptions and beliefs. Pure honesty, for example, may actually be falsification of a belief. You may believe that women are inferior to men at the hard job of managing a company. But unless you put this belief to an objective test, you have not acted with integrity.

When presented with the distinction between honesty and integrity, most of us can generally agree that there is a difference. But most will confess that they had not consciously thought about it. It is accurate to say many of us cannot name more than a handful of clearly articulated values. In many cases, contradictions remain on an unconscious level. A manager may profess that her three top organizational values are fairness, honesty, and equality. Yet in her everyday dealings with her subordinates and peers she is competitive, petty, and elitist. This manager is operating on the unconscious level of her true values, despite what she says is important to her.

Not thinking consciously about values can cause many problems for managers. Lack of an integrated value system (and thus integrity) results when we do not understand and clarify our values. Because of their importance in driving behavior, values are an essential part of management style. Just as organizations cannot operate without guiding principles, individual managers must have a sense of their own moral compass.

Values Clarification: Making the Hidden Visible

For organizations, the process of clarifying and stating their values is an important part of defining how they will operate. For example, the Levi Straus Company approached value clarification by establishing what they called an "aspiration statement," meaning a statement of what they hoped to achieve in the way they treated their employees. The company organized a number of off-site retreats to focus on unexamined assumptions regarding diversity and stereotypes about particular groups. At the same time, top management held their own forums on a broad range of workplace issues. From all these meetings came an aspiration statement that contained the statements of values and goals for realizing them:

> *New behaviors.* Leadership that exemplifies directness, openness to influence, commitment to the success of others, willingness to acknowledge our own contributions to problems, personal accountability, teamwork, and trust. Not only must we model these behaviors but also we must coach others to adopt them.

> *Diversity.* Leadership that values diversity in experience and perspectives and a varied work force (age, sex, ethnic group, etc.) at all levels of the organization, that takes full advantage of the rich backgrounds and abilities of all our people, and that promotes greater diversity in positions of influence. Differing points of view will be sought; diversity will be valued and honesty rewarded, not suppressed.

> *Recognition.* Leadership that provides greater recognition—both financial and psychic—for individuals and teams that contribute to our success. Recognition must be given to all who contribute: those who create and innovate and also those who continually support the day-to-day business requirements.

> Ethical management practices leadership that epitomizes the stated standards of ethical behavior. We must provide clarity about our expectations and enforce these standards throughout the corporation.

> *Communications.* Leadership that is clear about the company, units, and individual goals and performance. People must know what is expected of them and receive timely, honest feedback on their performance and career aspirations.

> *Empowerment.* Leadership that increases the authority and responsibility of those closest to our products and customers. By actively encouraging responsibility, trust, and recognition in the organization, we can harness and release the capabilities of our people.

This aspiration statement clearly addresses behaviors, if enacted, that qualify as values. The Levi Straus process can be contrasted with the situation in most organizations where everyone works under an invisible umbrella of unstated assumptions about ethical conduct. The danger of operating this way is the probability of inconsistency and, more importantly, contradiction. That is why it is so essential that organizations and individuals examine their values and the worldview and assumptions that have created those values.

Examining Our Assumptions about Life

No discussion of values can ignore the importance of worldview. For many people, including managers, their view of the world is limited to day-to-day subsistence concerns. To transcend this basic level of existence, we have to be educated to look at our assumptions about life. Until we do, it is impossible to understand the values that are driving us, much less write a value-oriented mission statement. When we actively explore our assumptions, we must examine a key set of critical issues, including:

Knowledge and information. How does the organization deal with the flow of information within its boundaries? Does information flow freely from the top down and back up or is there a lead ceiling that limits or prevents access to information about policy, mission statements, expectations, and values? Does the organization value individual development? Does it encourage and support its employees in expanding their knowledge base?

Leadership. Leadership calls for vision and decisiveness. Effective leaders should be able to articulate their values, their vision of the good life and a good society, the use of power, and a code of professional ethics. Leaders should make clear the values, models, and ideals they wish for individuals and for societies. Do they prefer an individualistic or a collective vision for society? Do they embrace an ascetic or a consumer-oriented lifestyle? Do they espouse hedonism or altruism?

The good life. Leaders bring into their work conceptions of what constitutes the good life, especially assumptions about people and their jobs. Is the idea of the good life promoted by a set of assumptions that is based on individualism, personal control, or reciprocity?

The good society. Similarly, we should know the implicit or explicit visions of leaders for what constitutes the good society. John Kenneth Galbraith, in his book *The Good Society* (1996), proposed that we, as citizens, ". . . explore and define what, very specifically, would be right. Just what should the good society be? Toward what, stated as clearly as may be possible, should we aim?" Leaders in support of the societal status quo adhere to individualistic conceptions of well-being, whereas those with more communitarian ideas will advance very different theories and interventions.

Power in relationships. Another revealing dimension of morality in leadership is the distribution of power in organizational relationships. The way that power is distributed affects the organization's ability to advance values such as self-determination, collaboration, and democratic participation. Are relationships based on egalitarian or paternalistic principles?

Professional ethics. What is the range of ethical behavior? Is it limited to compliance with government regulations? Does the organization take the customer into account? Is it concerned with distributive justice? Is the vision of professional ethics based upon an organizational set of values that determines its ethical stance?

Clarifying What Is Most Important

Social scientist Milton Rokeach, who has devoted his professional life to the study of values, states that humans differ from one another in the way they organize their values into hierarchies or priorities. All humans have both end values (beliefs about ultimate goals or desirable states such as happiness or wisdom) and instrumental values (beliefs about what we must do to achieve those end values, such as behaving honestly or responsibly). The range of both end and instrumental values has been found to be relatively small, in the dozens rather than in the hundreds or thousands. In addition, these values are more or less universal, for there are a limited number of needs that we seek to satisfy, just as there are only so many end states of existence that people everywhere can strive for and just so many ways to realize them. With just a small set of values, it is possible to account for the richness and variety of individual differences in behavior, attitudes, ideologies, judgments, evaluations, and rationalizations. A dozen and a half end values (see Table 8.1), for instance, can be ordered in trillions of different ways, enough to account for variations in values among individuals, groups, organizations, institutions, societies, and cultures across the world.

Clarifying Your Own Values

If you wish to begin clarifying your own values, follow Rokeach's list with these five steps:

Step 1. Start with the list of end values and rank them from most preferred to least preferred.

Step 2. Rank the instrumental values the same way. Do not mix values across the list.

Step 3. Look over the lists and reorder any values that you think need to be changed.

Step 4. Now do the same ranking process for your organization's end and instrumental values.

Step 5. Compare your personal values to the espoused values of your organization.

TABLE 8.1   END VALUES AND INSTRUMENTAL VALUES

End Values	Instrumental Values
A comfortable life A prosperous life	*Ambition* Hardworking and aspiring
Equality Brotherhood and equal opportunity	*Broad-mindedness* Open-minded; diversified
An exciting life A stimulating, active life	*Capability* Competent; effective
Family security Taking care of loved ones	*Cheerfulness* Light-hearted; joyful
Freedom Independence and free choice	*Cleanliness* Neat and tidy
Health Physical and mental well-being	*Courage* Standing up for your beliefs
Inner harmony Freedom from inner conflict	*Forgiveness* Willing to pardon others
Mature love Sexual and spiritual intimacy	*Helpfulness* Working for the welfare of others; caring and compassion
National security Protection from attack	*Honesty* Sincere and truthful; trustworthiness
Pleasure An enjoyable, leisurely life	*Imagination* Daring and creative
Salvation Saved; eternal life	*Intellectualism* Self-reliant; self-sufficient
Self-respect Self-esteem	*Logic* Consistent; rational
A sense of accomplishment A lasting contribution	*Ability to love* Faithful to friends or the group; respectful
Social recognition Respect and admiration	*Loyalty* Faithful to friends
True friendship Close companionship	*Obedience* Dutiful
Wisdom A mature understanding of life education	*Politeness* Courteous and well-mannered; respectful
A world at peace A world free of war and conflict	*Responsibility* Dependable and reliable
A world of beauty Beauty of nature and the arts	*Self-control* Restrained; self-disciplined

The end and instrumental values are listed in alphabetical order. There is no one-to-one relationship between end and instrumental values.

Your values and the organization's values should be largely congruent, otherwise you will experience a feeling of conflict between what you and the organization believe. When such dissonance arises, you have to somehow justify continuing to work there either by denial or by rationalization. Both of these defenses lead to an uncomfortable feeling of not doing what is instinctually right for you. When the engineer for Morton Thiokol stated that going with the disastrous launch of *Challenger IV* was not an act of goodness, he was expressing a personal value that conflicted with the value that the company and NASA placed on expediency. This is an existential bind that we all find ourselves in at times. In hindsight we often wish that we had stuck to our principles and not given into group pressure. Organizations should make sure that their decisions mirror what is good not just for their bottom line but also for the common good.

Each of Rokeach's thirty-six values appear in every developed society, although they vary considerably not only in the way they are ordered but also in the relationships among them. For example, in democratic societies, freedom and equality rank equally high, while in communistic countries equality is ranked higher than freedom. If freedom is ranked higher than equality, that is an aristocratic society, but if both freedom and equality are ranked low in importance, that indicates a totalitarian society.

It is important to stress the inadequacy of each value in and of itself. Values only have meaning when they operate as a set that forms a whole. Conflicts occur when people adhere closely to one value but neglect another equally important one. A typical case in organizations is the belief in autonomy and self-determination and the disregard for other values such as collaboration and fairness. To avoid this sort of conflict, we need to avoid becoming fixated on certain values to the exclusion of others. This is why it is important to regard values as complementary rather than mutually exclusive. A case in point is the dialectic between care and justice. Caring and compassion provide the basic motivation to look after someone else's well being, whereas the pursuit of social justice ensures that our compassion is extended to people beyond our immediate circle.

Table 8.2 presents five sets of patterns and hierarchies of end state values for different groups who participated in Rokeach's value clarification exercises. The data for the scientists, liberal politicians, educators, and British Tories (conservatives) come from the studies in Rokeach's book, *Understanding Human Values* (1979). The data for the business group is from a sample of two hundred managers in a high-tech industry survey in 1996–1997. These comparisons are presented to demonstrate that although diverse groups share common values, they give them different priorities, which can lead to value conflicts. For managers and their organizations, determining individual and group values can identify and head off potential value clashes. By clarifying value priorities, conflicting groups or individuals can work toward collaboration or compromise to resolve differences.

TABLE 8.2   EXAMPLES OF VALUE PATTERNS AND HIERARCHIES

Scientists	Businesspeople	Liberal Politicians	Educators	British Tories
A sense of accomplishment	Family security	A world at peace	A sense of accomplishment	Freedom
Self-respect	Health	Equality	Self-respect	Family security
Wisdom	Self-respect	Freedom	Wisdom	A world at peace
Family security	Wisdom	Family security	Freedom	Health
Freedom	A comfortable life	True friendship	Equality	True friendship
Equality	A sense of accomplishment	Self-respect	Inner harmony	Self-respect
A world at peace	Freedom	Happiness	A world of beauty	Social recognition

When we look more closely at Rokeach's data for the five groups, we find both common and unique values. The values most common over the five samples were:

- Freedom (all five samples)
- Family security (four groups)
- A sense of accomplishment (four groups)
- Self-respect (four groups)
- Wisdom (three groups)
- Equality (three groups)
- World at peace (three groups)

As for unique values, the business sample identified only two found in their top seven that differed from all the others: health and a comfortable life. The educator sample produced two unique values: a world of beauty and inner harmony. The British Tory sample had national security and social recognition as two values that did not show up in the top seven of the other samples. Liberal politicians had one value unique to them: true friendship. The scientist sample had no value that was not found on the other lists.

As we might expect, there were also value clashes among the groups. Equality was absent on the British Tory list while freedom was the number one value. The Tories would clash with the scientists, the liberals, and the educators over the role of distributive justice and freedom.

Organizational Values: The Ideal and the Real

Based upon the current literature on values in society and organizations, Tables 8.3 and 8.4 show the end and instrumental values that could be adopted by most organizations in a democratic society. These sets of values are based upon the need for organizations to develop their human capital. Robert Haas, of the Levi Straus Company, has stated: "We always talked about the 'hard stuff' and the 'soft stuff.' The soft stuff was the company's commitment to our workforce. And the hard

TABLE 8.3   THE BEST END VALUES FOR ORGANIZATIONS

End Values	Rationale
Wisdom Gain a mature understanding of life; education	To develop intellectual capital for the individual and the organization
A sense of accomplishment Make a lasting contribution	To involve people in meaningful and fulfilling tasks and projects for individual and organizational achievement
Equality Promote brotherhood and equal opportunity	To ensure a level playing field for all and to commit to diversity in the workforce
Self-respect Encourage self-esteem	To empower self and others in the organization
A world at peace Work toward a world free of war and conflict	Globalization and free markets can only work if this is a universal value
Freedom Promote independence and free choice	The linchpin of the democratic process in government and business
Health Encourage physical and mental well-being	To promote physical and mental health for the individuals within the organization
Family security Taking care of loved ones	To encourage the integration between work values and family values and prevent a conflict between the organization and the individual

TABLE 8.4   THE BEST INSTRUMENTAL VALUES FOR ORGANIZATIONS

Instrumental Values	Rationale
Honesty To be sincere and truthful; to be trust-worthy	To support a cornerstone of good business practice
Logic To be consistent; to behave rationally	To promote a principled approach to conflict resolution and problem solving
Responsibility To be dependable and reliable	To encourage teamwork and coope-ration among all participants in the organization
Helpfulness To work for the welfare of others; to be caring and compassionate	To provide a cooperative and collab-orative environment
Broad-mindedness To be open-minded; to have a diverse world view	To encourage acceptance and to take advantage of differences within the organization
Capability To be competent and effective	To ensure the development of individual and organizational talents
Ambition To be hardworking and aspire to achieve	To promote excellence within the individual and the organization

stuff was what really mattered: getting pants out the door. What we've learned is that the soft stuff and the hard stuff are becoming increasingly intertwined. A company's values—what it stands for, what its people believe in—are crucial to its competitive success. Indeed, values drive the company."

Clarifying Values in the Organization

It is possible for organizations to work with their members to explore and rank their values in order to come up with a more coherent picture of what is driving their assumptions and their behavior. The three-part process begins with individual value clarification, moves to a critique of the organization's internal and external values, and ends with work groups reporting their results to the entire organization. The following case shows an organization going through this process.

Ben Wilkenson, president of Zenon, decided it was time for the company to look at its mission statement and bring it up to date. The old mission statement did not indicate what the company stood for. Some of the board members had suggested that a clear mission statement for the annual report would impress the shareholders with Zenon's social responsibility. Cold numbers, they said, turned on accountants, but the company needed to define itself in more ways than just the bottom-line for both shareholders and employees.

Ben called together his eight direct reports for a meeting on company values. He thought that he would start at the top and then work the process throughout the company. He told them that they were a planning group for Zenon's mission and values statement and that they would be meeting once a month to complete the job.

Ben and his managers completed the Rokeach value inventory individually and then compared them as a group. The top end values were family security, respect, health, freedom, a sense of accomplishment, a world at peace, and national security. The group discussed their views on each value and what it meant to them individually. When it was clear that they had reached an understanding of their values, Ben asked them adapt these values to three key sectors of the organization: customers, shareholders, and employees. The group said that the end values were good but that the instrumental values really told them how to behave. After deliberating on this issue for two sessions they decided on the following values that pertained to customers, shareholders, and employees: Honesty, loyalty, responsibility, capability, broad-mindedness, and helpfulness. The group then decided that the six values, if applied in their working relationships with the three target groups, added up to integrity.

Keep in mind that a values framework or mission statement is not a dogmatic doctrine but an opportunity to explore and open a dialogue on what an organization stands for. The clarification process is most productive when members actively explore all facets, and the end product becomes something that everyone in the organization strives to act on in their daily work lives. The inevitable conflicts that occur are part of living in a pluralistic world. The conflicts can be resolved by the kind of principled bargaining we discussed in Chapter Seven. Values are concerns that individuals in the organization bring to a conflict; therefore, they must be respected and put on the table for discussion. Working through our assumptions and values allows everyone to become empowered and involved. It allows conflict to be handled in a more rational and productive manner.

Psychological Type and Values

Just as psychological type affects other aspects of management style, it also affects the way we view the world and our values. Thinking types believe very strongly in the power of pure reason and tend to disregard the feeling values. Thinking types, in fact, have a difficult time articulating their values. Because 80 to 90 percent of business executives are thinking types, this difficulty presents a serious problem for organizations trying to integrate personal values and organizational ethics. Most thinking types are not accustomed to allowing their feeling values to surface and be examined for consistency and appropriateness. Therefore the individual and organizational exercise in value clarification is all the more important for the thinking type manager.

Because feeling types use their personal values to judge the world, they are constantly ruminating on how their values fit in with a given circumstances. Thinking types try to rationalize and intellectualize most moral dilemmas by remaining outside the situation. By distancing themselves, they can remain detached and not become personally involved, as opposed to the feeling type who is acutely attuned to the values of the personalities involved. For example, the stockbroker in the film *Twelve Angry Men* tries to suppress any empathy for the defendant, who is accused of murder, because he believes in the power of logic and reason. His personal values never surface. The rational facade is broken only when he realizes a flaw in his thinking about one of the witnesses. At that point his tightly held logical superstructure starts to crumble. Had he paid more attention to the person and the emotions beneath the surface, his logic would not have been so blinding.

Introverted feeling types, who are most attuned to their inner world, may not be aware of the particular values they hold until one of their cherished beliefs is violated. Then they may burst out with emotion that may take others aback because they do not know what set them off. Being aware of their values may help avoid the confrontation or at least lead you to approach the subject more delicately. On the other hand, extroverts exhibit their values on their sleeves and espouse them in public. What you see is what you get with an extroverted feeling type.

Conclusion

Values are the part of management style that direct our ethical behavior. When we are motivated, we channel our needs toward the achievement of end values, toward our ideal of how we would like the world to be. Without values, our needs have no moral component and can be acted out in an indiscriminate fashion. When you value family security, freedom, and a sense of accomplishment, you can direct your needs for achievement and personal power towards these ends.

Values also form the basis for the underlying assumptions behind our conflict style strategies. There are times when our values hinder conflict resolution. For example, if we are too obedient, forgiving, or loyal, we may adopt a lose/yield strategy. On the other hand, being logical, capable, and broad-minded facilitates a collaborative or win/win strategy. As we saw in Chapter Seven, we need to change our assumptions in order to become wise problem solvers.

At this point we have discussed five management style factors: psychological type, needs, power bases, conflict style, and values. The sixth building block is the way we handle stress, an ability that can work strongly in our favor or sabotage our efforts. A stressed person who is unaware of the toll the stress is taking may fail to use all that he or she knows about consciously using an integrated management style. Therefore handling stress is the last element in our model—it is crucial to a manager's overall effectiveness.

CHAPTER NINE

STRESS: MANAGING WORK
AND DIFFICULT PEOPLE

John Harding is a senior manager in an electronics components firm that is growing rapidly as it makes the transition to globalization. His responsibilities have grown exponentially in the last year. John has always been an overachiever who cannot abide failure or loss of control, and in the past two years he has developed hypertension, sleep disturbance, and has frequent bouts of irritability.

His work day starts at 6:00 a.m. with a hasty breakfast, if any, and a labored commute to the office in his BMW. On the way to work John is constantly ruminating over the day's schedule of meetings and worries about the business plans. His confrontations begin on the road. The route to the office is packed with commuters, eighteen-wheelers, and pickup trucks. The pace of the driving is frenzied. John is acutely aware of every maneuver by his fellow lemmings. A pickup truck looms threateningly on his rear bumper. A woman is driving perilously close to his left side while singing along to some deafening music in her car. An eighteen-wheeler blasts its horn in response to a commuter who cuts it off. John responds aggressively to these threats, shouting at these scofflaws and cutting in and out to avoid their constant assaults. As he approaches his exit, he is sweating profusely and cursing at the maddening crowd.

When he finally parks his car in the underground garage, John has to pause to gain composure and walk to the elevator. It is 7:00 a.m. and he feels like he has done battle with the dragons of hell. The elevator to his office is crowded with grim-faced warriors who only acknowledge the floor indicator on the panels in front of them. John enters his office, drops his attaché case on the floor, and sinks into his chair. His next response is to reach for a cup of black coffee and a cigarette. After a few swigs and multiple drags, he is ready for work.

The first event on his daily calendar is an 8:00 a.m. meeting with the international marketing staff. John is wired for confrontation. The meeting goes badly when he is impatient and abrupt. The marketing representatives present a proposal that seems off base. He tells them it is totally unacceptable and abruptly ends the meeting. A few hours later, the senior manager of international marketing, upset by the earlier session, asks for a private meeting. John is irritated by the turn of events; his day has started disastrously. Saying he is stressed to the max is an understatement.

The Age of Stress

The 1990s might be viewed as the Age of Stress. The pressures of our occupations, the threat of war, the volatility of the economic market, the downsizing of organizations, and the uncertainties of life in general all contribute to feeling overwhelmed and besieged. Hans Selye, the noted stress researcher, first described the way we react to stress in scientific terms more than sixty years ago. We experience stress in response to a noxious agent with alarm (fight or flight) followed by resistance. Stress can come from lack of self-realization (physical immobility, boredom, sensory deprivation) or from instances where we have exceeded the limits and become overloaded or exhausted. A similar physiological reaction can also come from an exhilarating challenge and result in pleasure in what we are doing, giving flow to the experience. Stress can result when we perceive internal and external events as threats.

Our goals, of course, should be to strike a balance between the equally destructive forces of negative stress and to find as much positive stress as possible. That is not always easy or seemingly possible for managers in particular, but the purpose of this chapter is to deepen our understanding of stress and its manifestations in ourselves and others, and to look for ways to change our thinking so that we can work positively with it.

Challenges and Threats: Rethinking Stress

The distinction between challenge and threat is one of the crucial factors in learning to deal with stressors, those elements in our environment that elicit a stress response. The difference lies in the idea of mastery as opposed to threat. When you believe you are facing a challenge, you look for solutions to overcome the stressor. When you think you are facing a threat, you respond with flight or fight/defeat. If you experience a pervasive sense of threat, you may become physically ill; you may suffer increased risk of a number of psychological and physical disorders, including coronary heart disease, gastric ulcers, and disorders of the immune system.

When we look at the stress response in more detail, we see that it has several linked components:

1. We recognize stressors in a situation, as John did when he confronted heavy traffic on his commute and in his corporate environment when he got to work.
2. Our mindset mobilizes the stress response. John's confrontational survival of the fittest mindset was mirrored in his body through muscle tension, increased adrenaline flow, and increased blood pressure.
3. Our actions at this point depend on our state of mind. We may flee, attack, approach, or avoid. We may feel anxious, angry, affectionate, experience a sense of mastery, or feel sad and defeated. John's continued feelings of irritation and confrontation led to an agitated, anxious response.
4. The stressors disrupt normal activities. It is unlikely that John will think as clearly or get the productivity he wants from his staff if he continues to react in the same high-stress way.

People vary widely in their specific sensitivities; what is a stressor for one person may be a benign or challenging situation for another. Differences in personality structure—psychological type, need patterns, conflict style—account for some of the wide variations in our individual sensitivity to stressors. Someone who avoids conflict, for example, will feel stressed when confronted with a dispute. Feeling types will feel pressure when they have to give negative feedback to a subordinate. In addition, stressful interactions with other people form mutually reinforcing cycles of maladaptive behavior. If your boss is a command-and-control person who likes to micromanage, you will be drawn into that behavior by becoming overly compliant or avoiding contact.

Stressors may be purely internal or may come from external sources. Even under the most benign circumstances, some people can create their own stress. For example, someone could be sitting alone and ruminating over past, present, or future occurrences and find that he or she is very stressed. Internal conflicts and complexes involving authority figures and use of power can also determine our reactions. Because of past experiences with authority figures, some people become stressed whenever they are around their bosses. Others feel uncomfortable about using power in any form. On the other hand, we can be calm and relaxed when we are bombarded with external stress, as when an employee confronts a manager about a crisis that has come up on Friday afternoon.

Stress at Work

Work can be considered a mixed blessing and at worst an absolute curse. Some people work because they must satisfy their basic needs for food, shelter, and safety. Others work because it is a means to an end. A fortunate few work because it satisfies some intrinsic need. Even so, psychologist Robert Holt points out that all research on occupational stress is a pointer to the dark side of work. As competence seekers, we look to work for fulfillment, but work, with its power struggles and political battles, wears us down and causes stress.

Regardless of our attitudes toward work or its rewards, stress is a natural part of our experiences every day. There are at least six potential sources of stress at work:

1. *The characteristics of the job.* Too much or too little work, schedules and deadlines, pressure to make decisions, fatigue from the physical demands, excessive travel, long hours, constant changes in priorities, and micromanagement by domineering, task-oriented bosses.
2. *Problems in role clarification when roles are ambiguous, overlap, or create overload or competition.* If your boss gives you an assignment but at the same time gives your colleague the same task without telling you, you will be stressed when you find that your boss has put the two of you in role competition.
3. *The quality of relationships with bosses, subordinates, and peers.* Some organizations are overly task-oriented, to the point that the human side is overlooked or dismissed, as when employees are asked to work overtime and weekends without regard for their family lives. In addition, certain individuals may actually carry stress (we will discuss this in detail later in the chapter) because of their pathological personalities. Difficult people exist everywhere in life; organizations are no exception.
4. *Problems in career development.* Anxiety over job security, such as in reorganizations that may outsource or downsize your job, or cause obsolescence or early retirement, create stress. Disparity between your job and your sense of your capabilities or frustration from having reached a career ceiling are also related fears.
5. *The organization itself—its culture and norms.* Some organizations place severe restraints on autonomy, institute dress codes, place limitations on decision making, and foster an us-versus-them attitude of competition within organizational units.

6. *The conflict between organizational and personal life.* This is the most-often-cited problem by middle and upper managers. Family problems and loyalties clash with everyday demands and work priorities. Rigid rules may restrict the amount of time that a person can devote to family, hobbies, and self-development outside the organization.

We confront all of these stressors every day. We can accept them passively as part of the landscape, denying their existence, or we can choose to cope actively with them to reduce stress. The following sections outline steps that can be taken to deal productively with these sources of stress.

Key Ingredients of Stress: Assumptions, Perceptions, and Feelings

As we saw in Chapter Four's discussion of changing management style, assumptions, perceptions, and feelings are at the heart of the way we process information (including stressors) from our environment—and to the way we respond to that information. As you may recall, assumptions are taken-for-granted beliefs we develop from our experiences, while perceptions result from the way we process information that comes to us through our five senses. Psychological types differ in that sensing types rely on what they perceive as facts and details in the situation, while intuitive types can arrive at a perception without being aware of the concrete basis for it. When sensing types are called on to brainstorm without feeling they have enough facts, they become anxious and out of sorts. Intuitives will feel stressed when they are asked to deal with detailed presentations.

The third ingredient, feelings, are emotional reactions to specific situations. They are triggered by our perceptions and affected by our assumptions. If our assumptions are negative, we perceive the situation in ways that reinforce them, which leads to feelings of frustration, anger, and hatred. If our assumptions are positive and we perceive no stress in the situation, that triggers positive feelings such as joy, happiness, contentment, or exhilaration. Feelings are central to our ability to change our perceptions; for example, when we are stressed, benign perceptions can turn into catastrophic thoughts that bear little relation to reality.

Your Personal Response to Stress

The interaction of your ability to cope with stress and the external stressors you experience lead to your unique stress response. The tremendous variation in the way individuals react to stressors and the relationship of their response to performance were delineated by R. Yerkes and J. Dodson. Dodson and his colleagues demonstrated that as stress increases, so do efficiency and performance—up to a point, when there is a fall off in performance. If stress continues to increase, exhaustion can result. The Yerkes-Dodson curve (see Figure 9.1) shows the general pattern and average, not individual, behavior. Individual reactions may take several different forms.

The Stress Accumulator. Anyone who has seen Gregory Peck's portrayal of General Savage in the classic film *12 O'Clock High* can recognize that he accumulated stress until he reached a level of exhaustion and then blanked out. In the film, Savage assumes the almost impossible task of rebuilding the morale of the 918th squadron by himself. He bottles up his feelings toward his men and tries to avoid identifying too much with the flyers. He thinks that he has to remain aloof and impersonal at all times and takes on immense responsibility without an outlet for his feelings and his internal stress. Finally, his body shuts down in an effort to recharge. In technical terms, this is a form of psychological flight from unbearable stress.

The Stress Reactor. The opposite of the stress accumulator is the stress reactor who cannot stand any form of stress and shuts down. Their performance is like a spike on an EKG, rapidly moving up and down. Stress reactors are unlikely to be in executive positions; their vulnerability to stress would be too severe to be tolerated. Some individuals choose low-level, repetitive jobs that require little inter-

FIGURE 9.1 THE YERKES-DODSON CURVE

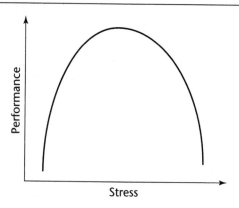

Source: Yerkes, R. M. and J. D. Dodson, "The Relation of Strength of Stimulus to Rigidity of Habit-Formation." Adapted from *Journal of Comparative Neurology and Psychology,* 1908.

action with others or change in the environment. Once there is a change in either the level of interaction or the task requirements, their inability to handle stress may emerge.

The Stress Resistor. This type needs a strong impetus to kick into gear. They are lethargic to a point but can show great intensity and high performance. They get the job done—after some procrastinating. They are tolerated in organizations because of their ability to eventually come through, but it is not a balanced approach to handling stress.

Not everyone is a pure type, of course. People who fall in the middle of all these types are known as generalized stress reactors. There are two additional stress reactor types that are based upon faulty assumptions and perceptions of some managers: the Right Stuff and the Keep Zapping types. The Right Stuff type supposedly needs little activation to kick into high gear and can sustain high levels of performance to infinity. The military, in its high performance flight schools, tries to shape this behavior, but the danger is that it can warp the personality and make it robot-like. Films such as *Robo Cop* and the older TV series, *The Bionic Man*, perpetuate the myth that there are no limits to performance.

The assumption behind the Keep Zapping type is that people are lazy and will not perform without external motivation; the more you put people under pressure the more they will respond. Although these assumptions fly in the face of research findings, some old-line managers cling to them. The result is a chaotic, anxiety-driven environment where hasty decisions are made and quality suffers in the long run. Individuals become fearful and try to hide mistakes. When the manager's expectations are unfulfilled, he or she projects anger onto the employees. The Keep Zapping type does not question his or her assumptions, believing that others cannot live up to what is expected of them.

The Yerkes-Dodson law demonstrates the relationship between stress levels and performance. What is lacking is the delineation of the types of stressors that give rise to the stress reaction. In the next section certain familiar stressors in the form of our needs will be isolated.

The Enemy Within: Needs and Stress

As we saw in Chapter Five, needs are the driving force behind individual competence. Most of the time, needs are a positive impetus towards attaining our goals, but if their intensity becomes overwhelming and pervasive, they can act as *internal stressors*. Certain, but not all, needs lead to personal stress. Here is a summary of needs that can become stressors under particular situations:

Achievement. Stress results when managers try to: reach higher levels of success without taking time to assess past achievements; set high standards; berate themselves when they perceive that they have not lived up to those standards.

Assistance. Assistance becomes stress when managers are acutely aware of rejection, exclusion, separation, and abandonment. Such people need others to reassure them regularly that they are all right.

Autonomy. Those with high needs for independence become stressed when they detect cues from the environment that suggest interference, intrusion, coercion, or restraint. They perceive the world as fencing them in and react with hostility or depression, depending on the circumstances. They can become extremely stress prone when they feel they have to conform.

Dominance. High needs for dominance make managers feel uncomfortable when they perceive they do not have control. They sense something catastrophic is going to happen or that they are losing the competitive edge and self-esteem.

Abasement. Stress results when super-responsible managers feel that they must conform to a high standard set by others. If they perceive that they have failed, they blame themselves and then feel worthless and need to atone.

Exhibition. In excess, such managers resort to dramatic efforts to meet this need. It can be self-defeating because they try so hard that they may alienate others. Then their stress level skyrockets.

Aggression. For these typical type A personalities, it is a dog-eat-dog world. Every encounter is competitive. In the organizational world, people respond to this type of aggressive behavior by resisting or pushing back. The person with this internal stressor, like John in our opening story, develops psycho-physiological reactions (such as muscle tension, headaches, and gastrointestinal symptoms) when thwarted.

Understanding the Effect of Needs on Stress

As a way of deepening our understanding of how assumptions, perceptions, and feelings interact with needs, let us examine types of stress-prone individuals: the autonomous and the succorant (or assistance-seeking) types. These types are most common in organizations and thus yield clear insights into the dynamics of how needs drive stress.

Extreme autonomous types react to any incursion on their life space as an obstacle. They become hostile if interrupted while talking, working, or daydreaming, and resent being held up in movie, checkout, gas station, or restaurant lines. Their assumptions are based on values of pure freedom, individuality, and preservation of autonomy. In common situations, they perceive only interference, intrusion, coercion, or restraint. Their sense of well-being depends on preserving the integrity and autonomy of their domain, and they need unrestricted freedom of choice, action, and expression. They want to direct their own destiny and attain their goals through individual action. If put under extreme pressure they can develop hostility, claustrophobia, eating disorders, and depression.

The autonomous type's basic assumptions are:

- I must stand alone.
- Individuality is the highest virtue in the world.
- I must fight any intrusion into my life space.
- I will be perceived as weak if I accept help.
- I should push people away if they crowd me.

To any perceived threat to their autonomy, they develop hostile responses, which may range from mild irritation to intense anger or rage. Their fight reactions are based on the assumption that they can counterattack and bully the other person to retreat.

A counterpart to the autonomous personality is the assistance-seeking person. Their assumptions, perceptions, and feelings cluster is based on receiving acceptance, intimacy, understanding, support, guidance, and positive feedback. If they do not receive these forms of self-validation and support, they can be passive and overly dependent and possibly develop a depressive reaction. In addition, they may become anxious and fearful. The assistance-seeking type is sensitive to perceived rejection, abandonment, and deprivation. Their main assumptions are:

- Everyone needs someone all the time.
- I am nothing without the approval of others.
- Life is meaningless without unconditional love.
- If I receive negative feedback, it proves I am unworthy.
- If I praise others, I will be given praise in return.

This type of person is hypersensitive to cues that signal danger to their self-esteem. As a result they try to flee from the situation physically or psychologically. They become inhibited, choke up, or block out the experience. Because of their perception of danger, they lose all ability to cope. They develop fears of being appraised, of encountering a dominant boss or a more expert peer or subordinate, and of making any mistake, no matter how small.

As we discussed, our needs can motivate us to be competent as well as impose a burden on us. In a similar vein, our psychological type can predispose us to unique stress reactions. The next section will deal with the facets of stress.

Handling Stress: The Psychological Types

Psychological type can predict our reactions to stress because it affects how we perceive and judge reality through sensing, intuition, thinking, and feeling. Because the functions are stable patterns of behavior, under stress we fall back on our strengths (dominant function) and are vulnerable to our weaknesses (inferior function). The extroverted intuitives (ENTP and ENFP), for example, become scattered and have trouble focusing when stressed. The introverted sensing types (ISTJ and ISFJ) become rigid about time, schedules, and procedures under stress. In the following sections, we explore the relationship between stress and the psychological types, give examples of those types under stress, and present tips to help each one handle stress more effectively. (Relaxation, including the practice recommended at the end of Chapter Four, can be helpful to all types.)

Extroverted Thinking Types (ESTJ or ENTJ)

In the best of circumstances, extroverted thinkers are principled, idealistic, dedicated, and rational. In a maladaptive mode, they are dogmatic, single-minded, intolerant, and cold. For example, Leo is an ESTJ. His conflict style is win/lose with colleagues and lose/yield with superiors. He has high needs for power, achievement, and recognition and conflicting needs for deference and abasement. He projects his less-obvious abasement needs on others by blaming and criticizing.

In his role as a human resources professional, Leo's power orientation and his deference needs have ensured his rise to upper levels in his company. But his subordinates and colleagues view him with suspicion. One remarked that Leo's intelligence is only "tacked on." He is on top of the latest concepts and methods, but he is superficial and dogmatic in his thinking about them. He usually rejects friendly criticism. Although Leo feels more threatened by women than by men, he sees himself as a champion of women's causes. As a master at stroking his bosses' egos, he has ingratiated and endeared himself to those in power.

Leo's most serious problems arise in group learning situations, where he lacks flexibility. Confronted by complex and open-ended problems, he cannot deviate from his own preconceived game plan. His behavior becomes condescending and rigid, his speech clipped and abrupt, as he seeks to prove others wrong. Colleagues who are not intimidated attack him, while others angrily withdraw.

Eventually Leo's behavior comes to the attention of his superiors, who confront him about it. Leo tries to rationalize and trivialize the poor evaluations he receives, arguing that others do not understand what they are doing, or do not know what is good for them, or that he resembles someone his superiors do not like. Nothing penetrates his armor, and no one is willing to persist in confronting his intense denial. His own behavior seals him off from help.

Tips for Extroverted Thinking Types (ESTJ or ENTJ)

Extroverted thinkers are formidable stress carriers because they insist that everyone else conform to their version of reality. They tend to repress feeling and thus lack empathy. Repressed feelings may become distorted, leading to high moral judgments of others' characters, which are then thrust upon them in a win/lose manner. Extroverted thinkers see others as adversaries who have to be put in their places. In addition, submerged feelings may gnaw at this type, giving rise to secret prejudices—a readiness, for example, to misconstrue any opposition as a personal attack. For these types, the best ways to reduce stress include:

- Reducing automatic thoughts (see Chapter Four's discussion of how to do this). Some of Leo's automatic thoughts are: "I have to know everything. There are threats to me everywhere. I know the perfect solution to all problems."
- Listing assumptions about stressful situations. Leo assumes all criticism must be attacked; his game plan is correct; no deviations are allowed; and women are a threat, so they can be defused by championing their causes.
- Listing counters (again, see Chapter Four) that help challenge dysfunctional perceptions of reality. Examples for Leo: "Criticism may be friendly. They are trying to help me. No one can devise a perfect plan; the best plans come from team efforts. Go with the group flow. Relax, women are no more or less a threat than men—treat them equally."

Extroverted Feeling Types (ESFJ or ENFJ)

In the best circumstances, extroverted feeling types are adaptive, realistic, sensible, and practical. When their dark sides emerge, they become demanding, reactive, shallow, and manipulative. Felicia, for example, is a public relations manager for a large financial institution. She enjoys her work because it allows her ample opportunity to exercise her extroverted, sociable nature. An ESFJ, she is highly affiliative, makes good use of reward and referent power, and delegates well. Her subordinates feel that she is a participatory manager.

In the middle of her fortieth year, Felicia's husband asks for a separation, throwing her into an acute depression that lasts for two weeks. She grows silent and morose; her colleagues cannot figure out what is wrong. But then a mercurial change takes place. She becomes her extroverted self again but is demanding and critical. She accuses her staff of being insensitive to her needs and undermining her efforts. She makes flip and inappropriate personal comments such as, "Gained some weight over the vacation, I see." Usually a stylish, professional, fastidious dresser, Felicia begins coming to work in wild, flamboyant, tight clothing. No one knows what to make of her.

During this time, Felicia's department is supposed to prepare an important proposal for a foreign investor. In such cases, Felicia usually organizes a team and works with them to assign tasks and meet collective goals. This time she hands out assignments without consulting anyone, giving jobs that conflict or overlap. She calls for daily instead of weekly meetings and overreacts to any statement she perceives as critical. The staff breaks apart into factions and the proposal is delayed.

Tips for Extroverted Feeling Types (ESFJ or ENFJ)

The extroverted feeling type's world is ruled by an external formula for what creates a harmonious sense of aesthetics. They reject anything that disrupts this balance (thinking is therefore repressed). When their sense of harmony or a value such as family security or self-respect is disturbed, they become stressed. For Felicia, she could ward off stress by:

- Separating work from her personal life. She has to deal with the trauma of her separation by confronting her feelings about it. Feeling types need a basic support system to air and vent their feelings. In most cases, it is better to do this outside of work (with a friend, clergy, or counselor).
- Listing her important values so that the basis for her judgment becomes clear. Doing so gives her a chance to reflect on what is important and what will prevent her from exploding when these values are questioned. In this case, the marital separation threatened her values of self-respect, family security, and inner harmony. By focusing on each value, she can work through the feelings associated with it. For example, she can realize that her self-respect is not tied just to a failed relationship or that her inner harmony can be disturbed by another person.
- Conveying to her staff and colleagues that she is going through a traumatic life crisis. This will help her find a support system at work so that her temporary mood swings can be tolerated and others can compensate for them.

- Working actively on these problems (preferably through counseling) rather than shelving them away.

Introverted Sensing Types (ISTJ or ISFJ)

Normally, introverted sensing types of people are calm, controlled, restrained, and innocuous. Their shadow side is defensive, cold, controlling, unsympathetic, perfectionistic, trivializing, and indecisive. Frederick, for example, is an ISTJ with high achievement, deference, and autonomy needs. As an accounting manager, he feels driven to control all tasks himself; he cannot delegate authority to his subordinates. Frederick rarely shows his emotions or motives, even under tremendous pressure from his superiors to keep overhead charges to a minimum. He has resolved to comply by any means.

Frederick's weekly staff meetings consist of recounting the previous week's accomplishments. He goes around the table asking each person what he or she has done. Group interaction is minimal, because most of the staff has fallen into the habit of not questioning or challenging Frederick, whose restrained manner discourages discussion. Meetings end politely, and work continues in an efficient vacuum.

Frederick's problems begin when government auditors run a routine check on the company's books. The auditors note a number of discrepancies and mischarges. Frederick panics. Outwardly, he seems controlled and even indifferent to the auditor's findings. But he orders his subordinates to check into every possibility that might allow them to continue with their current accounting procedures. He tells his staff that it is their responsibility to justify his position, not to conform to government regulations. Finally, a member of the staff rebels and complains to Frederick's boss, who confronts him with the allegations and explains that the auditors have found clear violations of the law. Frederick counters with a litany of contradictory statements that indicate he believes he has only been following orders to keep costs down and has done nothing wrong. He says that he can prove that he is being treated unfairly. His boss abruptly ends the meeting, convinced that Frederick should be relieved of his responsibilities.

Tips for Introverted Sensing Types (ISTJ or ISFJ)

The tendency of introverted sensing types is to be at the mercy of subjective perceptions—in Frederick's case, a misreading of the auditor's demands. Frederick had been ordered to reduce overhead, but not to disregard the law. When his methods are challenged, his defensive posture emerges. He uses every ploy to prove he is right, refusing to listen to anyone. Most of his arguments are based on petty details that only make him look foolish. Vacillating between stubbornness and utter ambivalence, he is the picture of the perfectionistic self-doubter.

Challenges to their highly developed inner concepts create stress for introverted thinking types (ISTJ and ISFJ). They become extremely annoyed when their thoughts or routines are questioned, upset, or even interrupted, or when they are forced to objectify their deep inner thoughts. If others do not receive their ideas with total acceptance, they become stubborn, headstrong, and resistant. The stress deepens when others intensify their demands for clarification. Then the introverted thinking types withdraw, possibly alienating the other party. In extreme cases, they can be the prototypical "clam." The following interventions are designed to identify faulty thinking and counter it with more balanced thoughts.

- Objectify the thoughts that are controlling the situation and determine whether they match facts that can be objectively verified. Without verifying the evidence for the thought, this type will wall himself or herself off, brood, and create internal tensions that can explode at any time.
- Explore their own feelings. Ask questions such as: "What am I feeling at this time? Can I describe these feelings? What caused me to feel this way? Do others in this conflict share these feelings? Are these feelings unusual or are they chronic to the situation?"
- Identify how their plans are affecting others. Frederick, for example, needs to get feedback from his boss on the company's position and expectations of him.
- Discuss the circumstances with others (such as staff, superiors, peers) who are part of the situation. In Frederick's case, he needs to involve the auditors in the process. He cannot stonewall the inevitable; he has to build a cooperative relationship with them.

Introverted Intuitive Types (INTJ or INFJ)

The introverted intuitive operates as a visionary, sensual, and prophetic person, but in darker moments can become grandiose, obsessive, exhibitionistic, self-absorbed, self-aggrandizing, or immersed in fantasy. For example, Peter, an INTJ who was trained as an electrical engineer and progressed through the ranks to become general manager for an electronics research and development company, has high needs for achievement, dominance, and autonomy. He has an uncanny sense of what is happening in the electronics field and is ahead of his colleagues in predicting events. Not content to be a visionary, however, when facing any new decision or product, Peter always asks, "What does it mean for me and the company?" His strategic orientation impresses the board of directors, while his colleagues and subordinates tolerate his self-centered and distant manner because his judgments are so often right.

Thanks to Peter's efforts, the company obtains a large government contract for developing state-of-the-art instrumentation for a new space vehicle. The project is Peter's baby, and he works feverishly to ensure its success. At times, he introduces new plans that substantially alter the current work but that are always instituted, much to the project officers' dismay. After end-of-the-year feasibility studies, the company builds a prototype vehicle and begins to test the instrumentation.

The initial test results are disastrous. Most of the components fail in the integrated system. The research staff grumbles, privately recounting their objections to the many radical changes Peter has pushed through. When Peter keeps looking for an answer that will prove him right but fails to find it, he grows stubborn. He obsesses over his original plan, sure that the test results are wrong. His manner becomes grandiose and inflated. He feels the gods are testing him but that he will not be denied his victory. He continues this approach as god-like expert even in the face of the government's observers and scientists who review the project. His tenacious attitude makes it more and more obvious that he is at fault. Finally, on orders from the government, Peter is transferred to a staff position.

Tips for Introverted Intuitives (INTJ or INFJ)

Peter demonstrates the classic dark side of the introverted intuitive. He walls himself off in his own world, making himself immune to outside judgment. Worst of all, he refuses to believe objective data. At best, an introverted intuitive's communication tends to be fragmented, episodic, and without personal warmth. They are so wrapped up in their own fascinating worlds that they are almost immune to external influence.

Introverted feeling types can reduce stress by:

- Recognizing that not everyone knows what is going on in their inner worlds. Introverted intuitives love to play with ideas and come up with intricate and complex plans and strategies. The problem is that they are not always conveyed in depth to others. Introverted intuitives need to open up their minds to others.
- Looking at their ideas as part of a broad network that involves other people and ideas. Introverted intuitives under stress feel rejected and become self-absorbed and self-aggrandizing. By involving others' input in their thinking, they diminish their sense of isolation.

- Using relaxation techniques to break the obsessive thinking that accompanies stress. Practicing these techniques during a stress attack reduces the power of their negative inner thoughts.
- Practicing role playing with a colleague who has an opposite view. By walking in another's shoes, an introverted thinker can break through the self-absorption and feelings of anger.

Extroverted Sensing Types (ESTP or ESFP)

At their best, extroverted sensing types are realistic, alert, jolly, and pleasant. At their worst, they become overly concrete, pedantic, resistant, hedonistic, stubborn, callous, and procrastinating. For example, Barbara, an ESTP, is a production manager in a publishing company. She has strong needs for personal achievement and autonomy and a win/lose conflict style. As the manager responsible for getting the books to the printer, she is under pressure to meet schedules and to please the editorial and manufacturing departments. Barbara finds her job exhilarating, even with its many problems. She likes dealing with pragmatic challenges that require her personal involvement. Although she is sometimes demanding, most of her coworkers like her. The match between her type and her job seems ideal.

Tough times arrive when problems crop up in the electronic production process on their best-selling biology textbook. Barbara feels it is a minor problem, stemming from a glitch in the software. Her colleagues and the typesetter do not agree. They insist on changes that will throw the schedule off by three weeks, possibly missing the fall selling season. Barbara refuses to comply. Eager for a showdown, she calls a meeting with the other production managers and the typesetter. She vows to win this fight, regardless of the consequences. She begins amassing reams of all kinds of information to buttress her case.

At the meeting, after a straightforward presentation by the typesetter, Barbara delivers a torrent of reasons why the problems should be circumvented and the book sent to the printer on schedule. She refuses to listen and keeps making disparaging remarks about everyone else. When asked about why her data are relevant, she merely repeats her position. When the meeting ends, everyone leaves feeling both embarrassed for and angry at Barbara.

The next day, during a confrontation with her boss, she again refuses to do more than rigidly repeat her position, even after her boss explains that the problem is not Barbara's alone but everyone's responsibility. Following more bitter words, her boss orders Barbara to handle the problem as the typesetter has suggested. Barbara and her boss are angry, upset, and demoralized. Her promising career prospects are considerably dimmer after this episode.

Tips for Extroverted Sensing Types (ESTP or ESFP)

Barbara's personal goals and the overall goals of the project are obviously in conflict. Her job and the typesetter's responsibilities were never clearly defined. When faced with what seemed like personal failure, she can only react by marshalling concrete data and resisting others' solutions—and neither of those actions solves the problem.

Extroverted sensing types aim to live life to its fullest through the accumulation of new experiences (sensations). They love tangible reality and are not inclined to reflection (intuition), so they are stressed when the situation calls for deep reflection and making connections that are not immediately apparent. Under these conditions, they grasp any apparent facts and narrowly focus on them for confirmation. They have great difficulty in defining their underlying assumptions and become stressed when they are pressed to do so. Extroverted sensing types can try these stress-reducing tips:

- Stepping back and looking at the big picture. Like other extroverted sensing types, Barbara focuses on her own set of details. At meetings, she could sit in and learn more about all the other elements in the production of this biology project—for example, its timing, and the sales and marketing campaign.
- Asking others involved in their work how they view their list of priorities.
- Becoming more sophisticated in problem-solving techniques, particularly focusing on concerns and interests rather than on winning.
- Practicing relaxation techniques immediately before going into potential conflict situations to encourage a more open frame of mind.

Extroverted Intuitive Types (ENTP or ENFP)

Extroverted intuitive types are normally enterprising, outgoing, expansive, and unrestrained. Their dark side is to be defiant, irresponsible, unstable, ruthless, and irritable. Martha, an ENFP, is a successful marketing manager for a large computer software company. Open and jovial, she is well liked by her staff, even though sometimes they think her ideas are a little risky. Her highest needs are for dominance, achievement, and autonomy. She uses referent, reward, affiliation, and authority power. Martha's bosses see her as a great idea person who can bring out the best in people. Most of the time, they leave her alone. Her staff supports her by restraining her from acting on all her intuitive impulses and by supplying the details and fine tuning for which she has no patience.

Martha's dark side emerges at the beginning of a marketing campaign for a new line of software. She assumes that because of her previous successes, she will be put in charge, but instead is only a player, while a deputy to the vice president takes the lead. She resents the deputy for receiving more responsibility, because she thinks he is inexperienced. Work on the campaign demands many collaborative problem-solving sessions that irritate Martha because she resents the deputy's role as leader (*she*, after all, is the expert in group process).

From the first meeting, Martha's irritation is obvious. Instead of her usual light-hearted self, she is caustic and sullen. She finds opportunities to snipe at the deputy, making sarcastic remarks about his past accomplishments and criticizing his handling of the brainstorming sessions. She obsesses about details and blows disagreements out of proportion. Her free-wheeling intuitive style has vanished.

When Martha goes to the senior vice president, who is a personal friend, she uses inflated and fabricated information to prove that the deputy is completely inept. The senior vice president, believing everything Martha says, goes to the president, who calls a meeting with the marketing campaign committee. He dresses down the deputy for lack of progress and puts Martha in charge. Now totally demoralized, her staff is unlikely ever to trust Martha again.

Tips for Extroverted Intuitives (ENTP or ENFP)

Martha exemplifies what can happen when authority, power, and competence are threatened. Martha uses her contacts in high places to sabotage the deputy. Extroverted intuitives—the entrepreneurial types in American business—can be ruthless in their obsession with their goals. Martha had no regard for the people or the campaign once she was not put in charge. In the past she could afford to be expansive and outgoing because she was driving the process, but not any more. Extroverted intuitives can try these stress-reducing tips:

- Looking at the implications of their actions. Martha could ask herself about her goals. She is so focused on revenge for a slight that she thinks nothing of taking it out on the deputy. Under stress, she substituted lethal short-term gains for her long-term goals and lost the trust of her staff.
- Building a working relationship with others. In Martha's case, she needs to work with the deputy and understand that he needs her to be successful. Building this relationship would negate her bad feelings toward the deputy.
- Blocking out the task into manageable sections. This helps reduce the feeling of too many details, which can seem overwhelming and create stress for this type.
- Intermingling detail work with intuitive work. This reduces the pressure to focus only on sensing (this type's inferior function).

Introverted Thinking Types (ISTP or INTP)

In the best circumstances, introverted thinkers are independent, vulnerable, tenacious, and uncompromising. Under stress, they may become defensive, tragic, fearful, hypersensitive, reluctant, stubborn, and withdrawn. Tony, an INTP, manages the research division of a health-care benefits company. In his position, he initiates, reviews, and coordinates all the research his organization sponsors. He uses mainly expert power and prides himself on being an innovative manager who can sense the most important issues in the health-care industry. Less interested in financial or administrative details, Tony's allegiance is to the academic research communities that his organization funds. He identifies with the poor and the vulnerable and is most interested in their access to health care.

When Tony took over as manager of the research division, there was no money crunch. He could pursue projects that he thought had merit and enjoyed the sense of fulfilling his needs. His subordinates saw him as a talented director, though a bit of a bleeding heart and at times overly sensitive to criticism. When questioned at staff meetings, he sometimes withdrew.

Tony's dark side emerges when the parent company begins to curtail some of the research ventures and shifts priorities away from some of his favorite endeavors. At first he blames his boss for a lack of support. She tries to reason with him, but Tony becomes a zealot, refusing to listen and trying to justify funding for certain projects. After a short time, he withdraws, sequestering himself in his office surrounded by data printouts and books on social injustice. He keeps it up until he is transferred to another department.

Tips for Introverted Thinking Types (ISTP or INTPs)

Tony has fallen into the introverted thinker's abyss of idiosyncratic thinking. Lacking skills in referent power, he finds himself alone when he needs help. He cannot accept certain political realities and sees no constructive way to change the system. His only defense is withdrawal. Even if he leaves this position for one that is more in line with his political values, he may continue the same maladaptive behavior if he does not find ways to confront his stressors. Stress-reducing tips might include:

- Working through ideas with others. A good exercise is to make an outline of your thoughts as if you were writing a chapter for a book. Tony could use this technique and present the material to a friend, who would be encouraged to ask questions. This would train Tony to focus ideas outward.

- Becoming aware of the impact of your decisions on others. Ask yourself, "Who is affected by this decision? Do I need to clear this with anyone? Are there political implications?" Feeling is the weakest link in the introverted thinker's approach to making decisions.
- Recognizing a tendency to hypersensitivity under stress. The best way to avoid taking things too personally is to follow the procedures in Chapter Seven on conflict resolution, especially separating the people from the problem. Recognize the role of your perceptions and emotions.
- Using the techniques in Chapter Six on building referent power. Tony needed to realize he could not operate in a vacuum without others' support and goodwill.

Introverted Feeling Types (INFP or ISFP)

In their normal state, the introverted feeling type is sympathetic, harmonic, reserved, and inaccessible. When adversity strikes, he or she can become dependent, secretive, melancholy, and helpless. Jung (who, as you may recall, developed the theory on which the types are based) said the introverted feeling type has the capacity for unscrupulous ambition and mischievous cruelty. Janet, an ISFP, is a group manager in the data-processing department of a large corporation. She and her staff of twenty provide the company with all of its management information and financial data. A quiet, sympathetic woman, Janet tries to create harmony by pleasing everyone. Her subordinates complain, however, that she is psychologically distant and hard to draw out on important issues. She rarely holds staff meetings, preferring to have her subordinates come to her with minor problems, while she tends to avoid or ignore larger problems. Because of her mastery of facts and details and her quick attention to minor problems, she is considered a valuable manager.

Janet's dark side emerges when her boss announces that her department has to shift to a new computer system within a very short period of time. Janet does not question the rationale or the urgency of the switch and says nothing to her boss, but inwardly she feels overwhelmed. She takes the new computer documentation to her office, sets it to one side, and goes back to reviewing project logs from her programmers and attending to other minor tasks for the rest of the day.

The next day she calls three trusted employees into her office and complains to them that the new system is useless, the change is a stupid upper management decision, and her boss is completely unreasonable. Urging them not to mention the meeting to anyone, she announces her intention to send a report to the president and CEO (but not to her boss) explaining why the department should not switch to the new system. She spent the next day composing her report and by evening had put it in the interoffice mail.

Meanwhile, Dick, Janet's boss, assumed that she concurred with both the decision and the timetable. When the president received Janet's letter, he called Dick into his office in consternation. Dick felt sabotaged and amazed by Janet's behavior. He told the president he would meet with her right away and try to solve the problem. The president reminded Dick that the project would go ahead regardless of Janet's objections.

As a thinking type, Dick was determined to maintain a rational, objective manner. When he went to her office for an explanation, he was not prepared for Janet's initial coldness or for the torrent of repressed rage that followed. After her outburst, Janet became resigned and helpless. Dick suggested she take some time off and let him put someone else in charge of the project. That left Janet feeling even more depressed.

Tips for Introverted Feeling Types (INFP or ISFP)

Introverted feeling types usually give an impression of outward harmony and pleasantness and express no outward desire to control others. But under stress, when someone threatens their domain, that harmony is disrupted. Beset by their internal rage, they feel helpless and compelled to instigate their own devious strategies or to escape. These types can handle stress more effectively by:

- Taking an assertiveness training course. Because Janet's tendency is to become dependent and secretive under stress, she needs to learn to express her thoughts and feelings externally. In this case, she has to learn to confront her boss directly about the new computer system.
- Outlining feelings and the rationale behind them in order to give them a more concrete and analytical form. Because they ruminate over their feelings and suffer in silence, these types need to learn to objectify their feelings and make them more rational so that they can be examined with some sense of psychological distance.
- Practicing relaxation to help improve composure and to develop more of an ability to analyze their feelings.
- Reading and studying techniques for encouraging analytic thinking (e.g., James Adams' *Conceptual Blockbusting* (1986) and Richard Leviton's *Brain Builder* (1995) give valuable exercises for strengthening left-brain thinking).

Organizational Pains in the Neck: Stress Carriers

Stress carriers are people who, through repeated behavior, cause distress in others. They are not always aware of their behavior and may act out of unconscious needs and psychological factors. Eric Berne, founder of transactional analysis, talks about feeling states such as "I'm OK, you're OK"; "I'm not OK, you're not OK." Difficult people have the perception that "I'm not OK and you're not OK" (*Games People Play*, 1964). When they are stressed, the not-OK feeling sets in, and they want to make sure you are not OK as well. Once they have disempowered you, their own feelings of powerlessness are reduced. As managers, our job is to cope with the stress carrier by righting the power balance, a task that begins with understanding the types of difficult people and how to deal with each of them.

Difficult People: The Fourteen Types

Sherman Tanks come out charging, on the attack. Aggressiveness is their main need, and they are arbitrary and arrogant. They attack the person, not the problem, and in this sense seek to humiliate or spur a counterattack. Humiliation only fuels their attack, because Sherman Tanks love to step on the squeamish. One of the distinguishing factors in the Sherman Tank is the constant barrage of verbal and nonverbal threats. Some Sherman Tanks are crass; others are subtle and smooth in their attacks. Either way, the victim is robbed of power.

Snipers do not attack directly. They wait for a convenient time, such as a meeting, and then constantly attack by sidetalk and subtle nonverbal gestures of disdain. Another form of sniping is talking behind your back to your colleagues or boss.

Unlike Sherman Tanks, *Exploders* are unpredictable and intermittent. When something triggers the adult tantrum in the Exploder, he or she erupts like a volcano. An almost trance-like quality comes over them. It is as if they are under the spell of a demon. When the tantrum is over, they may blink and feel remorseful or just go on as if nothing has happened.

Complainers constantly find fault with procedures, policies, workload, and people. Everything becomes a problem for them. They are not people who see legitimate problems but are constantly whining about something. Some have a pet complaint that they lock on to and beat to death. They are adept at putting people on the defensive, and when this happens, all participants are caught in the accusation-defense-reaccusation game.

Clams are silent and unresponsive. They shut up when you need a response to a problem that you are both involved with, so the conversation becomes asymmetrical: you are doing all the talking, pleading, digging, and responding. The behavior is a learned response to a number of predisposed conditions: avoiding commitment to painful interpersonal situations, expressing calculated aggression, and evading the situation or interaction.

Superagreeables tell you what they think you want to hear: "The component will be ready tomorrow. You can count on that." They are stress carriers because you believe them, but they invariably let you down. They tell you all the good things you want to hear because they seek approval from you while ignoring the realities of the problem. By saying gratifying words to you, they unconsciously think they have pleased you and that by being nice you will ignore the inevitable: They do not perform.

Negativists' favorite phrase is, "There's nothing we can do." It is an unconditional negative, backed up with previous experiences, selected data, and firm conviction. The effect of the negativist is that problem solving is derailed because the phrase, "Here is a solution to the problem," is not in their vocabulary. Negativists suffer from a pervasive sense of powerlessness and project this feeling onto others. Sometimes the recipients of negativists' remarks fall into the trap of agreeing with them.

Bulldozers are know-it-all experts. They are usually highly trained in their specialty and exude a sense of superiority that overwhelms people. In contrast to some of the other stress carriers, Bulldozers are highly productive. What makes them difficult is that their expertise spills over into all areas. Their tone of absolute certainty, desire to one-up other people, and use of paralogic make others look incompetent and stupid, causing feelings of resentment. They leave little room for anyone else's judgment, creativity, or resourcefulness. In psychologist Albert Ellis's terms, they suffer from the irrational belief that they must be perfect and try to accomplish that state by being expert in everything. They want to be in control of the world. A Bulldozer high in need for achievement and dominance can be the worst stress carrier.

Balloons are phony know-it-all pseudoexperts. They are often curious people who collect scraps of information and proceed to expound upon them in order to get admiration from others. They are not liars or con artists, people who know they are skillfully manipulating you. Balloons, because of a faulty ego system, are fooling themselves. The Balloon is more of an irritant than a serious problem (unlike other stress carriers). If you know you are dealing with a Balloon, the best strategy is not to take the person seriously.

Stallers are indecisive and hold off making decisions while hoping that the problem will go away. Eighty percent of the time, this works. (Pareto's Law states that 80 percent of organizational decisions are trivial and only 20 percent count.) The underlying concern of the indecisive Staller is not to hurt anyone by making an unpleasant decision. They try their best to avoid the problem and they are the ultimate conflict avoiders.

Micromanagers under stress constantly remind you that: "I'm in charge here!" These high achievers and dominant managers get into the smallest details of projects that they previously delegated to others. Once a problem, big or small, surfaces, they are in everyone's hair. What was once delegated is snatched back and micromanaged. They make subordinates feel diminished and incompetent. To cope with micromanagers, you need to control yourself, prevent problems, and be prepared.

Stone Tablets are the rule carriers of the organization. They use regulations and policy as weapons and want to leave no room for discussion. Not only are they inflexible in their quest for adherence to the rule but they will close down when you ask, "Why?"

Type A Stress Carriers drive peers and subordinates to fits of anxiety and despair. Their competitive, hostile, and arbitrary behavior invokes anxiety and hostility. They interrupt in mid-sentence, challenge every point, make problem solving a contest, become hostile when confronted, and react strongly to any stimulus.

The *"ain't it awful" Game Players* want to suck you into their pathetic lives and make you one of them. They sidetrack problem solving and burden you with the woes of their personal and organizational life. They blame everything on the system, boss, peers, and subordinates and bring in the smallest details to support their position.

Coping with Stress Carriers

Stress carriers are not going to change, no matter how much you would like them to. To some degree they are like various personality disorders that any clinical psychologist or psychiatrist will tell you are the hardest to treat and create the greatest frustration for therapists. If you accept this principle, you can then gain control over your responses and reactions to them.

The second most important aspect of dealing with stress carriers is to understand the behavior pattern, isolate the diagnosis, and treat the problem. In medicine there is no magical cure for all diseases; treatment is specific to the illness. The same principle applies to stress carriers. By isolating the behavior, you can develop a plan that fits the specific situation.

The third key to handling stress carriers is to practice your own new behaviors and responses to gain proficiency. Any new behavior is acquired at a slow rate during the first ten or so attempts before it becomes natural. So resist the temptation to give up when the behavior does not seem to work.

The final thing to remember when dealing with stress carriers is that your management style may be contributing to the problem with a particular person. What are your stress reactions? Do you explode at an Exploder? Clam up when faced with a Sherman Tank? Knowing your own style and understanding how it interacts with the other person's will help you manage your own stress and your reactions to stress carriers.

The following methods for coping with the various stress carriers come from Robert M. Bramson (*Coping With Difficult People*, 1981) and other leading experts who deal with personality and character disorders.

Because Sherman Tanks are hostile-aggressives on the attack, you must not back down or flee. If you remain calm, you are in a good position to cope with them. Remember that they have a strong need to prove themselves and believe they know what should be done. They value aggression and assertiveness in themselves. By staying in charge of your internal reactions, you can balance the Sherman Tank's power ploy. You can:

- Give them time to run down.
- Get their attention. Change your posture. State their name. If possible, get them to sit down.
- Maintain eye contact and sit or stand in a calm, receptive manner.
- Do not argue or counterattack.
- Try to get into the problem-solving mode. Proceed in an adult-to-adult manner.

Snipers need a different approach because they are subtle and cunning. Because they see themselves as victims, they avoid face-to-face confrontations, do not reveal problems, want you to explode so you lose face, and try to one-up you to regain power. In coping with snipers, follow these steps:

- Ask questions that will bring the attack to the surface.
- Provide an alternative to open warfare. Ask snipers if they can share their thoughts with the rest of the group to help solve the problem. That uncovers the snipers and puts them on the spot to contribute actively to the group.
- Seek group confirmation of the covert attack if the sniping takes place in a meeting. You can state that they have made a very interesting point and invite the rest of the group to comment on it. You remove yourself as the focus and shift it to the group.
- Deal with the underlying problems in a private meeting.
- In general, try to remain in the questioning mode until the issue comes clearly to the surface.

Because Exploders erupt without much warning, you will feel rocked back on your heels and will have to recover. Remember, however, that Exploders blow up when they feel threatened and powerless. They secretly blame and are suspicious of others. Use these coping suggestions:

• Give the Exploder time to run down.
• If the explosion continues, ask the Exploder to stop.
• Try to get at the reason for the explosion. Recognize their concerns.
• Perhaps get some distance from the problem and deal with the Exploder in private. Tell the Exploder that you would like to meet with him or her in thirty minutes. That accomplishes two purposes: It gives the person time to calm down and lets you deal with him or her in private.

Remember that Complainers need to be understood as powerless people trying to make you feel responsible for their plight. They see the world only in terms of "oughts" and "shoulds," internal moral imperatives, and catastrophic thinking. These issues can be dealt with by getting Complainers into an active, problem-solving mode. You should:

• Listen attentively to what they are saying.
• Acknowledge their perceptions by paraphrasing what you heard.
• Ask pertinent questions such as, "What is the specific problem you are addressing?" Always come back to specifics.
• Do not agree or disagree.
• Try to bring out objective facts and move into the problem-solving mode. For example, ask, "Now let's see . . . The report on November 7 did not include what tables?"
• Try to get agreement on limited tasks. For example, say "Let's focus on the specifications for the XYZ project, especially section X."
• Do not be persuaded by "never" or "always." Try to question the validity of these statements.
• Remain calm under all circumstances.

Silent and unresponsive Clams may have three underlying motivations for being a difficult person: (1) clamming up is a way of avoiding a potential conflict; (2) they can be aggressive in a passive way and hook you into feeling frustrated and angry; or (3) they seek to avoid potential failure, which they fear. Regardless of their motivations, the Clam must be coped with through:

• Asking open-ended questions such as, "Can you tell me who you would approach about the problem? Any suggestions? You can start anywhere."

- Waiting for them to open up.
- Not trying to give them a response.
- Coping with your own inner frustrations. Do a quick five-second relaxation response by taking three deep breaths.
- When they open up, allow them to say whatever they want.
- Restate what they have agreed to do, and ask for their agreement.
- If they remain closed, end the meeting with an intention to continue at another time.

Superagreeables desperately need your approval at all costs. They will say anything to please you, even if it is impossible to deliver. Your goal is to make honesty nonthreatening. This is not an easy task because Superagreeables have brainwashed themselves to believe that they must please. Because they view unpleasant news as a potential rebuke and a threat, they want to avoid conflict. They will use humor to avoid harsh realities and dodge straight talk as a way of masking the problem. You must:

- Try to understand the underlying issues that feel threatening and that keep Superagreeables from being straightforward.
- Build a personal relationship with them on some aspect of their lives that is important to them. You show them that you see them as people in whom you are interested. That makes them feel accepted so they can bring out any hidden problems. They can then confide more in a friend than just a business associate.
- Listen to and interpret their humor. Usually Superagreeables are giving you a message about how they feel about *you*. They use humor rather than direct statements because they can deny the true meaning of the humorous message. Deciphering their humor gives you insight into their true feelings.
- Look for openings to get at what the Superagreeable is avoiding. If they allude to a problem say, "Sounds like you've really been thinking this over. Now let's see what this means for you and me." Then let the Superagreeable open up. You can now do some problem solving.

Negativists want everyone else to buy into their state of despair. All of us have suffered from the slings and arrows of fate and, consciously or unconsciously, we can empathize with these types of negativity. If you do that too much, though, Negativists will hook you into their game and gain control by blocking you. Keep in mind that they feel a lack of power and control. They may be embittered by past disappointments and prey to an internal stream of negative selftalk: "OBSTACLES AHEAD—DANGER!" Negativists do not trust anyone. The key to dealing with Negativists is to empower them:

- Avoid getting drawn into their state of mind. Say to yourself, "OK, here he goes again. A Negativist at work!" Be alert to your own feelings and others' reactions. This awareness prevents you from being drawn in.
- Be optimistic about the possibilities of solving the problem.
- Focus on the realistic steps that can be taken to solve the problem.
- Dream up a worst-case scenario and discuss it with them.
- Analyze the problem by listing the forces against and in favor of any alternative(s).
- Do not argue, or they will dig in more firmly.
- In extreme cases, go around them and accomplish the task yourself or through others.

Bulldozers have supreme confidence in their expertise, but overwhelm others and micromanage any task. Their internal scripts tell them they cannot settle for anything less than perfection, so they search for the solution that they believe they alone have the power to deliver. They see others as incompetent. It is no wonder that the person facing the Bulldozer is left with little sense of competence and a high degree of frustration. Coping with Bulldozers requires the following steps:

- Do some serious research so that you are on top of the problem and are not put on the spot.
- Listen to and acknowledge what Bulldozers say.
- Question them in an adult-to-adult manner.
- Avoid trying to be more expert than they are.
- If the behavior is incessant and the Bulldozer is your boss, let the matter go.
- If the Bulldozer is a peer, seek out other colleagues' input. If possible, leave the Bulldozer out of the problem solving.

Because Balloons need and seek admiration and respect from others, they compile a great deal of extraneous and esoteric information. Their internal script (of which they are unaware) tells them that to be loved, they must be an expert, so they put bits and pieces of information together in a collage of self-determined knowledge. They may read an article on the new information network in the *New York Sunday Times Magazine*. From that moment on they become self-appointed experts, ready to advise everyone on the subject. The problem is they have not fully assimilated or really learned much about the topic. These curious people, armed with partial information, are not aware when they are out of their depth. The coping steps for Balloons are:

- State the facts as an alternative version.
- Do not call them on their bluff.
- Give them a tactful way out—postpone in-depth discussion of the topic for another time.
- Cope with Balloons alone. Groups allow them to feed on their need for admiration.

Stallers postpone decisions and hope problems will go away. Their internal script tells them to be superhelpful and to deliver the highest-quality product, but in situations where a problem has developed they put off decisions. Stalling keeps them from failing. To cope with Stallers:

- Try to get them to give you reasons for delays.
- Look for indications that help to expose the problem, such as avoiding face-to-face contact, neglecting to return phone calls, and shifting topics in a meeting.
- When the underlying issue is on the table, try to suggest ways of proceeding with the task.
- If a Staller tries to indict you as part of the problem, accept it and try to work things out, looking forward rather than backward.
- Always give positive reinforcement to the Staller's attempts to get on with the task.
- Establish a decision-making chart and timetable on which you both agree.

Micromanagers, with their "I'm in charge here!" attitude, are always on the alert for problems in projects that they delegate. They hover and interfere when they suspect things are going wrong. The smallest glitch will send them into a frenzy and lead them to take over the project. Micromanagers fear failing and being out of control, and they may secretly blame themselves for trusting you. They believe that their ego is on the line. Keeping problems from them early on in projects creates enormous trouble, so the key to handling them is disclosing all information and keeping them up to date. To cope with Micromanagers:

- Be in charge of yourself—be positive to yourself and others.
- Keep records of progress and problems.
- Immediately alert everyone involved if problems develop.
- Be prepared—do not be taken by surprise.
- Have alternative solutions ready.
- Do not give in to panic.

- Do not act like a victim.
- Do not try to control the uncontrollable; accept that some micromanagers are uncontrollable.
- Control yourself.

Type A Stress Carriers are like electric charges waiting to go off. Unlike Sherman Tanks, they move randomly. You feel their energy charge being transferred to you—and it is very uncomfortable. The fact is that Type A's are overwhelmed by perfectionism, fear of failure, and catastrophic thinking, and they project their anxiety onto you. To cope with Type A Stress Carriers:

- Do not get hooked into their behavior. Remain calm. Say to yourself, "Relax. Relax. Relax." If you are in a group and happen to be sitting next to a Type A, move to another seat.
- Do not feed on your own anxiety. When you start to feel anxious, take five deep breaths, exhaling slowly after each one.
- Do not placate Type A's. If you try to calm them down, they will take that as an attack or argue or get more agitated. Let them run their course.
- Practice relaxation techniques before encountering Type A's.
- Do not try to change them.
- Look upon them as a challenge.

Stone Tablets are the Moses's of the organization. They have the "shoulds" and the "oughts" under their control and feel it is their duty to make sure you follow every rule to the letter. There is no room for interpretation except theirs. Stone Tablets are super-perfectionists whose "us versus them" mentality is symptomatic of their hidden hostility to perceived "outgroups." They are anxious about being wrong, probably as a result of being punished in early life for deviating from the rules. To cope with Stone Tablets:

- Remain calm.
- Say, "That is very interesting."
- Do not argue—that is what they want.
- Do your homework—gather data that confirms your interpretation of the rules.
- Present your findings in a factual, low-key manner.
- Emphasize fairness.
- If all else fails, get a third-party arbitrator.

The "ain't it awful" Game Players take advantage of your need to be sympathetic and helpful about their personal problems. They need someone to verify that they are as powerless and hopeless as they feel, and they want others to feel as "not OK" as they do. To cope with "ain't it awful" Game Players:

- Do not play the game. Avoid agreeing with them.
- Say, "I see. Now let's see how we can solve the problem."
- Focus on a specific task—one that they can master.
- Reinforce problem solving—ignore victim talk.
- Always speak as an adult to an adult.

Difficult people are the only ones who can will themselves to change. Your job as a manager is to cope with them and get on with the job. Distance helps, achieved through accurately assessing the behavior and separating the people from the problem. As you gain insight into their assumptions, you can follow the coping steps for each type.

Conclusion

Psychobiologist Robert Sapolsky studied a group of baboons living in the Serengenti of East Africa. He looked at their social structure and how they reacted to stress. He found significant differences in their biochemical levels that were related to social rank, mirroring other findings in humans. The tests showed that baboons that rank lower on the social scale are under chronic stress, which leads to overproduction of hormones that affect blood pressure, cholesterol levels, and the effectiveness of their immune systems. Like humans, the baboons react to being on the bottom of the totem pole, to the loss of control, and to the loss of the ability to predict future events when others rule their lives. Such conditions are crucial factors in inducing and sustaining prolonged stress, as well as in promoting an unhealthy aging process in the brain and the body's systems. But there is a positive aspect to this. As Sapolsky says, "We have a tremendous power to affect whether or not these disease states come about in the first place. How we live our lives, how we perceive the events that happen to us, are very important. If you can't control events—and how many of us can control all the stressful events that occur in our lives?—then it is very important to work on changing your perception of the events."

Sapolsky's research leads not to a fatalistic acceptance or resignation, but to the kind of good advice that wise men and women have suggested for centuries: "It's ironic that after all of this laboratory work, all the biochemistry coupled with all the work with something as unlikely as a troop of baboons, that the take-home message is something that our grandmothers told us. We should be happy, we should relax, we should take things in stride. Maybe that's basically the final lesson."

His findings also suggest that reactions to stress may be one factor in the wide variability found among the elderly. Those who utilize the coping experience of a long life to adapt positively to tension and change are likelier to maintain their vigor than those who let the stress of these factors overwhelm them.

The final word on managing stress is that you can only control yourself. You can only change what you are aware of. This book contains many tips on managing stress. Each chapter has outlined the pitfalls of ineffective use of the building blocks of management style and the strategies for improving your use of them. In essence, the skillful and informed use of these building blocks decreases stress by increasing competence and awareness. The next and final chapter shows you how to develop a complete action plan for assessing and improving your own management style.

CHAPTER TEN

PUTTING IT ALL TOGETHER: DEVELOPING AN ACTION PLAN FOR YOUR MANAGEMENT STYLE

A s fascinating as they are, most manager case histories and explanations of the ingredients of management style stop short of providing personal answers to the questions they raise. Even after reading this book, you may still wonder exactly how to apply the concepts and practices to your own management style. You may not be entirely clear about your psychological type (but suspect you know what type you are) or you may have found that certain aspects of the needs and conflict management chapters rang true. But how can you put all this information together to figure out (or even verify) your current management style so that you can take advantage of the benefits of developing one that is stronger and more integrated? This chapter is designed to guide you through a series of assessments and tests that you can use to get a more specific sense of your configuration of the six building blocks of management style and how that affects the ways you behave as a manager. Then, you can develop a personal action plan that will help you to make the changes that are important to you and that will help you grow and develop. You can also use these assessment tools with people you manage to guide them through the same process.

What Is Your Psychological Type?

In Appendix B, you will find the Assessment of Psychological Type. In it, you will be asked to compare the paired words or phrases and check the appropriate box for the one that best describes you. Try to answer the questions as you prefer to be—not what your job or anyone else demands of you. This is important because it will allow you to determine your true type rather than to respond to pressures from your environment. Use the following worksheet to record the results. Tally the number of your responses as indicated, then circle the appropriate letter (such as E or I, S or N, and so on).

Number of Extrovert Boxes Checked	Number of Introvert Boxes Checked
E	I

Number of Sensing Boxes Checked	Number of Intuition Boxes Checked
S	N

Number of Thinking Boxes Checked	Number of Feeling Boxes Checked
T	F

Number of Judging Boxes Checked	Number of Perceiving Boxes Checked
J	P

What is your type? _____

A Note about Psychological Type

The question always arises, "What does it mean when my scores are close on one or more preferences?" This can occur on this test or the full Myers-Briggs Type Indicator. We make the assumption, based on theory and observation, that type is fixed but can vary in strength based on a number of factors such as internal conflict or external pressures at the time or the person's attitude toward test taking. Under normal conditions, when our type is well balanced, we develop our favorite function and use it effortlessly and supplement it with the auxiliary function. (See Chapter Two for a review of these concepts.) But when we face external pressures early and later in life to be different from what we are, our type may become distorted. An introvert will be forced to be more outgoing or an intuitive to be more detailed-oriented than he or she wants to be. In addition, we may lack the opportunity to exercise the processes or attitudes that make up type. As Isabel Myers states, "Unknowingly parents frequently refuse their children the conditions necessary for good type development; the young introverts who get no peace or privacy, the extroverts shut off from people and activity, the intuitives tied to routine matters of fact, the sensing children required to learn everything through words with nothing to see or handle, the young thinkers who are never given a reason or permitted an argument, the feeling types in a family where nobody cares for harmony, the judging types, for whom all decisions are handed down by an excessively decisive parent, and the young perceptives, who are not allowed to run and find out."

All of these factors lead to internal conflict that distorts our natural type. External pressures from our job or our relationships can also force us unconsciously to bend our types out of shape. An intuitive in a job requiring excessive detail and factual orientation may reluctantly stress an undeveloped sensing function. An extrovert married to an introvert may turn his or her psychic energy inward. In addition to these developmental and external pressures, the way we take the test can influence the outcome. If we are unsure of the concepts in the items, the results may reflect that feeling. If we take the test while we are tired or distracted, the results may not be clear. The net result can be answers to items that cancel each other out and produce ambivalent results. The remedy for distorted results is honest introspection and a clear head. Try not to let job pressures and relationships determine your preferences. As much as you can, respond from your own feelings and inclinations.

Determining Your Other Functions

The next step in analyzing your psychological type is to determine your dominant, inferior, and auxiliary functions. The following chart will help you identify both the dominant, and auxiliary functions:

I**ST**J	I**SF**J	I**NF**J	I**NT**J
IS**T**P	IS**F**P	IN**F**P	IN**T**P
E**ST**P	E**SF**P	E**NF**P	E**NT**P
ES**T**J	ES**F**J	EN**F**J	EN**T**J

The underlined function is your dominant function. The auxiliary is the other function. For example an ISTJ has S (sensing) as the dominant function and T (thinking) as the auxiliary function. The inferior function (that is, the least developed one) is the opposite of the dominant, in this case N (intuition).

List your dominant, auxiliary, and inferior functions in the following chart:

Dominant	
Auxiliary	
Inferior	

Now look up your psychological type's profile in Chapter Two. Fill in your strengths, behavior under stress, and areas to develop in the following chart:

Strengths	Behavior Under Stress	Areas to Develop

Use the following charts to record any fusion or crossover factors:

FUSION FACTORS

Achievement with Dominance	
Achievement with Autonomy	
Dominance with Autonomy	
Dominance with Exhibition	
Dominance with Aggression	

CROSSOVER FACTORS

High Assistance and Low Nurturance	
High Autonomy and Low Deference	

What Is Your Needs Profile?

The next building block of management style is the assessment of your needs profile. (See Chapter Five if you need to review the information on needs.) Complete the Assessment of Needs in Appendix C, then transfer the ratings for each need to the following chart:

NEEDS

Achievement	
Dominance	
Affiliation	
Deference	
Autonomy	
Nurturance	
Assistance	
Abasement	
Change	
Order	
Endurance	
Intensity	
Introspection	
Aggression	
Exhibition	

How Do Your Psychological Type and Needs Interact?

The next step is to identify any psychological type interactions with the needs. If your answer is "Yes" to any of the interactions listed below, check the box. The following chart will help you identify these interactions:

Psychological Type	Needs	Check if Yes	Implications
Thinking	Dominance (high)		
Thinking	Aggression (high)		
Thinking	Aggression (low)		
Thinking	Dominance (low)		
Thinking	Deference (low)		
Feeling	Dominance (high)		
Feeling	Aggression (high)		
Sensing	Achievement		What are your job requirements? Are they S or N?
Intuition	Achievement		What are your job requirements? Are they S or N?
Extroversion	Aggression (high)		
Extroversion	Recognition (high)		
Introversion	Autonomy (high)		

Now list how your needs make you stronger as a manager:

1.
2.
3.
4.
5.

List areas where you want to improve as a manager:

1.
2.
3.
4.
5.

What needs do you want to modify?

1.
2.
3.
4.
5.

See Chapter Five for suggestions on modifying needs.

What Power Bases and Influence Style Are You Using?

To determine your power bases and influence style, fill out the Influence Inventory in Appendix D. Put the ratings into the following summary chart:

POWER BASES

Authority	
Reward	
Discipline	
Expert	
Information	
Referent	

Power Patterns for Different Types of Managers

Keep in mind that the types of power that are most suitable vary depending on your level as a manager. The following charts show the power patterns that are appropriate for a first-line supervisor, a middle manager, and a manager in a matrix organization. Find the one that seems to fit your situation best.

Power Patterns for a First Line Supervisor

Authority	Reward	Discipline	Expert	Information	Referent

The first line supervisor must balance authority, reward, and expertise (leading by example) with moderate use of discipline (when necessary) and information (as needed) and make minimal use of referent power.

Power Patterns for a Middle Manager

Authority	Reward	Discipline	Expert	Information	Referent

The middle manager's power profile shifts to an equally high use of reward, information, and referent power. There is less use of authority, discipline, and expert power.

Power Patterns for a Project Manager in a Matrix Organization

Authority	Reward	Discipline	Expert	Information	Referent

The project manager must use referent power heavily along with information power. Authority and discipline power are seldom used. Expert power should be used only in cases where clarification is needed, as the expertise should lie in the hands of the task managers.

How does your use of power compare with these three management power templates?

What changes do you want to make to be more effective in your job?

See Chapter Six for suggestions on modifying your power bases.

What Is Your Conflict Resolution Style?

The next step is to take the Conflict Resolution Style Assessment in Appendix E and record the results in the following worksheet.

Style	Rating
Win/Lose	
Lose/Leave	
Compromise	
Lose/Yield	
Collaborate	

Effective conflict managers have a high rating for collaborate style, followed by a strong compromise style. If your rating differs from this pattern, you can become more effective by adjusting your assumptions about conflict and use the techniques outlined in Chapter Seven.

What Are Your Problem-Solving Preferences?

After filling out the Four-Quadrant Inventory in Appendix F, record your scores for the four dimensions and put them in the following chart:

Instructions: Subtract the total for TW (Theoretical World) from RW (Real World). If the value is negative, use a minus sign to show that. Subtract the total of AE (Active Experimentation) from RO (Reflective Observations) and use a minus sign to show a negative value.

Real World (RW)	Theoretical World (TW)	(RW) minus (TW)
		=

Reflective Observation (RO)	Active Experimentation (AE)	(RO) minus (AE)
		=

Plot your scores on the two axes in the Four-Quadrant Chart that follows:

THE FOUR-QUADRANT CHART

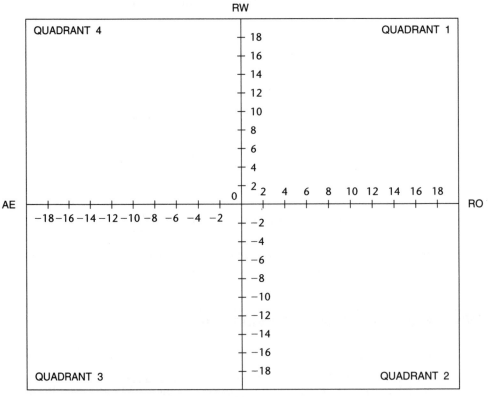

List the qualities of your conflict resolution style here. (Refer to Chapter Seven if necessary.):

Strengths
1.
2.
3.

Weaknesses
1.
2.
3.

How does your style affect your approach to problem solving?

What about your style would you like to modify or adapt?

What Are Your Values?

Complete the Values Assessment in Appendix G. Then list both the top seven end values and instrumental values in the following chart:

Your Top Seven Values

End Values	Instrumental Values
1.	1.
2.	2.
3.	3.
4.	4.
5.	5.
6.	6.
7.	7.

What are the implications of your values for you as a person and a manager? (See Chapter Eight for a review of the issues involved here.)

What Are Your Stress Reactions

Complete the three tests in Appendix H: The Stress Type Inventory, the Life Events Inventory (Holmes Stress Point Scale), and the Index of Beliefs.

Evaluating Your Responses to the Index of Beliefs

Check the beliefs where you circled two or more "Agree"s in the Index of Beliefs assessment in Appendix H.

If you agree on two items, you have a tendency to hold this belief.

If you agree on three items, there is a strong likelihood that you hold this belief.

If you have circled two or more answers for a given belief you need to develop counters to modify the belief. See Chapter Nine for developing effective counters.

Worksheet for Developing Counters to Irrational Beliefs

Beliefs	Check if two or more agree	Counters
Everyone must love me.		
One's self-worth is tied to his or her achievements.		
Some people are wicked and must be punished for their villainous behavior.		
Unless conditions are just right, it is catastrophic and I cannot function.		
Unhappiness is caused by external events; we have no control over anything.		
I need to worry about the possibility of some future catastrophe happening.		

Beliefs	Check if two or more agree	Counters
It is easier to avoid certain difficult or unpleasant events in life than face them.		
I need to be dependent upon someone else.		
We are all products of our past history; we cannot change anything.		
There is a right and perfect way to do everything, and it is disastrous if we do not find that way.		

Your Stress Assessments

Record the results of your stress assessments in the following chart.

Stress Reactions	Score
Stress Type Inventory Score	_____
Holmes Stress Point Scale	_____

What Is Your Susceptibility to Stress?

If you have a Stress Type Score equal to or greater than 100, you have a tendency to be a stress reactor.

If your score on the Holmes Stress Point Scale is 300 or more, you probably run a risk of developing some kind of stress-related illness in the next year. If your score is 200 to 299, your illness risk is moderate, and if your score is between 150 and 199, your risk is mild.

What actions do you need to take to lessen or modify your response to stress?

Summary

Now that you have analyzed your results on the six factors of management style, you need to summarize your findings. This snapshot can help you create a complete action plan for further personal development. You can also use this process to look at your management style in an integrative way. As you ponder the results, your strengths and weaknesses, and areas where you would like to improve, pick out the three most salient points for each of the management style factors. Transfer them to the Management Style Matrix Worksheet on the following page in the strengths, weaknesses, and areas to develop columns. Then review your personal management style matrix and determine your priorities for each factor. Rate the priorities as low, medium, or high.

Management Style Matrix Worksheet

Management Style	Strengths	Weaknesses	Areas to Develop	Priority
Psychological Type				
Needs				
Power Bases				
Conflict Style				
Four-Quadrant Problem-Solving Approach				
Values				
Stress				
Reactions				

The next step is to go back to the chapters that address the management style factors given a high priority rating. Management style develops over a long period of time. In many cases, we build up a workable and effective style, while others, because of life scripts, organizational pressures, and lack of training, need further work. Attaining competence requires more than a "three-minute" approach. Change takes time, practice, and commitment. The exercises and plans for the development of management style throughout this book should serve as your basis as you start your program.

Developing an Action Plan

As you go about recognizing and developing the elements of management style that you wish to work on, remember that no two managers have the same configuration. Every one of us has priorities that change and our sense of what we need to work on evolves over time as well. The best approach to developing an action plan is to begin by looking at the assessment of priorities that you have created. Start by focusing on one area for each day of the week. Keep the number of areas manageable, because trying to do too much can create stress. Always try to pick out critical incidents where you have encountered a need for modification. For example, if you are an extroverted thinker who needs to modify your interactions with others, think of the times you have felt this need in the past month. Keep a log of these incidents. Do the same for the other management factors where you see the need for modification. Work on one factor at a time.

Use the following chart as a quick review of the purpose and method for working on each element of your management style, as well as a reference to chapters in this book that can help you through the process.

Management Style	Focus	Method
Psychological Type	Strengthening inferior function and developing weaknesses.	Psycological Type exercises. Chapter Two.
Needs	Needs that get you into trouble.	Cognitive restructuring using counters. Chapter Five.
Power Bases	Power bases related to your job.	Development of influence skills. Chapter Six.
Conflict Style	Moving toward win/win (collaborative) approach.	Restructuring assumptions and following the three step approach. Chapter Seven.

(Continued)

(Continued)

Management Style	Focus	Method
Four-Quadrant Problem-Solving Approach	Using all the quadrants in problem solving and conflict resolution.	See Chapter Seven.
Values	Understanding your values and their impact on your life.	Clarification of personal values. Chapter Eight.
Stress Reactions	Coping with stress.	Relaxation training, restructuring of irrational beliefs, both internal and external. Chapter Nine.

In conclusion, the pursuit of a more effective and satisfying management style can be a rewarding adventure that will enrich your life and your work. As you gain understanding and mastery over your management style, you will develop a natural flow that becomes second nature. And you will feel like—and be told—that you are indeed a "good manager."

THE INTEGRATED MANAGEMENT STYLE MODEL

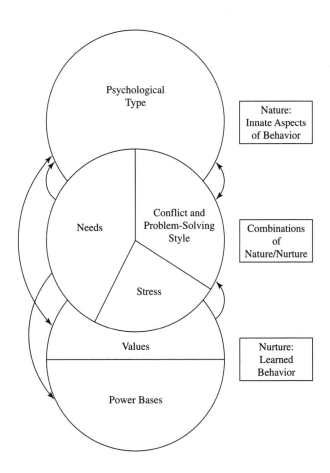

ASSESSMENT OF PSYCHOLOGICAL TYPE

Determining Your Psychological Type

EXTROVERT OR INTROVERT

	E	I
1. I am gregarious. I am reserved.	✓	
2. I am relaxed. I am intense.		✓
3. I am enthusiastic. I am aloof.	✓	
4. I speak out in groups. I absorb information in groups.	✓	
5. My energy grows at parties. My energy wanes at parties.		✓
6. I have a large group of friends. I have a selected few friends.	✓	
7. I think out loud. I think inside my head.		✓

(Continued)

EXTROVERT OR INTROVERT (*Continued*)

	E	I
8. I look for activity. I seek quiet time.		√
9. I like to talk. I like to listen.	√	
10. I share my personal experiences. I am unapproachable.	√	
11. I like new experiences. I like stability in my inner life.		√
12. I want to be with people. I take a detached approach.	√	
13. I am influenced by external opinions. I am inner directed.	√	
14. I show emotions. I exercise restraint.	√	
15. I respond quickly. I respond warily.	√	
Total number of checks in each column.	10	5

The column with the larger number of checks indicates your attitude of either extroversion or introversion. See the worksheet in Chapter Ten that helps you further specify aspects of your type.

SENSING OR INTUITION

	S	N
1. I am realistic. I am inspirational.		√
2. I like routine. I like variety.		√
3. I think about facts. I think about possibilities.		√
4. I like precision. I like brainstorming.		√

(Continued)

SENSING OR INTUITION (*Continued*)

5. I am concerned with the present.
   I am concerned with the future.   ✓

6. I use my five senses.   ✓
   I rely on my sixth sense.

7. My feet are on the ground.   ✓
   My head is in the clouds.

8. My mind is literal.
   My mind is figurative.   ✓

9. I make direct statements.   ✓
   I make allegorical statements.

10. I pay attention to basics.   ✓
    I pay attention to overtones.

11. I use learned skills.
    I acquire new skills.   ✓

12. My focus is on reality.
    My focus is on inspiration.   ✓

13. I am steadfast.   ✓
    I am mercurial.

14. I work on solving problems.   ✓
    I discover problems.

15. I like details.
    I like the big picture.   ✓

Total number of checks in each column.   6   9

THINKING OR FEELING

	T	F
1. I am logical and analytical. I have a personal value orientation.		✓
2. I am critical. I am personable.		✓
3. I am firm on policy. I bend the rules.		✓
4. I have an impersonal orientation to problems. I have a strong personal involvement in problems.		✓

(Continued)

THINKING OR FEELING (*Continued*)

	T	F
5. I am direct. I am tactful.	✓	✓
6. I show justice. I show mercy.		✓
7. I am hard-headed. I am soft-headed.		✓
8. I am fair-minded. I am sympathetic.		✓
9. I focus on ideas. I focus on ideals.		✓
10. I am firm. I am empathetic.		✓
11. I am unaffected by atmosphere. I am tuned into atmosphere.		✓
12. I concentrate on the task. I concentrate on the relationship.		✓
13. I prefer the honest truth. I avoid unpleasantness.	✓	
14. I live by logic. I live by values.		✓
15. I am tuned into designs. I am tuned into people.		✓
Total number of checks in each column.	2	13

JUDGMENT OR PERCEPTION

	J	P
1. I am deliberate. I am spontaneous.	✓	
2. I prefer structure. I prefer to be unstructured.	✓	
3. I am decisive. I am cautious.		✓
4. I voice my opinions openly. I am open-minded.		✓

(*Continued*)

JUDGMENT OR PERCEPTION (*Continued*)

	J	P
5. I persevere.	✓	
I do not worry about time.		
6. I am organized and systematic.		
I am flexible.		✓
7. I am self-regimented.	✓	
I like to freewheel.		
8. I am punctual.	✓	
I am leisurely.		
9. I am systematic.	✓	
I am impulsive.		
10. I aim to be right.		
I aim to be fair.		✓
11. I am geared to morality.	✓	
I am geared to the existential.		
12. I am determined.	✓	
I am easy going.		
13. I live up to standards.	✓	
I am open to new experiences.		
14. I like the deliberate.	✓	
I like the whimsical.		
15. I live to plan.	✓	
I like unplanned activities.		
Total number of checks in each column.	11	4

My type is: _____

See the corresponding worksheets in Chapter Ten to help you flesh out your assessment of your type.

ASSESSMENT OF NEEDS

R ead the following statements and rate them as needs that you express on a 1 to 5 scale (1 = low, 5 = high). Try to be objective. If you are in doubt, ask someone who knows you. Try not to be influenced by what you think you should be or by what others want you to be.

Overall Management Needs

Need for Achievement	Rating
1. I like to do my best in whatever I undertake.	5
2. I like to be able to say that I have done a difficult job well.	4
3. I like to be able to do things better than other people.	5
4. I like to accomplish tasks that others recognize as requiring skill and effort.	5
5. I enjoy work as much as play.	4
TOTAL:	23

Need for Dominance   Rating

1. I argue with zest for my point of view against others.   2

2. I feel I can dominate a social or business situation.   3

3. I like to be one of the leaders in the organizations
   and groups to which I belong.   1

4. I usually influence others more than they
   influence me.   2

5. I enjoy the sense of power when I am able to control
   the actions of others.   2

TOTAL   10

Need for Affiliation   Rating

1. I like to be loyal to my friends and colleagues.   5

2. I like to do things for my colleagues and workers.   5

3. I share things with my friends and colleagues.   5

4. I enjoy cooperating with others more than working
   by myself.   3

5. I like to hang out with a group of congenial people
   and talk about things.   2

TOTAL   20

Boss's/Peers/Subordinates Relations Needs

Need for Deference   Rating

1. I conform to custom and avoid the unconventional.   3

2. I accept suggestions rather than insist on working
   things out in my own way.   3

3. I seek the advice of older people and follow it.   2

4. I like to follow instructions and do what is expected
   of me.   2

5. I like to accept the leadership of my superiors.   3

TOTAL   13

Need for Autonomy	**Rating**
1. I am unable to do my best work when I am in a subservient position.	3
2. I like to come and go as I please.	2
3. I resist people who try to assert their authority over me.	4
4. I am apt to criticize, openly or covertly, people who are in positions of authority.	3
5. I like to be independent of others in deciding what I want to do.	3
TOTAL	16

Need for Nurturance	**Rating**
1. I take pains not to hurt the feelings of my subordinates.	
2. I like to help people when they are in trouble.	
3. I give my time and energy to those who ask for it.	
4. I like to show a great deal of affection toward my colleagues and subordinates.	
5. People are apt to tell me their innermost secrets and troubles.	
TOTAL	

Need for Assistance	**Rating**
1. I like my colleagues or workers to encourage me when I meet with failure.	
2. I think of myself as neglected when things go wrong.	
3. I like sympathy when I am sick or depressed.	
4. I am rather easily discouraged when things go wrong.	
5. I experience a vague feeling of insecurity when I must act on my own.	
TOTAL	

Need for Abasement	**Rating**
1. When things go wrong, I feel personally responsible.	_____
2. I undertake more than I can handle.	_____
3. My friends think I am too humble.	_____
4. I think that charity should begin with your enemies.	_____
5. I feel depressed by my inability to handle various situations.	_____
TOTAL	_____

Task Factor Needs

Need for Change	**Rating**
1. I like to travel and experience new things.	_____
2. I like to experience novelty and change in my daily routine.	_____
3. I like to meet new people.	_____
4. I like to experiment and try new things.	_____
5. I like to try new and different jobs, rather than do the same old thing.	_____
Total number of always responses:	_____

Need for Order	**Rating**
1. Any written work that I do I like to have precise, neat, and well-organized.	_____
2. I like to plan and organize the details of any work that I have to undertake.	_____
3. I like things to run smoothly without any hitches.	_____
4. My work station is neat and well organized.	_____
5. If I have to take a trip, everything has to be planned and programmed in advance.	_____
TOTAL	_____

Need for Endurance	Rating
1. I like to work hard and long on any job I do.	_____
2. I like to stay late working in order to get a job done.	_____
3. I like to stick at a job or problem even when it may seem as if I am getting nowhere.	_____
4. I like to complete a single job or task before taking on others.	_____
5. I dislike being interrupted while at my work.	_____
TOTAL	_____

Need for Intensity	Rating
1. I can expend a great deal of effort in a short time.	_____
2. I am intense with the tasks that interest me.	_____
3. I work hard when I work, and play hard when I play. Then I feel drained.	_____
4. Long stretches of tedious work bore me and make me feel frustrated.	_____
5. I feel fresh, vigorous, and ready for anything, most of the time.	_____
TOTAL	_____

Interpersonal Modifiers

Need for Introspection	Rating
1. I like to observe how another individual feels in a given situation.	_____
2. I like to put myself in someone else's place and to imagine how I would feel in the same situation.	_____
3. I like to think about the personalities of people and try to figure out what makes them tick.	_____
4. I like to understand how my colleagues feel about various problems they have to face.	_____

(Continued)

Need for Introspection (*Continued*)	Rating
5. I like to judge people by why they did something—not by what they actually did.	_____
TOTAL	_____

Need for Aggression	Rating
1. I treat a domineering person as rudely as he or she treats me.	_____
2. I feel like getting revenge when someone has insulted me.	_____
3. I like to tell people what I think of them.	_____
4. Sometimes I use threats to accomplish my purpose.	_____
5. I am apt to express my irritation rather than restrain it.	_____
TOTAL	_____

Need for Exhibition	Rating
1. I like to tell amusing stories and jokes.	_____
2. I like people to notice me when in public.	_____
3. I am apt to show off in some way if I get a chance.	_____
4. I love to talk, and it is hard for me to keep quiet.	_____
5. I like to use words of which other people often do not know the meaning.	_____
TOTAL	_____

Scoring the Assessment of Needs

- A need can be considered as high if a rating between 20–25 is recorded.
- A need can be considered as medium if a rating between 11–19 is recorded.
- A need can be considered as low if a rating between 5–10 is recorded.

See the worksheets in Chapter Ten to see how to work with and modify those needs that are important to your success and effectiveness as a manager.

INFLUENCE INVENTORY

Directions

As a leader, you are faced with many situations in which you must seek the cooperation of subordinates or colleagues to get the job done. In these instances you must influence them to do what you perceive is necessary. In influencing others, we have certain assumptions about how to accomplish this task.

The Influence Inventory has a number of paired statements that reflect various assumptions about the use of power. Please circle the A or B statement that is more characteristic of your management style. In some instances, both choices may suit you. In this case choose the one that is more characteristic of you.

INFLUENCE INVENTORY

1. A. They do it because I have status in the organization.
   B. They do it because I usually reward them.

2. A. I use my expertise to influence them.
   B. I give as much information as I can to help them.

3. A. I praise their abilities to accomplish the task.
   B. I set high standards and expect performance.

4. A. I use my rights as boss to decide the issue.
   B. I persuade them by emphasizing my camaraderie with them.

5. A. I use my knowledge about policy and procedures to help them.
   B. I believe in running a tight ship. Procedures must be followed.

6. A. They do it as part of a reciprocal relationship.
   B. My specialized competence is the key.

(Continued)

INFLUENCE INVENTORY (CONTINUED)

7. A. I usually provide positive incentives to do the job.
    B. I use information and data to help them.

8. A. Procedures must be enforced.
    B. My judgment is usually superior to theirs.

9. A. They listen and cooperate because of mutual respect.
    B. They do it because I usually reward them.

10. A. I provide them with the big picture and explain my reasons.
    B. They work with me because of our rapport.

11. A. My competence in this area is well respected.
    B. They feel formally obligated to follow my lead.

12. A. I set high standards and expect results.
    B. I promise them future rewards.

13. A. I keep them fully informed about what is going on.
    B. I use my expertise to influence them.

14. A. I lead by example and good faith.
    B. I use all my information to persuade them.

15. A. I am firm with them and expect results.
    B. My rank is all I need.

16. A. I give as much information as I can to help them.
    B. They know I will reward them.

17. A. My official authority usually carries the weight.
    B. I believe discipline shapes character.

18. A. I set high standards and expect performance.
    B. I give as much information as I can to help them.

19. A. I am responsible. Therefore, I have the authority.
    B. My expert qualifications are the driving force.

20. A. I use my expertise to influence them.
    B. I am firm with them and expect results.

21. A. They know I will reward them.
    B. They respect my authority.

22. A. They listen and cooperate because of mutual respect.
    B. I impress them with consequences of failure.

23. A. I usually provide positive incentives to do the job.
    B. They do it as part of a reciprocal relationship.

24. A. My judgment is usually superior to theirs.
    B. They recognize that teamwork and cooperation will bring rewards.

25. A. They respect my authority.
    B. I give as much information as I can to help them.

26. A. They do it because we are part of a team.
    B. They respect my authority.

27. A. I am firm and enforce strict compliance.
    B. They work with me because of our rapport.

28. A. I provide them with the big picture and explain my reasons.
    B. Lines of authority must not be violated.

29. A. They respect my ability to make the right decision.
    B. I have built a strong relationship with them.

30. A. I promise them future rewards.
    B. I use my expertise to influence them.

INFLUENCE INVENTORY ANSWER SHEET

Circle the letters that you selected on each item in the inventory.

Item	Authority	Reward	Discipline	Expert	Information	Referent
1.	A	B				
2.				A	B	
3.		A	B			
4.	A					B
5.			B		A	
6.				B		A
7.		A			B	
8.			A	B		
9.		B				A
10.					A	B
11.	B			A		
12.		B	A			
13.				B	A	
14.					B	A
15.	B		A			
16.		B			A	
17.	A		B			
18.			A		B	
19.	A			B		
20.			B	A		
21.	B	A				
22.			B			A
23.		A				B
24.		B		A		
25.	A				B	
26.	B					A
27.			A			B
28.	B				A	
29.				A		B
30.		A		B		
TOTAL						

Scores: 7–10 = high, 4–6 = medium, 0–3 = low.

The results of this test show your power bases. See Chapter Ten for more information on how to modify your use of power as part of your management style and your level in your organization.

CONFLICT RESOLUTION STYLE ASSESSMENT

The assessment instrument contains questions about our assumptions and our tactics in dealing with conflict. The items are grouped in sections containing five questions. Rank order the five questions in each section:

5–Highly agree

4–Agree

3–Neutral

2–Slightly disagree

1–Totally disagree

Transfer the rankings for each item onto the summary of rankings sheet on page 256. Then obtain the total for each of the five conflict styles.

Assumptions about Conflict

1. Competition breeds success. Without healthy competition, groups stagnate.
2. Conflict runs a predictable course. Why sweat the issue?
3. It is impossible to satisfy everyone's needs. We can resolve conflict by give-and-take.

4. People have an underlying dark side that emerges during conflict. This is why most conflicts remain unresolved.
5. Conflict can be difficult to bear, but it can lead to increased creativity.

Item	1	2	3	4	5
Rank					

6. The task comes first; people must accommodate.
7. Most of the time, conflict will be resolved at top levels. I see any energy expended on the conflict as wasted.
8. There are too many differences among people to please everyone. You have to reach a settlement.
9. Negotiations should be undertaken with the serious intent of minimizing disruptions.
10. The assumption that someone has to win and someone has to lose leads to destructive competition.

Item	6	7	8	9	10
Rank					

11. Conflict is inevitable. Others want to win, and we must face a battle.
12. Most conflicts should be resolved by third-party intervention.
13. I believe groups should identify those issues on which compromise is impossible and those issues that they can use to reach a compromise.
14. Emotions have no place in a conflict. Feelings should be controlled when a dispute arises.
15. Conflict is natural and contains positive and negative energy. It is our job to harness these forces.

Item	11	12	13	14	15
Rank					

16. Compromise leads to more problems than it solves. Strong leadership is the only remedy to long-standing conflicts.
17. Most of the time conflict will be resolved at top levels. I see any energy expended on the conflict as wasted.

18. I don't mind conflict as long as we maintain our heads and give and take a little.
19. Self-interest and narrow-minded attitudes drive people apart. We should all try to minimize differences.
20. Conflict can be healthy. Mutual goals would be our criteria for judgment.

Item	16	17	18	19	20
Rank					

21. The decision rests on my superior knowledge and experience. Facts and logic will prevail.
22. Most of the time conflict will be resolved at top levels. I see any energy expended on the conflict as wasted.
23. I like someone who is skilled in negotiating from strength and has the ability to strike meaningful compromises when needed.
24. Self-interest and narrow-minded attitudes drive people apart. We should all try to minimize differences.
25. Different concerns can lead to new possibilities and new mutual options.

Item	21	22	23	24	25
Rank					

Tactics

26. People should face facts that one answer is better than others. It is my job to convince them of the right position.
27. I like to keep any encounters impersonal and let others fight it out.
28. The best way to resolve conflict is by expressing agreement with the other parties and offer suggestions on issues we both can live with.
29. I empathize with their position and give the other party support where I can.
30. I try to get the group to explore the concerns behind the various points of view. From this point we can move on to alternatives to the problem.

Item	26	27	28	29	30
Rank					

31. The decision rests on my superior knowledge and experience. People will follow the lead.
32. Conflict is destructive, and we should try to avoid confrontations that increase tensions.
33. We should rule out the extremes and settle on middle-ground agreements.
34. I think conflict is frightening. Differences should be discussed without people blowing up and attacking someone else.
35. I try to bring to the surface how others are really feeling and thinking. All issues must be brought out in the open and discussed.

Item	31	32	33	34	35
Rank					

36. I stand by my convictions and press hard to get them across.
37. I don't like people who cause anxiety and tension. When this happens, I try to avoid the situation.
38. I emphasize the team concept and implore the other side to get on the band-wagon.
39. I usually go along with the rest of the group to avoid being a barrier to problem solving and to maintain harmony.
40. I try to get people to explore their concerns with the rest of group. I then ask the rest of the group to address these concerns.

Item	36	37	38	39	40
Rank					

41. I am a hard battler, and I like to win. This tactic usually benefits my group.
42. I like people who are civil and understated when a conflict arises.
43. The leader should convince dissenters that the majority see it differently and to go along at this time. Compromise is in our best interest.
44. The best characteristics for a facilitator are moderation and harmonious accord.
45. A leader should present the concerns of our group, explore the other group's concerns, and not press for our group's position.

Item	41	42	43	44	45
Rank					

46. I like a leader who represents our position, someone who does not compromise and holds fast.
47. I refuse to take sides and let the others argue and settle their own disputes.
48. I appeal to the logic of the situation and try to persuade the group that we can come up with a compromise in spite of our differences.
49. Facilitators and team leaders must use strict rules to prevent strong feelings from erupting.
50. As a leader I try to put on the table all our concerns, see where we agree and disagree, then strive for mutual options.

Item	46	47	48	49	50
Rank					

SUMMARY OF THE RANK ORDER OF THE ITEMS

Win/Lose		Lose/Leave		Compromise		Lose/Yield		Collaborate	
Item	Rank	Item	Rank	Item	Rank	Item	Rank	Item	Rank
1		2		3		4		5	
6		7		8		9		10	
11		12		13		14		15	
16		17		18		19		20	
21		22		23		24		25	
26		27		28		29		30	
31		32		33		34		35	
36		37		38		39		40	
41		42		43		44		45	
46		47		48		49		50	
TOTAL									

Maximum score = 50   Mid-range score = 30   Minimum Score = 10
36 to 50 = High   25 to 35 = Medium   10 to 24 = Low

See Chapter Ten for more information on how to put the information on your conflict style together with other elements of your management style.

FOUR-QUADRANT PROBLEM-SOLVING PREFERENCE ASSESSMENT

This inventory assesses your approach to problem solving. Think of how you problem solve. Circle either A or B to describe the style that most closely fits you.

1. A. Practical
   B. Analytical

2. A. Factual
   B. Conceptual

3. A. Scheduling
   B. Planning

4. A. Immediate
   B. Long-term

5. A. Specific
   B. Abstract

6. A. Bottom-line
   B. Intangibles

7. A. Receptive
   B. Experimenting

8. A. Discerning
   B. Judging

9. A. Watchful
   B. Active

10. A. Reflecting
    B. Responding

11. A. Questioning
    B. Doing

12. A. Cautious
    B. Risk taking

13. A. Practical
    B. Judging

14. A. Experiencing
    B. Doing

15. A. Scheduling
    B. Experimenting

16. A. Concrete
    B. Evaluative

17. A. Cost
    B. Design

18. A. Bottom-line
    B. Quality

(Continued)

(Continued)

19. A. Analytical
    B. Receptive
20. A. Conceptual
    B. Observant
21. A. Planning
    B. Questioning
22. A. Perceiving
    B. Thinking
23. A. Generalizing
    B. Reflecting
24. A. Abstracting
    B. Watching
25. A. Reacting
    B. Reflecting
26. A. Factual
    B. Observant
27. A. Practical
    B. Questioning

28. A. Scheduling
    B. Discerning
29. A. Bottom-line
    B. Open-ended
30. A. Concrete
    B. Hidden
31. A. Conceptual
    B. Evaluative
32. A. Planning
    B. Experimenting
33. A. Generalizing
    B. Judging
34. A. Analyzing
    B. Risk taking
35. A. Abstracting
    B. Designing
36. A. Thinking
    B. Doing

Four-Quadrant Inventory Answer Sheet

Step 1. Circle the letters that you selected for each item in the inventory. Then add up the number of responses in each column.

	Real World RW	Theoretical World TW	Reflective Observation RO	Active Experimentation AE
1.	A	B		
2.	A	B		
3.	A	B		
4.	A	B		
5.	A	B		
6.	A	B		
7.			A	B
8.			A	B

(Continued)

(Continued)

	Real World RW	Theoretical World TW	Reflective Observation RO	Active Experimentation AE
9.			A	B
10.			A	B
11.			A	B
12.			A	B
13.	A			B
14.	A			B
15.	A			B
16.	A			B
17.	A			B
18.	A			B
19.		A	B	
20.		A	B	
21.		A	B	
22.		B	A	
23.		A	B	
24.		A	B	
25.	A		B	
26.	A		B	
27.	A		B	
28.	A		B	
29.	A		B	
30.	A		B	
31.		A		B
32.		A		B
33.		A		B
34.		A		B
35.		A		B
36.		A		B
TOTAL				

VALUES ASSESSMENT

Carefully assess the following lists of end and instrumental values. Rank order each list separately (1 being your most dearly held value, 18 being least important to you) on the Values Worksheet on page 262. Start with the end values, then do the instrumental values.

End Values	Instrumental Values
A comfortable life A prosperous life	*Ambition* Hardworking and aspiring
Equality Equal opportunity for all	*Broad-mindedness* Open-minded
An exciting life A stimulating, active life	*Capable* Competent; effective
Family security Taking care of loved ones	*Cheerful* Lighthearted; joyful
Freedom Independence and free choice	*Clean* Neat and tidy
Health Physical and mental well-being	*Courageous* Standing up for your beliefs
Inner harmony Freedom from inner conflict	*Forgiving* Willing to pardon others

(Continued)

(Continued)

End Values	Instrumental Values
Mature love Sexual and spiritual intimacy	*Helpfulness* Working for the welfare of others
National security Protection from attack	*Honest* Sincere and truthful
Pleasure An enjoyable, leisurely life	*Imaginative* Daring and creative
Salvation Saved; eternal life	*Intellectual* Self-reliant; self-sufficient
Self-respect Self-esteem	*Logical* Consistent; rational
A sense of accomplishment A lasting contribution	*Loving* Affectionate and tender
Social recognition Respect and admiration	*Loyalty* Faithful to friends or the group
True friendship Close companionship	*Obedient* Dutiful; respectful
Wisdom A mature understanding of life	*Polite* Courteous and well-mannered
A world at peace A world free of war and conflict	*Responsibile* Dependable and reliable
A world of beauty Beauty of nature and the arts	*Self-controlled* Restrained; self-disciplined

Values Worksheet

End Values	Instrumental Values	
		1.
		2.
		3.
		4.
		5.
		6.
		7.
		8.
		9.
		10.
		11.
		12.
		13.
		14.
		15.
		16.
		17.
		18.

APPENDIX H

STRESS ASSESSMENTS

Stress Type

Below is a group of statements related to everyday living. On a scale of 1 to 5, indicate the degree to which each one applies to you personally:

1. Never   2. Rarely   3. Sometimes   4. Frequently   5. Always

1. I want to be the best at everything I do.   _____

2. I get annoyed in traffic jams.   _____

3. I become impatient when waiting in line (queuing).   _____

4. I am annoyed when kept waiting for an appointment.   _____

5. I drive aggressively.   _____

6. I get annoyed with people who are inefficient.   _____

7. I try harder than others to accomplish things.   _____

8. I put more effort into my tasks than other people.   _____

9. I get annoyed when others don't take their work seriously.   _____

10. I am competitive and try to win when playing games.   _____

11. I enjoy competition.   _____

(Continued)

(Continued)

12. I don't like playing games with children because I shouldn't win. _____

13. I move, walk, talk and eat faster than others. _____

14. I feel pressure because of time constraints. _____

15. I think about my work most of the time. _____

16. I need to be busy and do things most of the time. _____

17. I can be short with other people when things go wrong. _____

18. I seem to have little spare time. _____

19. I need to work fast in order to accomplish everything. _____

20. I enjoy discussing my achievements. _____

21. I become upset with significant others who disappoint me. _____

22. At times I brood over failures. _____

23. I take life very seriously. _____

24. I show my anger, verbally or nonverbally, very easily. _____

25. I take on more than I can accomplish. _____

26. I don't like interruptions when I am working. _____

27. I don't like to depend on others. _____

28. If I need to get a job done I do it myself. _____

29. Too much relaxing makes me nervous. _____

30. I skip meals to get things done. _____

31. I do extra work to please myself and others. _____

32. I make mistakes under pressure. _____

33. People put great pressures and expectations on me. _____

34. Everything I do has to have serious purpose. _____

TOTAL _____

100 and greater = strong reactivity—stress proneness
85–99 = moderate reactivity to stress
70–84 = mild reactivity to stress
Less than 70 = low reactivity to stress

Holmes Stress Point Scale

Life's pressures can have an effect on your physical health. The following scale, developed by Thomas H. Holmes, M.D., measures the relative impact of a variety of stressful events. Check the events that have occurred to you within the last twelve months and then add up the numerical value attached to each of the events.

Life Events	Value	Your Score
Death of a spouse	100	_____
Divorce	73	_____
Marital separation	65	_____
Jail term	63	_____
Death of a close family member	53	_____
Personal injury or illness	50	_____
Marriage	47	_____
Retirement	45	_____
Change in health of family member	44	_____
Pregnancy	40	_____
Sexual difficulties	39	_____
Gain a new family member	39	_____
Business adjustment (merger, downsizing, etc.)	39	_____
Change in financial status	38	_____
Death of a close friend	37	_____
Change to different kind of work	36	_____
Change in communications with significant other	35	_____
Mortgage or loan more than $100,000	31	_____
Foreclosure of mortgage or loan	30	_____
Change in responsibilities at work	29	_____

(Continued)

(Continued)

Life Events	Value	Your Score
Son or daughter leaving home	29	_____
Trouble with in-laws	29	_____
Outstanding personal achievement	28	_____
Spouse beginning or stopping work	26	_____
Beginning or ending school	26	_____
Change in living conditions	25	_____
Revision of personal habits	24	_____
Trouble with boss	23	_____
Change in work hours or conditions	20	_____
Change in residence	20	_____
Change in schools	20	_____
Change in recreation	19	_____
Change in spiritual activities	19	_____
Change in social activities	18	_____
Loan for major purchase (car, appliance, school)	17	_____
Change in sleeping habits	16	_____
Change in number of family get-togethers	15	_____
Change in eating habits	15	_____
Vacation	13	_____
Christmas/Chanukah	12	_____
Minor violation of the law	11	_____
TOTAL		_____

If your score is 300 or more, you are at a very high stress level and probably run a major risk of illness in the next year. If your score is 200 to 299, your stress and illness risk are moderate, and if you score between 150 to 199, your stress and risk are mild.

Index of Beliefs

Place a checkmark in the appropriate column: "Agree" or "Disagree."

	Agree	Disagree
1. I want other people to approve of me.	_____	_____
2. I strongly dislike failing at anything I undertake.	_____	_____
3. There are bad people in the world who get away without punishment.	_____	_____
4. I very much like hearing favorable opinions of me.	_____	_____
5. There's nothing anybody can do about life's circumstances—it's the system.	_____	_____
6. If everything isn't right, I can't work.	_____	_____
7. I depend upon someone else for strength in handling life's problems.	_____	_____
8. I try to avoid doing unpleasant tasks whenever I can.	_____	_____
9. I always seek others' opinions before I do something.	_____	_____
10. It's okay to put off doing the things you dread.	_____	_____
11. I expect to be the best at anything I undertake; if not, I want to try.	_____	_____
12. I often get upset when situations aren't as I think they should be.	_____	_____
13. There is a perfect way to solve most problems.	_____	_____
14. I tend to put off making tough decisions.	_____	_____
15. We are what we are, and we can't change.	_____	_____
16. Most people suffer unhappiness through no fault of their own.	_____	_____

(Continued)

(*Continued*)

	Agree	Disagree
17. I worry about risky things that could happen to me.	_____	_____
18. The only way to understand present events is to understand past events.	_____	_____
19. I consider all possible alternatives to find the perfect solution.	_____	_____
20. I get upset when someone else is better than I am at things that matter to me.	_____	_____
21. I hate to see people get away with stupid, wicked behavior.	_____	_____
22. I worry about future events—even those that are outside my control.	_____	_____
23. It bothers me when people criticize me.	_____	_____
24. If I can't change the way things are, I get upset.	_____	_____
25. Fear of some awful future makes me anxious.	_____	_____
26. I like people to take care of me.	_____	_____
27. The way we behave now is determined early in our lives.	_____	_____
28. The fear of being punished keeps people from being bad.	_____	_____
29. Things are distressing in and of themselves—we can't do anything about them.	_____	_____
30. I remain anxious until I find the perfect solution.	_____	_____

The Key to the Index of Beliefs

Check the items that you agreed with.

Items			# Items Checked	Belief
1	4	23	_____	Everyone must love me.
2	11	20	_____	One's self-worth is tied to his or her achievements.
3	21	28	_____	Some people are wicked and must be punished for their villainous behavior.
6	12	24	_____	Unless conditions are just right, it is catastrophic and I can't function.
5	16	29	_____	Unhappiness is caused by external events; we have no control over anything.
17	22	25	_____	I need to worry about the possibility of some future catastrophe happening.
8	10	14	_____	It is easier to avoid certain difficult or unpleasant events in life than face them.
7	9	26	_____	I need to be dependent upon someone else.
15	18	27	_____	We're all products of our past history; we can't change anything.
13	19	30	_____	There is a right and perfect way to everything, and it's disastrous if we don't find that way.

Agree on two items: Tendency to hold the belief.
Agree on three items: Strong likelihood of holding the belief.

REFERENCES

Adams, J. *Conceptual Blockbusting: A Guide to Better Ideas.* Menlo Park, Calif.: Addison-Wesley Publishing Company, 1986.

Athos, A. G. and J. J. Gabarro. *Interpersonal Behavior.* Upper Saddle River, N.J.: Prentice Hall, 1978.

Bandura, A. *Social Learning Theory.* Upper Saddle River, N.J.: Prentice Hall, 1977.

Beck, A. T. "Cognitive Approaches to Stress." In *Principles and Practice of Stress Management,* edited by R. L. Woolfolk and P. M. Lehrer. New York: Guilford Press, 1984.

Benfari, R. C. *Understanding Your Management Style.* New York: Lexington Books, 1991.

Benfari, R. C., H. E. Wilkinson, and C. Oreh. "The Effective Use of Power." *Business Horizons,* May–June 1986.

Benfari, R. C. and H. E. Wilkinson. "Intelligence and Management." *Business Horizons.* May–June 1988.

Benson, H. *Beyond the Relaxation Response.* New York: Berkeley Books, 1985.

Benson, H. *The Relaxation Response.* New York: Morrow, 1975.

Berne, E. *Games People Play: The Psychology of Human Relations.* New York: Grove Press, 1964.

Bramson, R. *Coping with Difficult People.* New York: Anchor Press, 1981.

Bett, J. M., S. B. Goldberg, and W. L. Ury. "Designing Systems for Resolving Disputes in Organizations." *American Psychologist,* 45 (1990).

Camus, A. *The Myth of Sisyphus.* Translated by Justin O'Brien. New York: Alfred A. Knopf, Inc., 1955.

Carter, S. "The Insufficiency of Honesty." *Harper's.* May 1997.

Covey, S. R. *The 7 Habits of Highly Effective People.* New York: Simon & Schuster, 1989.

Crum, T. *The Magic of Conflict.* New York: Simon & Schuster, 1987.

Csikszentmihalyi, M. *Flow: The Psychology of Optimal Experience.* New York: HarperCollins, 1990.

Drucker, P. F. *The Effective Executive*. New York: HarperCollins, 1968.

Elgin, S. H. *The Last Word on the Gentle Art of Verbal Self-Defense*. Upper Saddle River, N.J.: Prentice Hall, 1987.

Ellis, A. *Reason and Emotion in Psychotherapy*. New York: Lyle Stuart, 1962.

Festinger, L. *A Theory of Cognitive Dissonance*. New York: Row, Peterson, 1957.

Ficino, M. *The Book of Life*. Dallas, Tex.: Spring Publications, 1988.

Fisher, R., and W. Ury. *Getting to Yes*. Boston: Houghton Mifflin, 1981.

Fisher, R., A. Kopelman, and A. K. Schneider. *Beyond Machiavelli*. New York: Penguin, 1996.

Fisher, R. and D. Ertel. *Getting Ready to Negotiate*. New York: Penguin, 1995.

Frankl, V. *Man's Search for Meaning: An Introduction to Logotherapy*. New York: Simon & Schuster, 1980.

Galbraith, J. K. *The Good Society*. Boston: Houghton Mifflin, 1996.

Goldman, D. *Emotional Intelligence*. New York: Bantam Books, 1995.

Goldman, D. *Working with Emotional Intelligence*. New York: Bantam Books, 1998.

Gould, S. J. "Biological Potential vs. Biological Determinism." In *The Sociobiology Debate*, edited by Arthur Caplan. New York: HarperCollins, 1978.

"The Nonscience of Human Nature." In *Ever Since Darwin: Reflections in Natural History*. New York: W. W. Norton, 1977.

Gregory, R. L. *The Oxford Companion to the Mind*. New York: Oxford University Press, 1987.

Heitler, Susan M. *From Conflict to Resolution*. New York: W. W. Norton, 1990.

Hogan, R., G. J. Curphy, and J. Hogan. "What We Know about Leadership: Effectiveness and Personality." *American Psychologist*, 49 (1994).

Holt, R. "Occupational Stress." In *Handbook of Stress*, edited by Leo Goldberger and Shlomo Breznitz. New York: The Free Press, 1982.

Howard, R. "Values Make the Company." *Harvard Business Review*. Sept.–Oct. 1990.

Ivancevitch, J. M., M. T. Matteson, S. M. Freedman, and J. S. Phillips. "Worksite Stress Management Interventions." *American Psychologist*, 45 (1990).

Janis, I. *Victims of Groupthink: A Psychological Study of Foreign Policy Decisions and Fiascos*. Boston: Houghton Mifflin, 1972.

Jung, C. *Psychological Types*. Princeton, N.J.: Princeton University Press, Bollingen Series, 1971.

Kagan, J. and N. Snidman. "Temperamental Factors in Human Development." *American Psychologist*, 46 (1991).

Kelman, H. "Negotiation as Interactive Problem-solving," *International Negotiation 1*, 1996.

Kluckhohn, F. R. "Dominant and Variant Cultural Value Orientations." In *Human Relations*, edited by H. Cabut and J. A. Kahl. Cambridge, Mass.: Harvard University Press, 1953.

Kluckhohn, F. R. and F. Strodtbeck. *Variations in Value Orientations*. New York: Alfred A. Knopf, Inc., 1982.

Kohlberg, L. "Moral Stages and Moralization: The Cognitive Development Approach." In *Moral Development and Behavior: Theory, Research, and Social Issues*, edited by T. Lickona. New York: Holt, Rinehart and Winston, 1976.

Kohn, A. *No Contest*. Boston: Houghton Mifflin, 1986.

Levinson, H. "Why the Behemoths Fell: Psychological Roots of Corporate Failure." *American Psychologist*, 49 (1994).

Leviton, R. *Brain Builders!* West Nyack, N.Y.: Parker Publishing, 1995

Lykken, D. T., M. McGue, A. Tellegen, and T. J. Bouchard, Jr. "Emergenesis: Genetic Traits That May Not Run in Families." *American Psychologist*, 47 (1992).

McClelland, D. *Power: The Inner Experience*. New York: Irvington, 1975.

McMullin, R. E. *Handbook of Cognitive Therapy Techniques.* New York: W. W. Norton, 1986.

Myers, L. *Gifts Differing.* Palo Alto, Calif.: Consulting Psychological Press, 1980.

Paine, L. S. "Managing for Organizational Integrity." *Harvard Business Review.* Mar.–Apr. 1994.

Rapaport, R. "To Build a Winning Team: An Interview with Head Coach Bill Walsh." *Harvard Business Review,* Jan.–Feb. 1993.

Restack, R. M. *The Mind.* New York: Bantam Books, 1988.

Rokeach, M. *Understanding Human Values.* New York: The Free Press, 1979.

Sapolsky, Robert. In *The Mind* by Richard M. Restak. New York: Bantam Books, 1988.

Satir, V. *Peoplemaking.* Palo Alto, Calif.: Science and Behavior Books, 1972.

Schein, E. H. "Organizational Culture." *American Psychologist,* 45 (1990).

Seligman, M. *What You Can Change and What You Can't.* New York: Alfred A. Knopf, Inc., 1994.

Selye, H. "The Stress Concept Today." In *The Handbook on Stress and Anxiety,* edited by L. L. Kutash, L. B. Schlesinger, and associates. San Francisco: Jossey-Bass, 1980.

Selye, H. *The Stress of Life.* New York: McGraw-Hill, 1976.

Skinner, B. F. *Beyond Freedom and Dignity.* New York: Alfred A. Knopf, Inc., 1971.

Slater, P. and W. G. Bennis. "Democracy is Inevitable." *Harvard Business Review,* Sept.–Oct. 1990.

Sternberg, R. and R. K. Wagner. *Practical Intelligence.* New York: Cambridge University Press, 1986.

Stewart, T. A. *Intellectual Capital.* New York: Doubleday, 1997.

Tichy, N. M. and M. A. Devanna. *The Transformational Leader.* New York: John Wiley & Sons, 1990.

Toffler, A. *Power Shift.* New York: Bantam Books, 1990.

Von Franz, M. and J. Hillman. "Jung's Typology." *Spring Publications,* 1971.

Weeks, D. *The Eight Essential Steps to Conflict Resolution.* New York: G. P. Putnam's Sons, 1992.

Wriston, W. B. "The State of American Management." *Harvard Business Review,* Jan.–Feb. 1990.

Yerkes, R. M. and J. D. Dodson. "The Relation of Strength of Stimulus to Rigidity of Habit-Formation." *Journal of Comparative Neurology and Psychology,* 1908.

INDEX

658.409
B4658

LINCOLN CHRISTIAN COLLEGE AND SEMINARY

9857

3 4711 00151 8952